play guitar with...

the best of metallica

AF133503

part 1
- 12 **ain't my bitch**
- **enter sandman** 24
- 36 **fade to black**
- **nothing else matters** 3
- 56 **the unforgiven**
- **welcome home (sanitarium)** 44

part 2
- 78 **carpe diem baby**
- **creeping death** 66
- 87 **leper messiah**
- **the memory remains** 106
- 98 **seek and destroy**
- **whiskey in the jar** 114

124 **guitar tablature explained**
translations 126 & 127

To access audio visit:
www.halleonard.com/mylibrary

3423-7752-3051-7252

This book © Copyright 2007 Wise Publications,
a part of HAL LEONARD LLC

*Music arranged by Arthur Dick (Part 1) and Martin Shellard (Part 2) Music
processed by Seton Music Graphics / Andrew Shiels
Cover Photo courtesy Ross Halfin / Idols
Printed in the UK.*

*Recorded by Passionhouse Music
All guitars by Arthur Dick*

Order No. AM988900

ISBN: 978-1-84609-874-2

For all works contained herein:
Unauthorized copying, arranging, adapting, recording, internet posting, public performance,
or other distribution of the music in this publication is an infringement of copyright.
Infringers are liable under the law.

Visit Hal Leonard Online at
www.halleonard.com

Contact us:
Hal Leonard
7777 West Bluemound Road
Milwaukee, WI 53213
Email: info@halleonard.com

In Europe, contact:
Hal Leonard Europe Limited
42 Wigmore Street
Marylebone, London, W1U 2RY
Email: info@halleonardeurope.com

In Australia, contact:
Hal Leonard Australia Pty. Ltd.
4 Lentara Court
Cheltenham, Victoria, 3192 Australia
Email: info@halleonard.com.au

nothing else matters

Words & Music by James Hetfield & Lars Ulrich

© Copyright 1991 Creeping Death Music, USA.
PolyGram Music Publishing Limited, 47 British Grove, London W4.
All Rights Reserved. International Copyright Secured.

2 bar count in

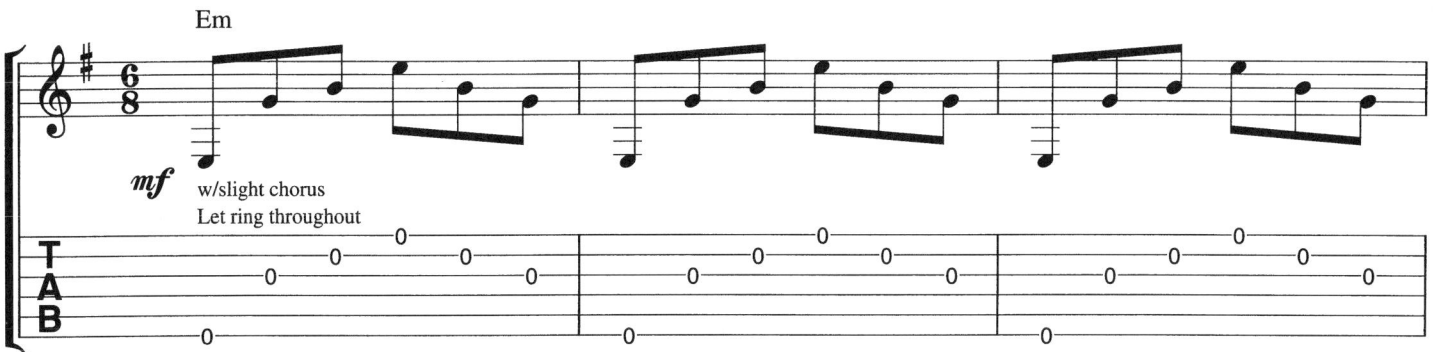

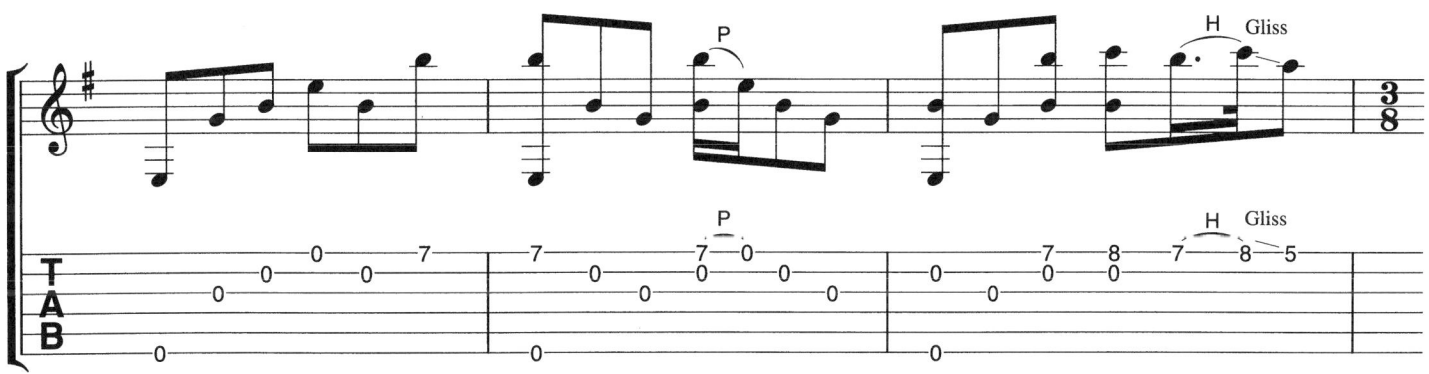

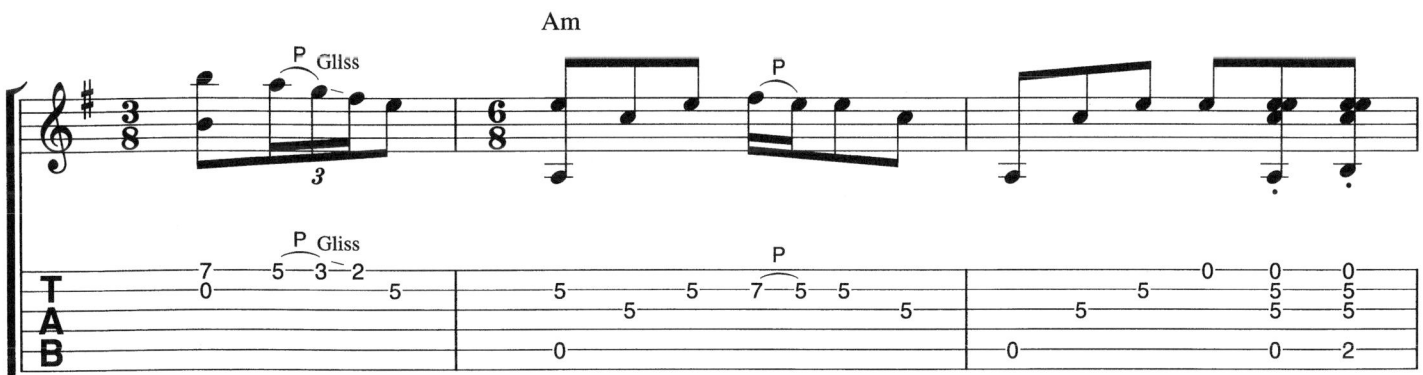

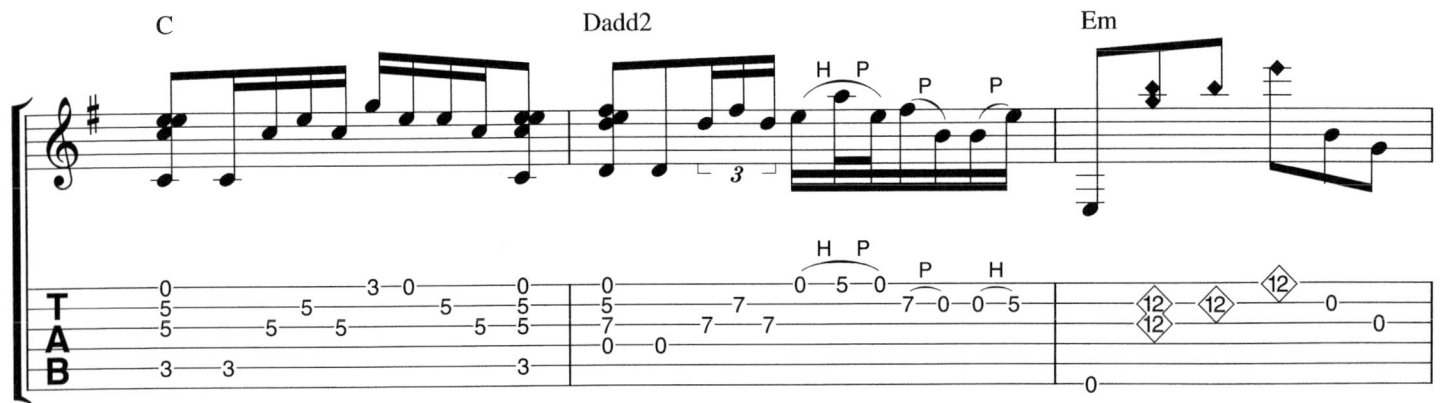

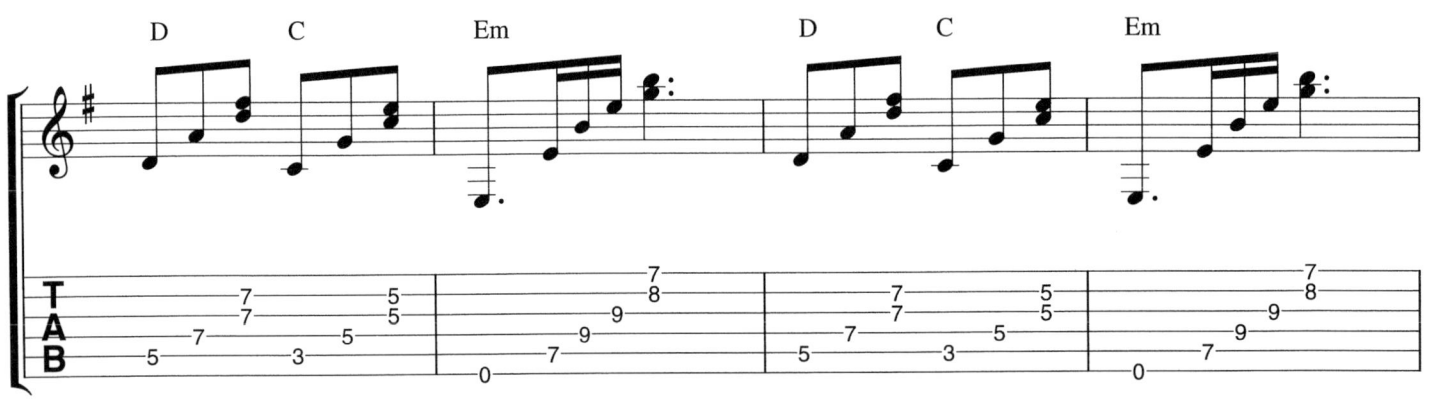
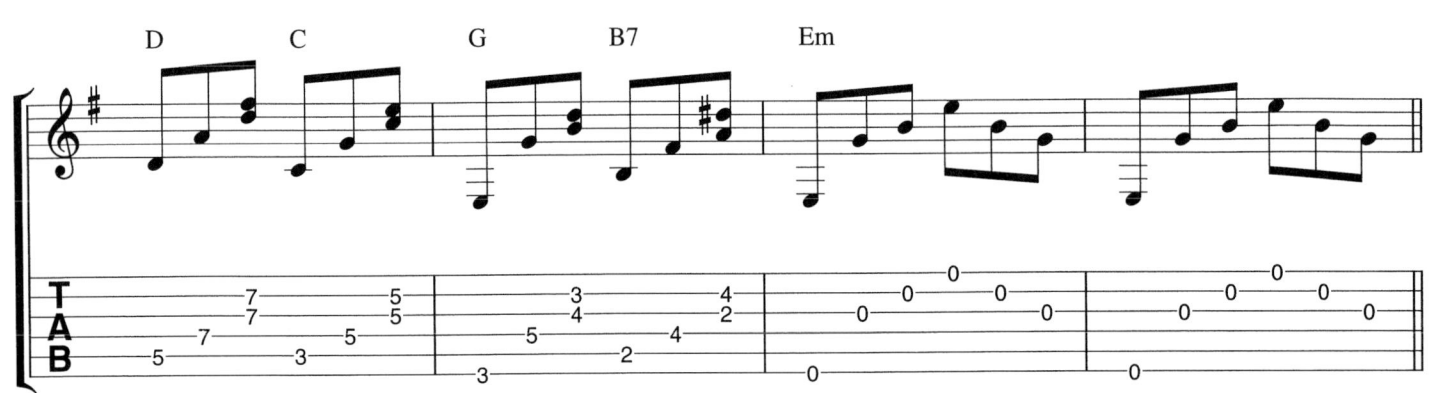

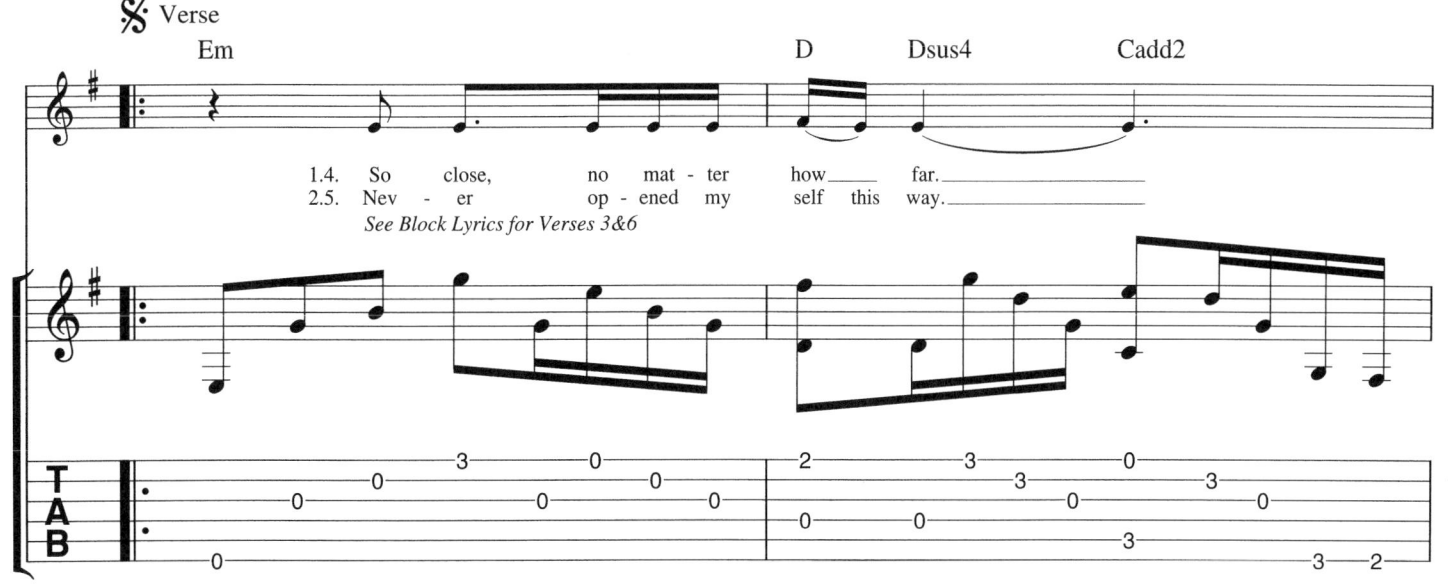
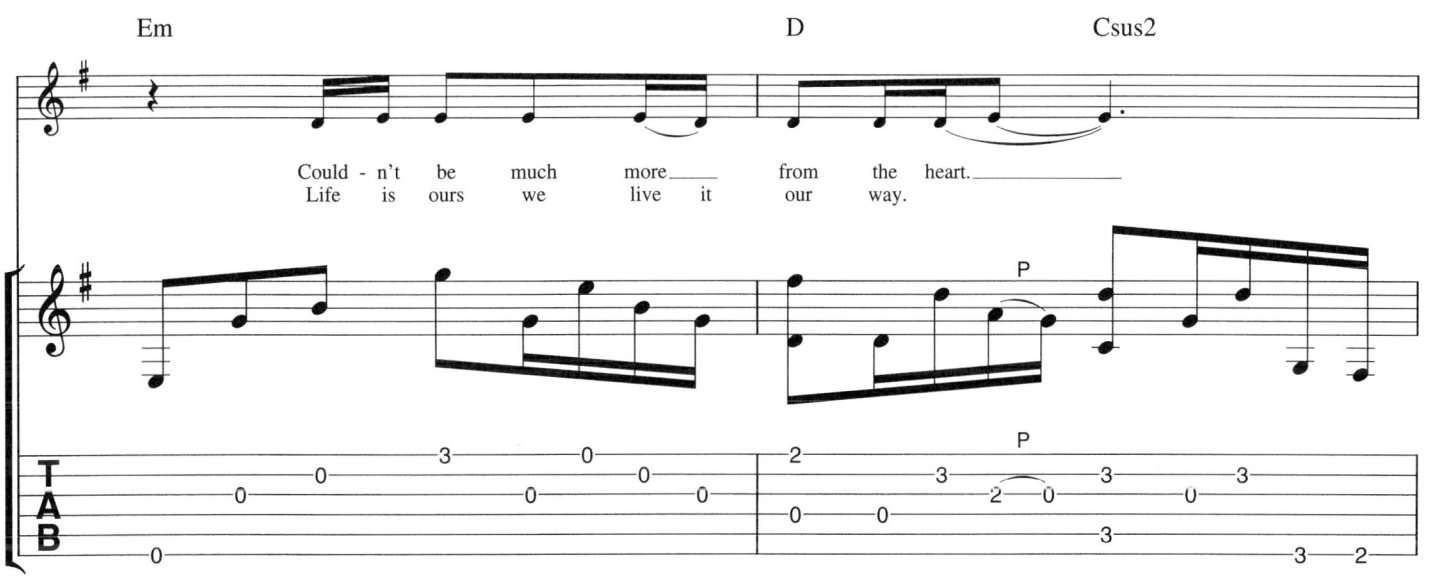
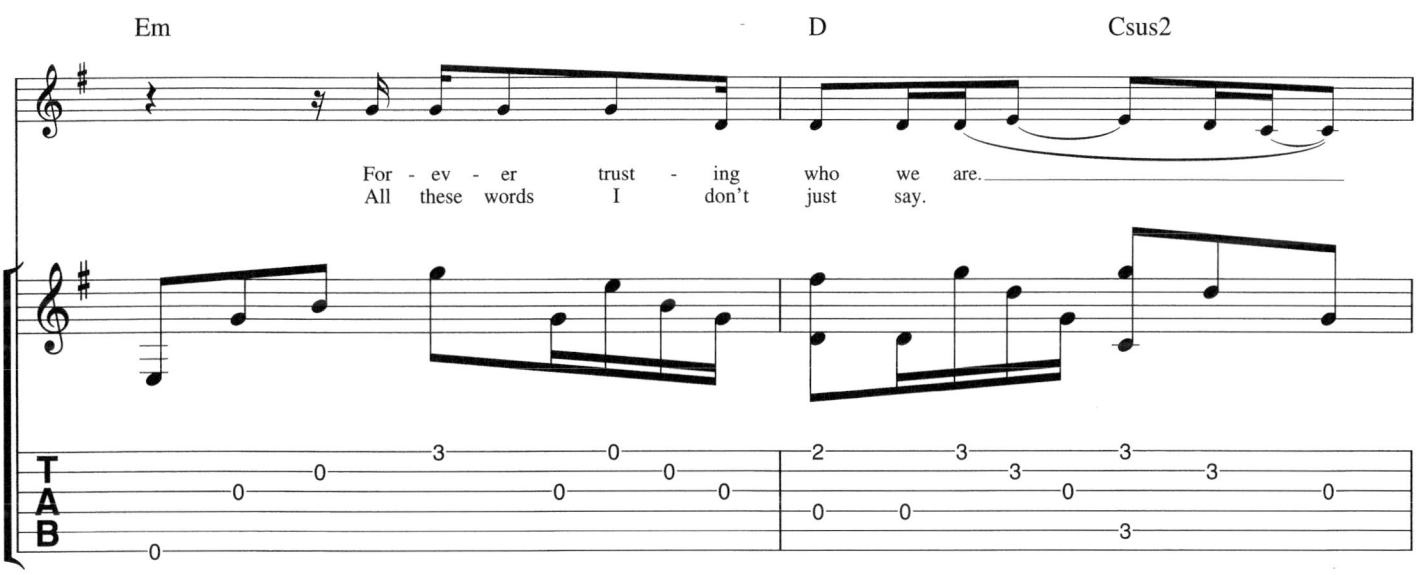

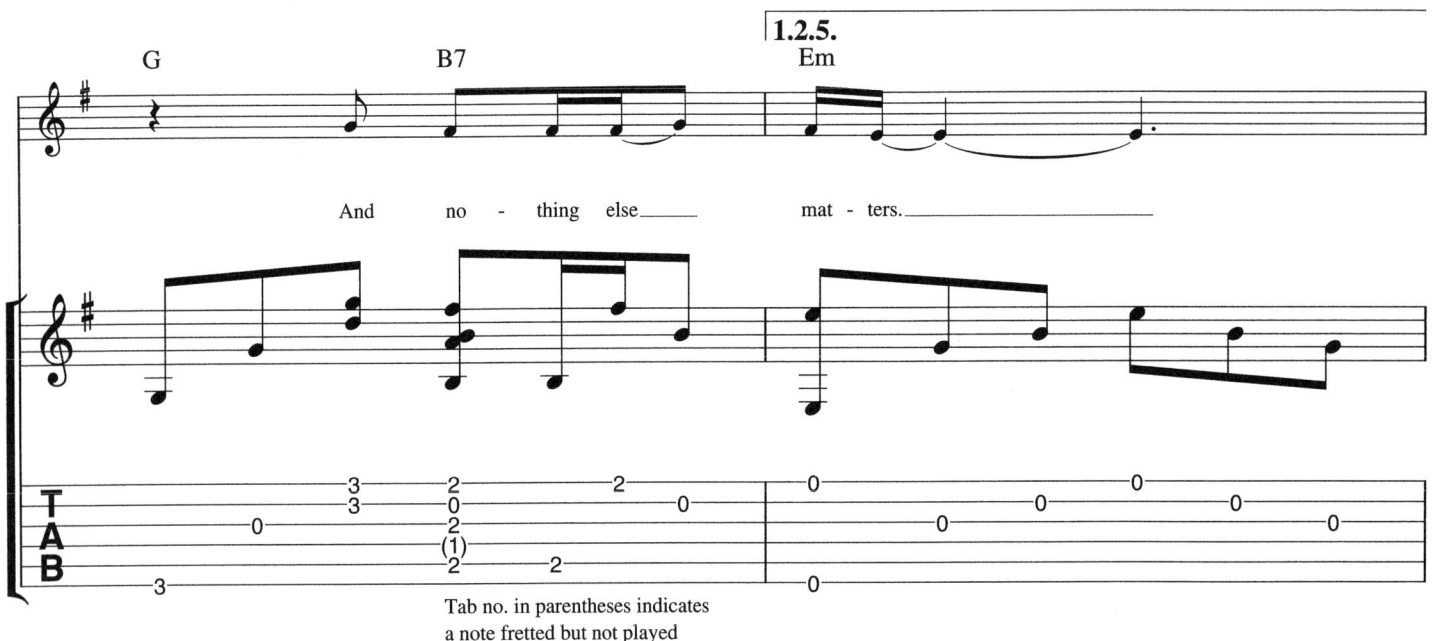
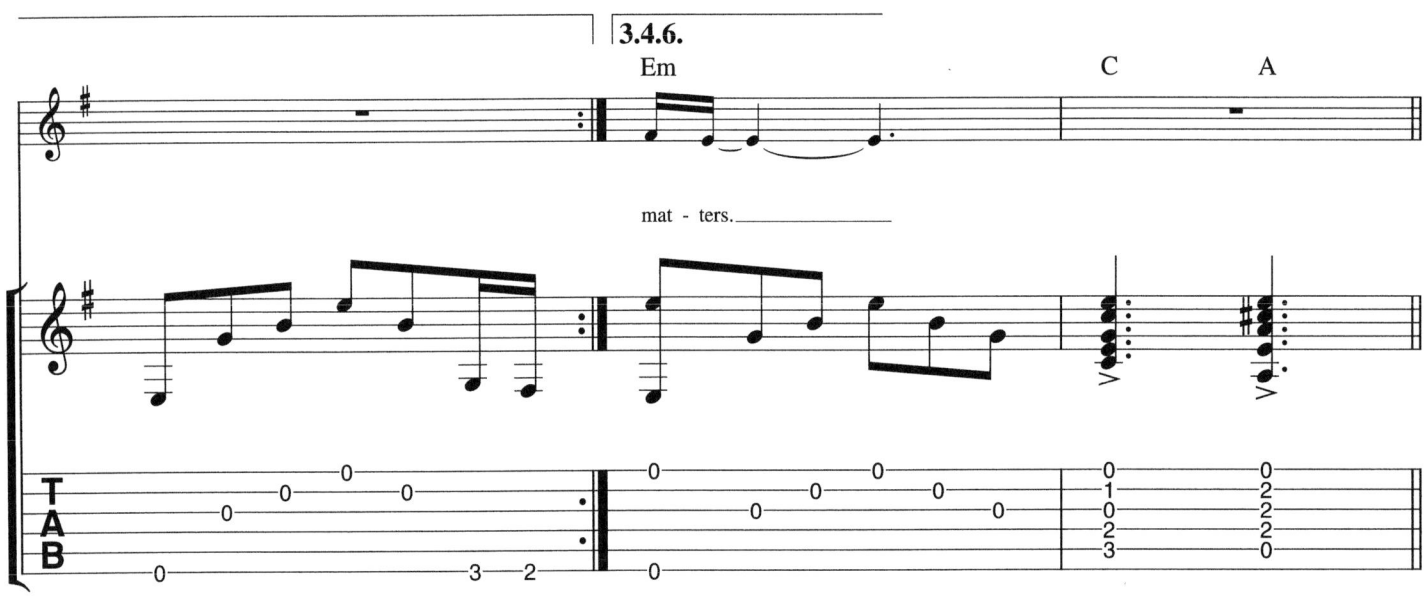
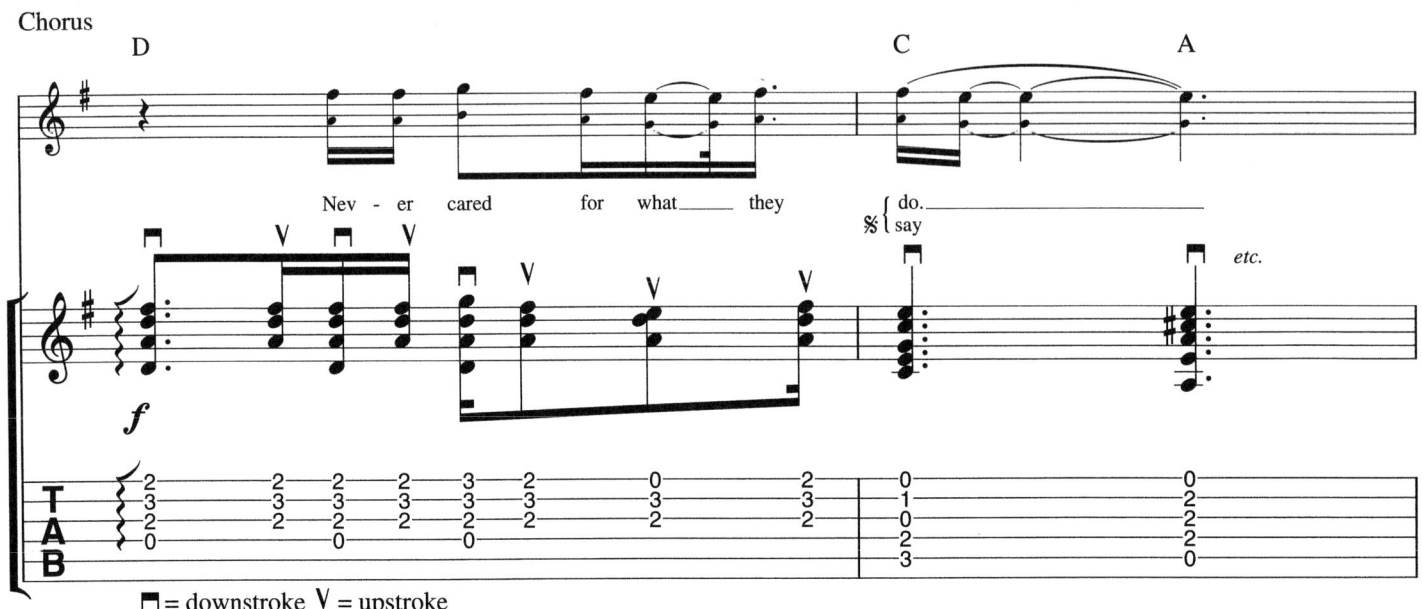

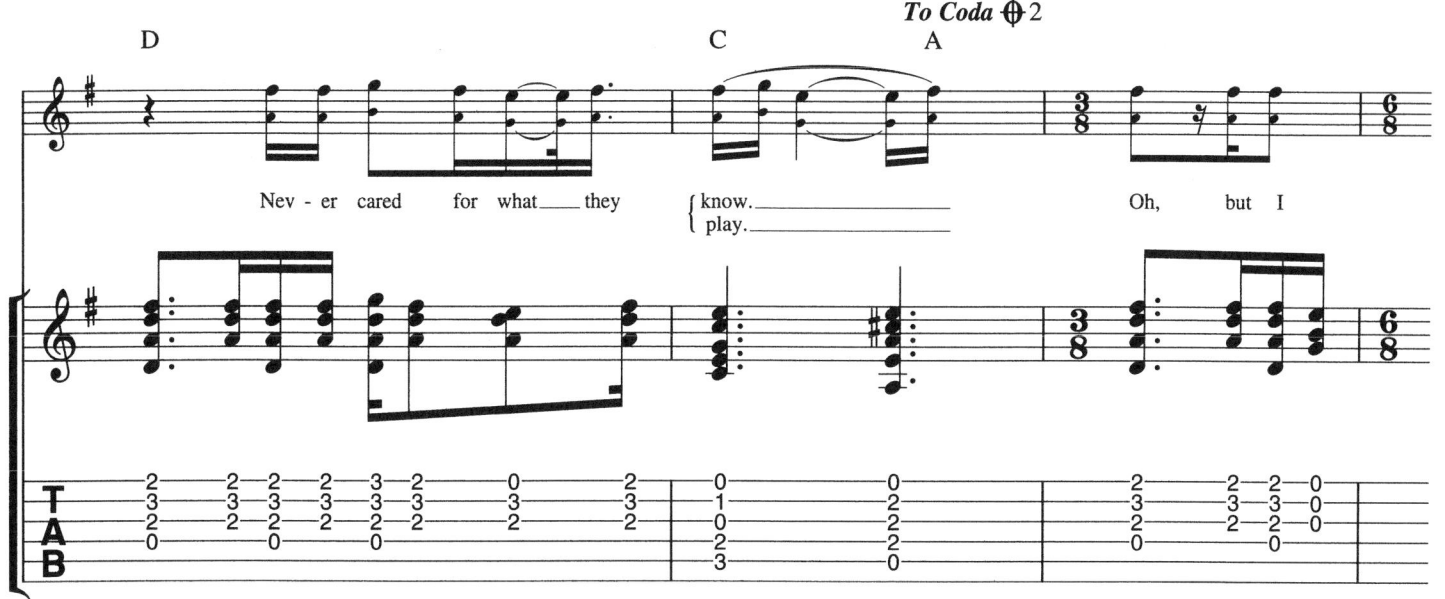
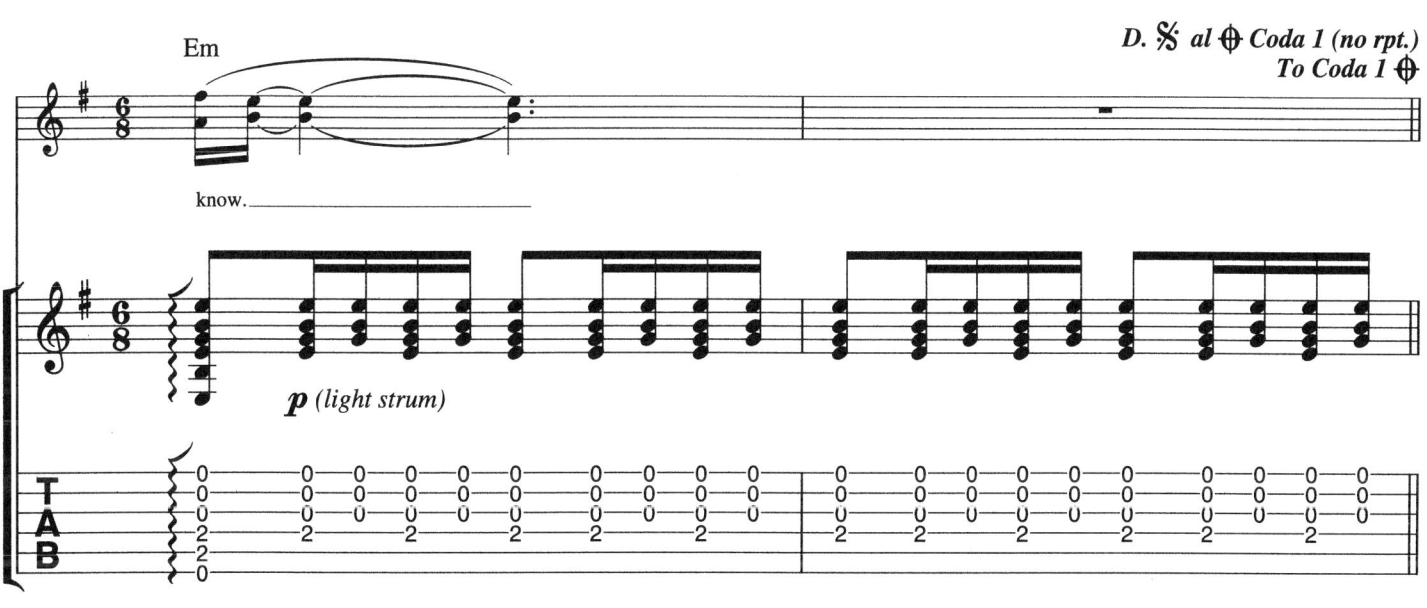
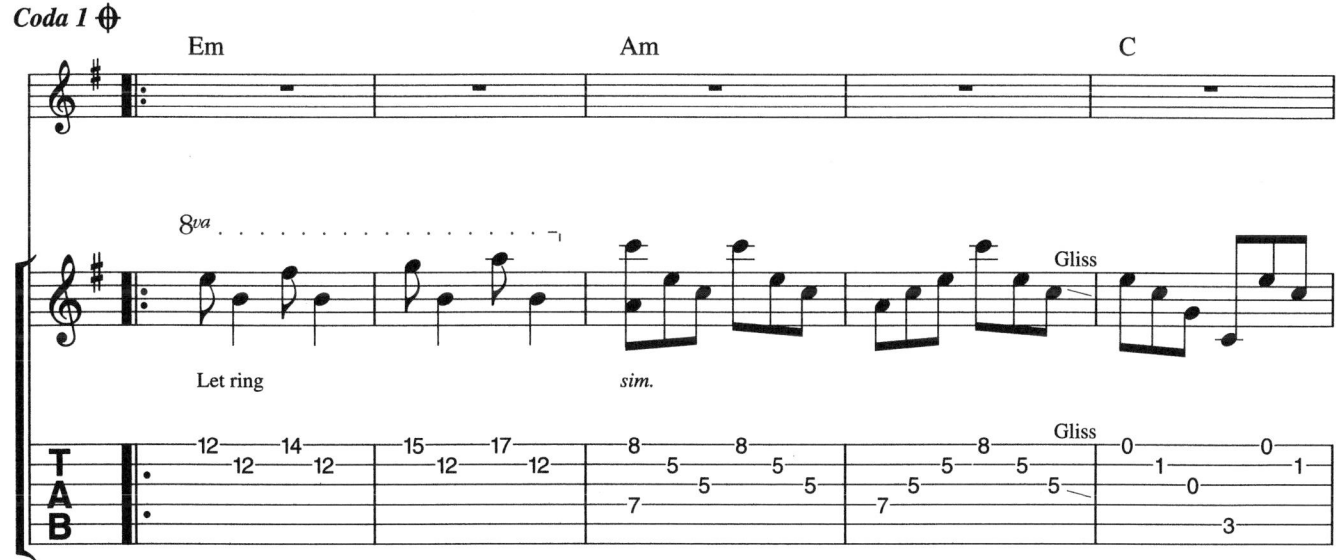

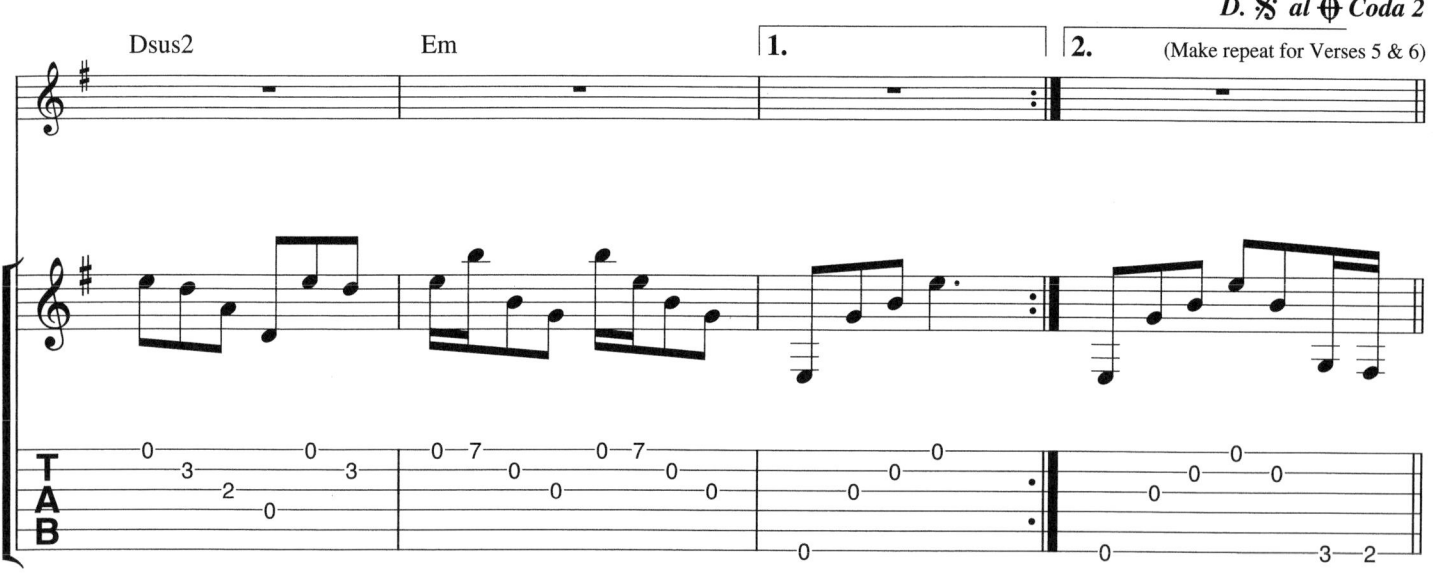
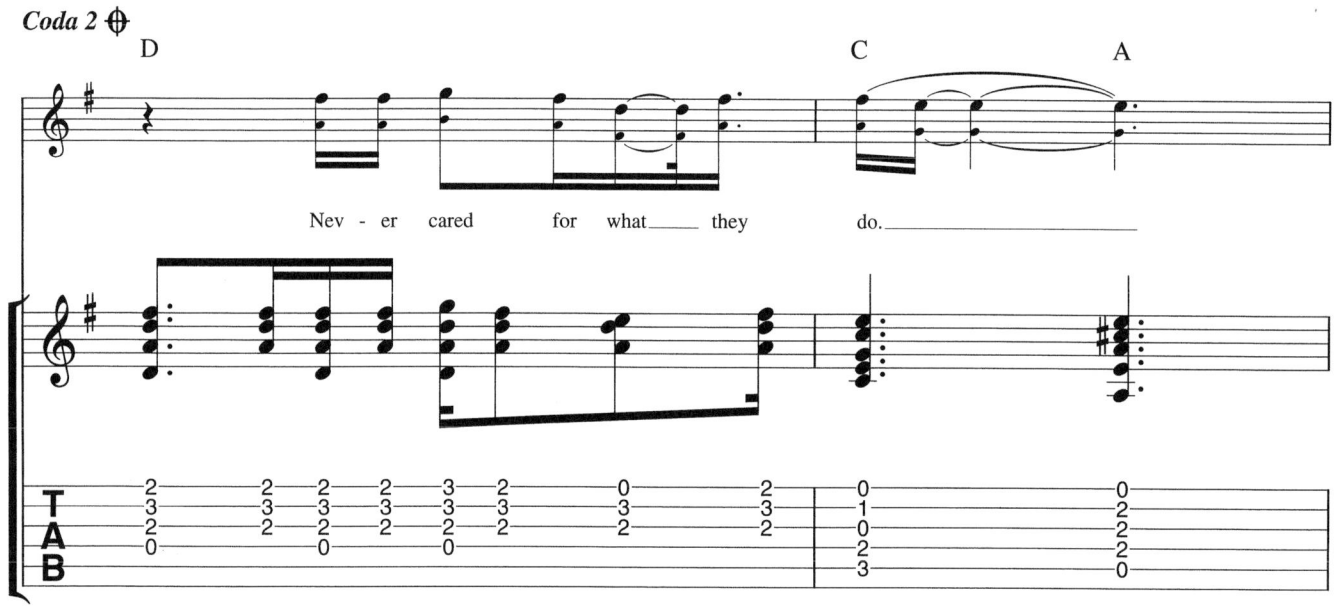
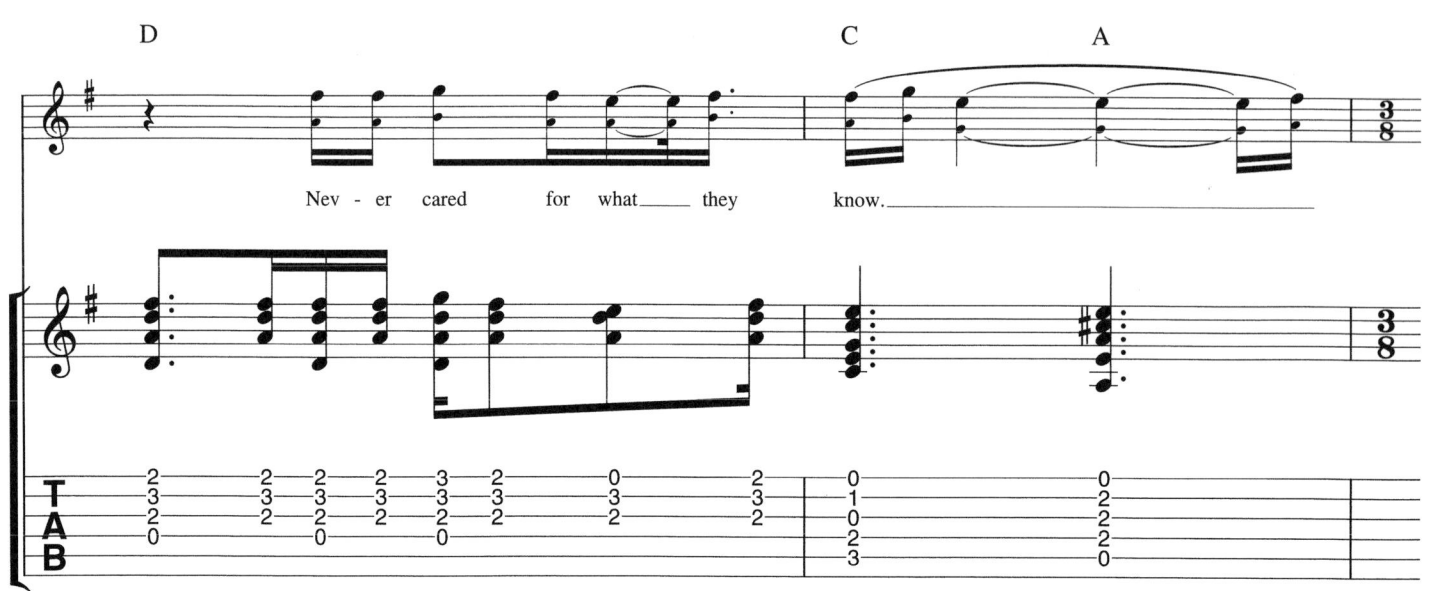

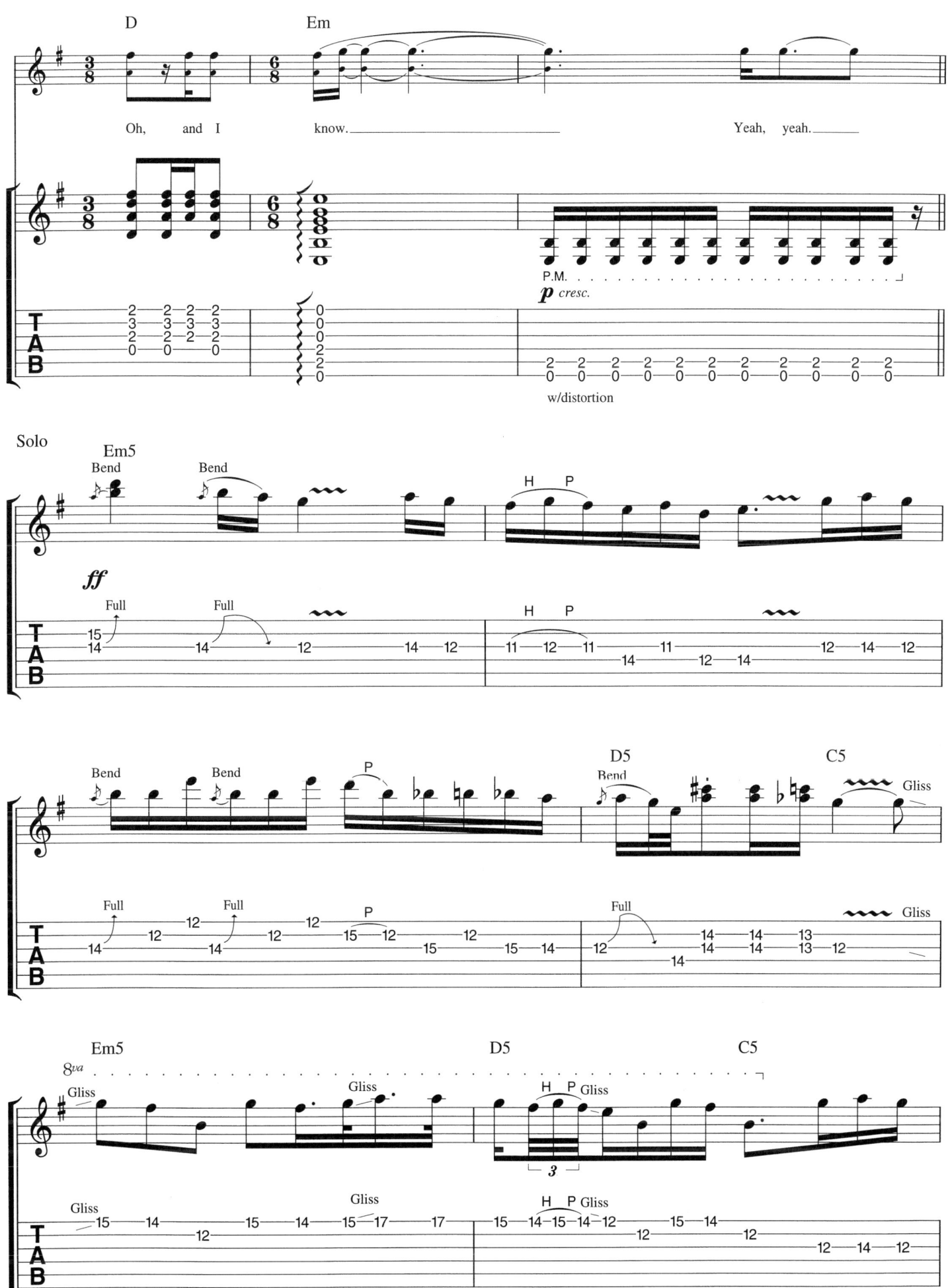

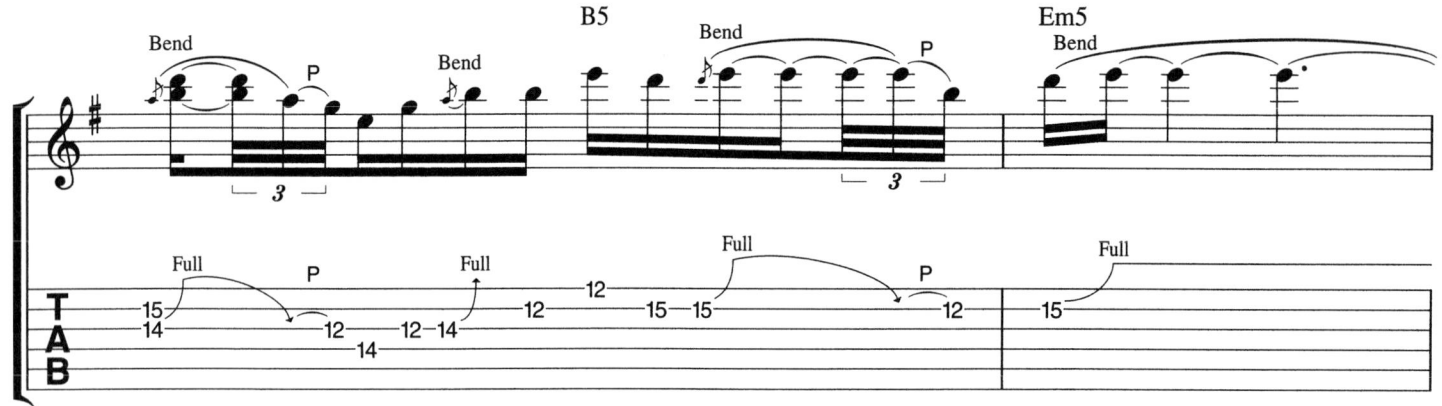
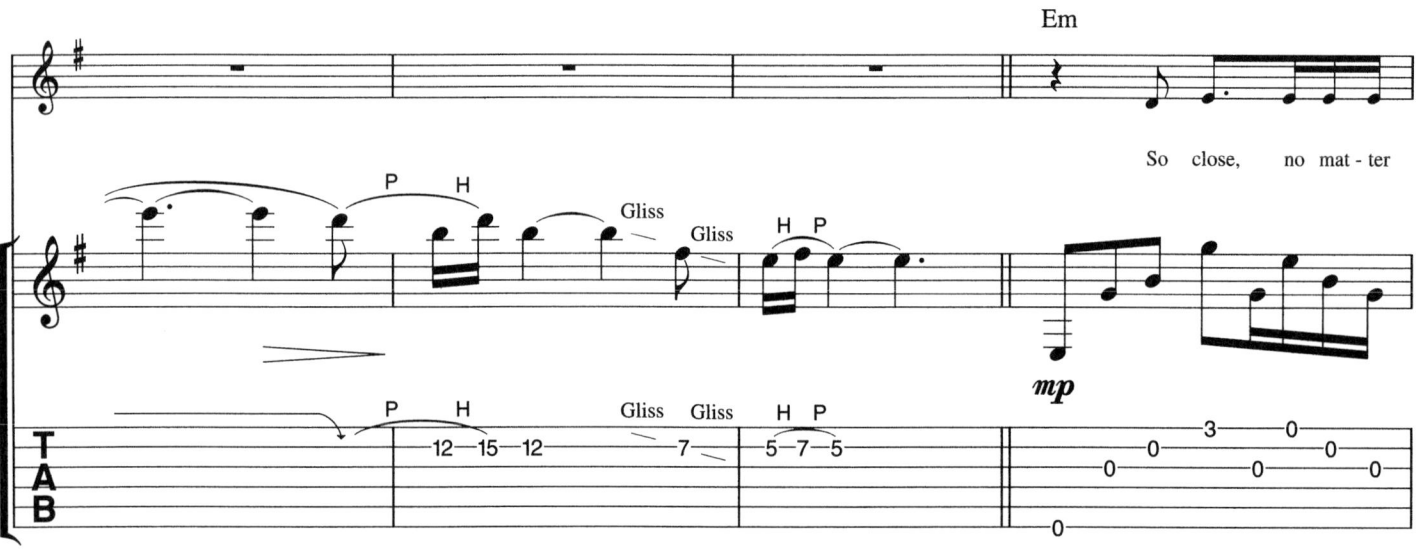

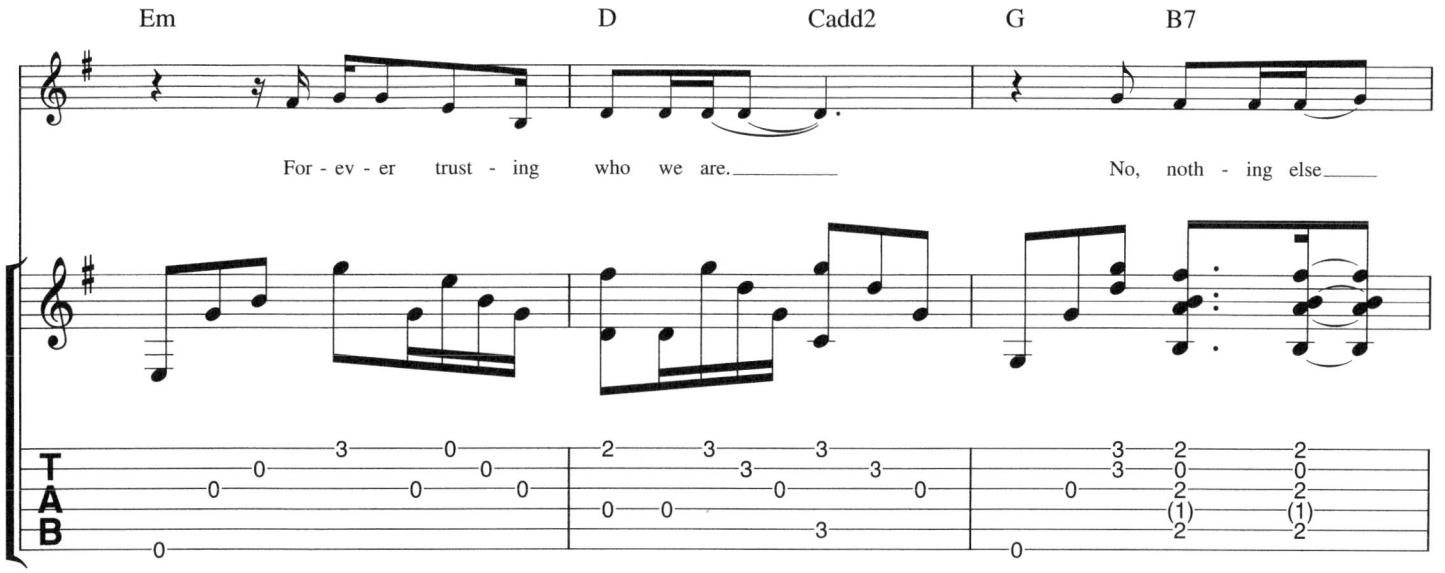
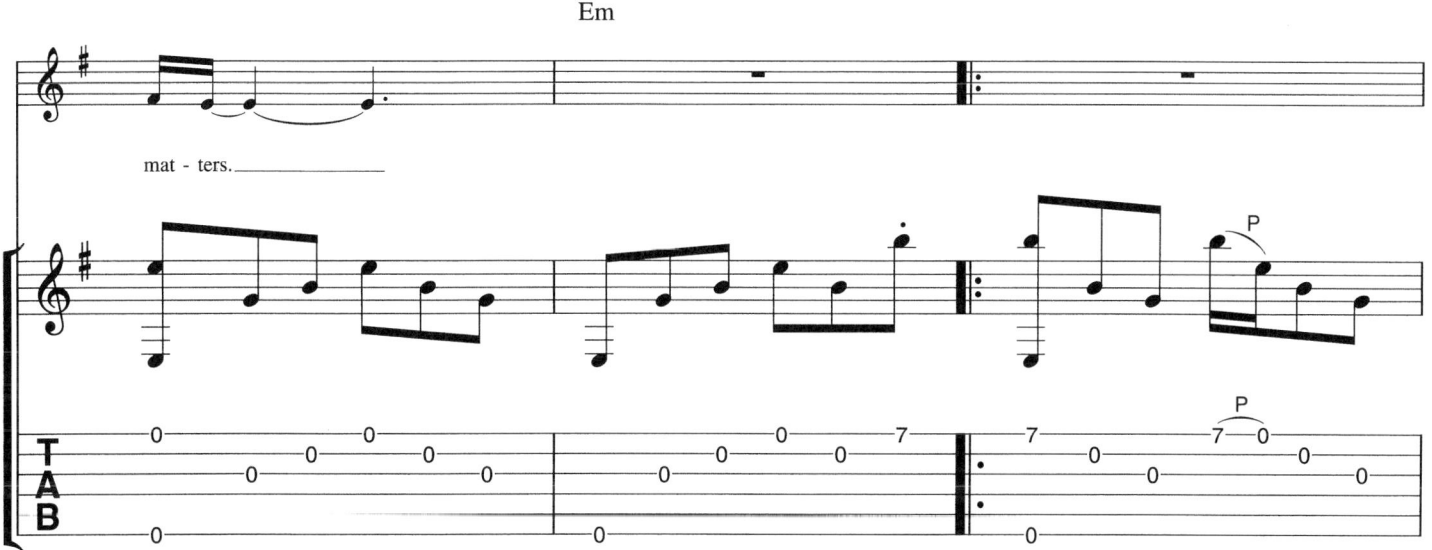
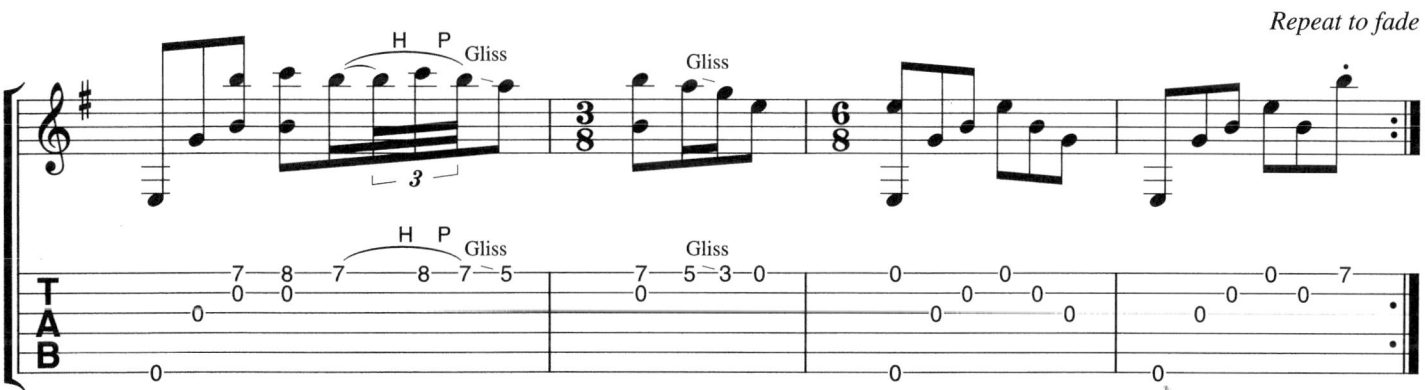

Verse 3 & 6   Trust I seek and I find in you
Ev'ryday for us something new
Open mind for a diff'rent view
And nothing else matters.

ain't my bitch

Words & Music by James Hetfield & Lars Ulrich

© Copyright 1996 Creeping Death Music, USA.
PolyGram Music Publishing Limited, 47 British Grove, London W4.
All Rights Reserved. International Copyright Secured.

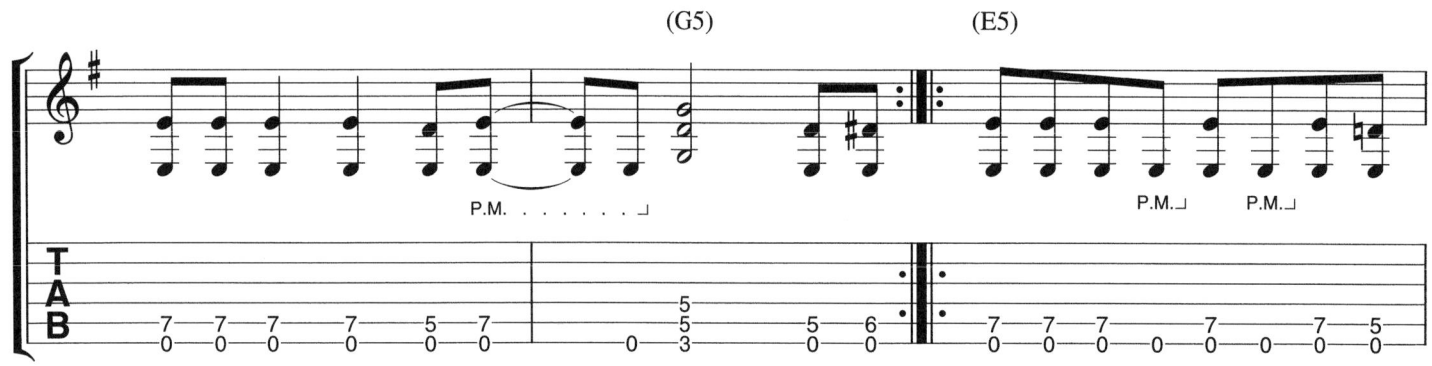

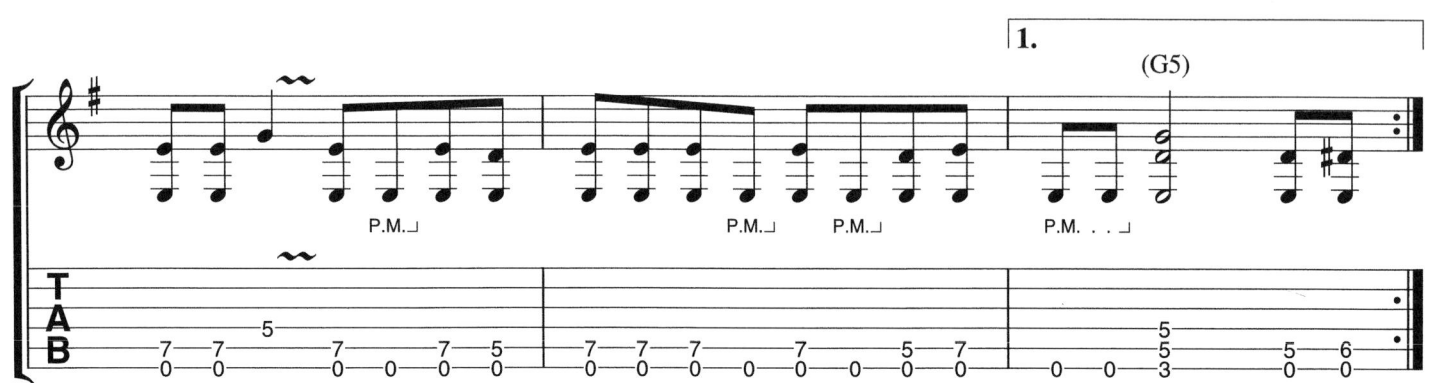

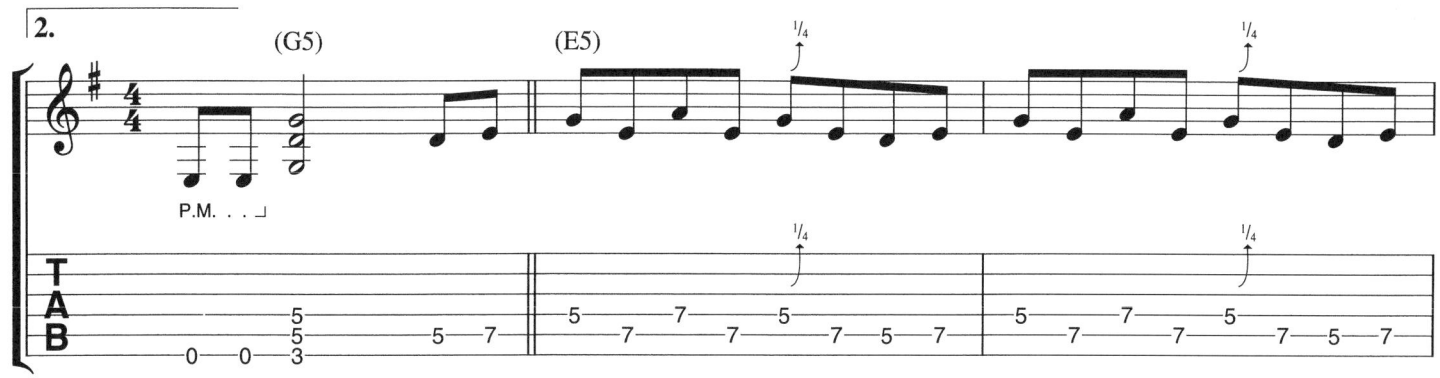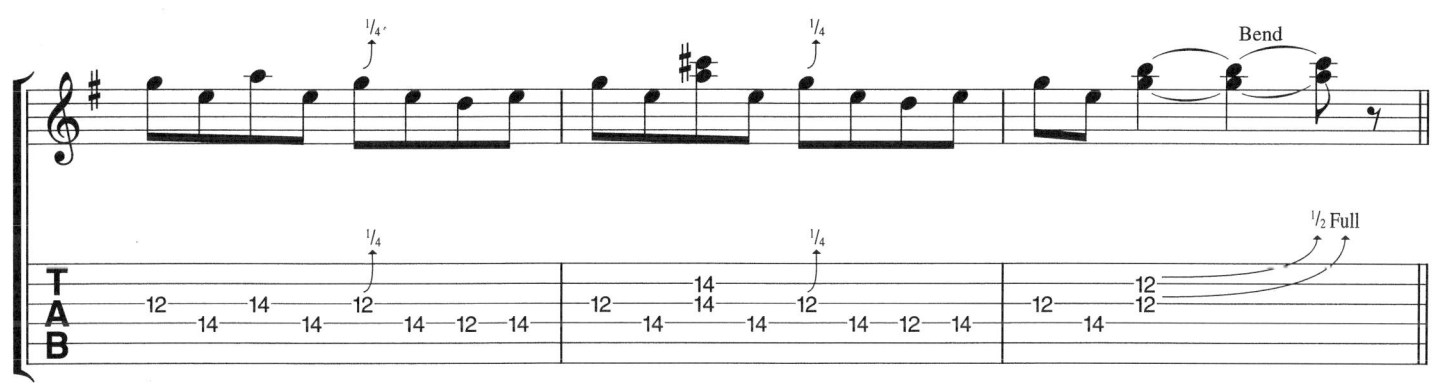

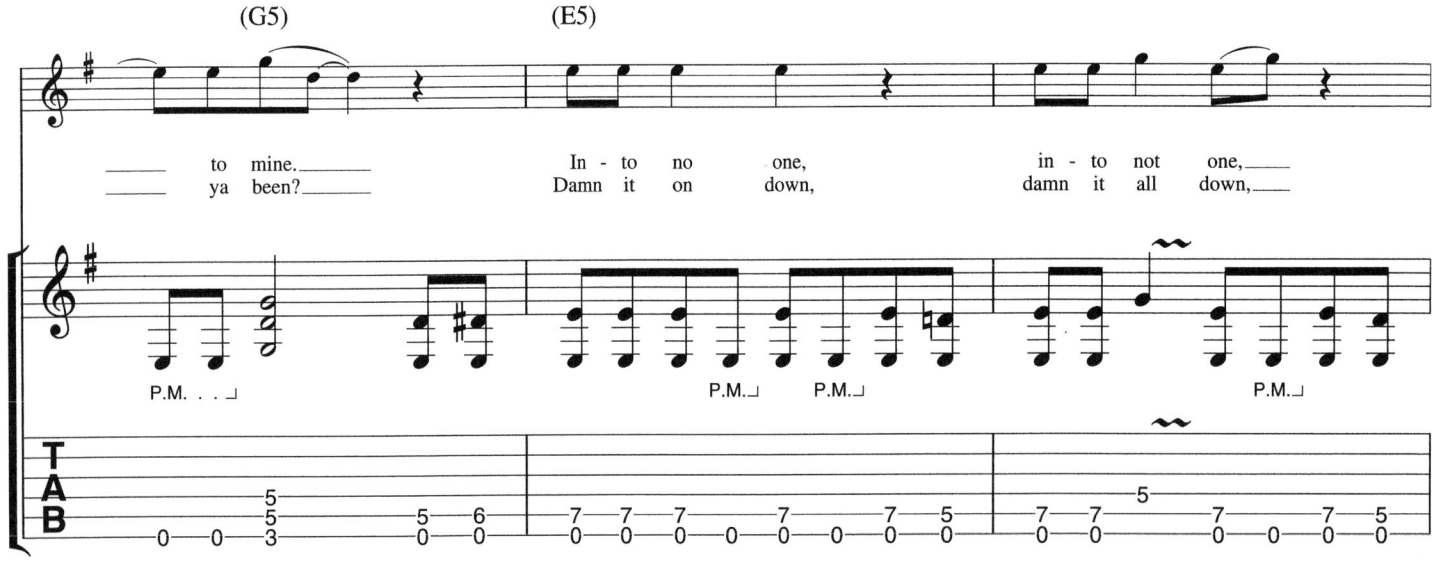
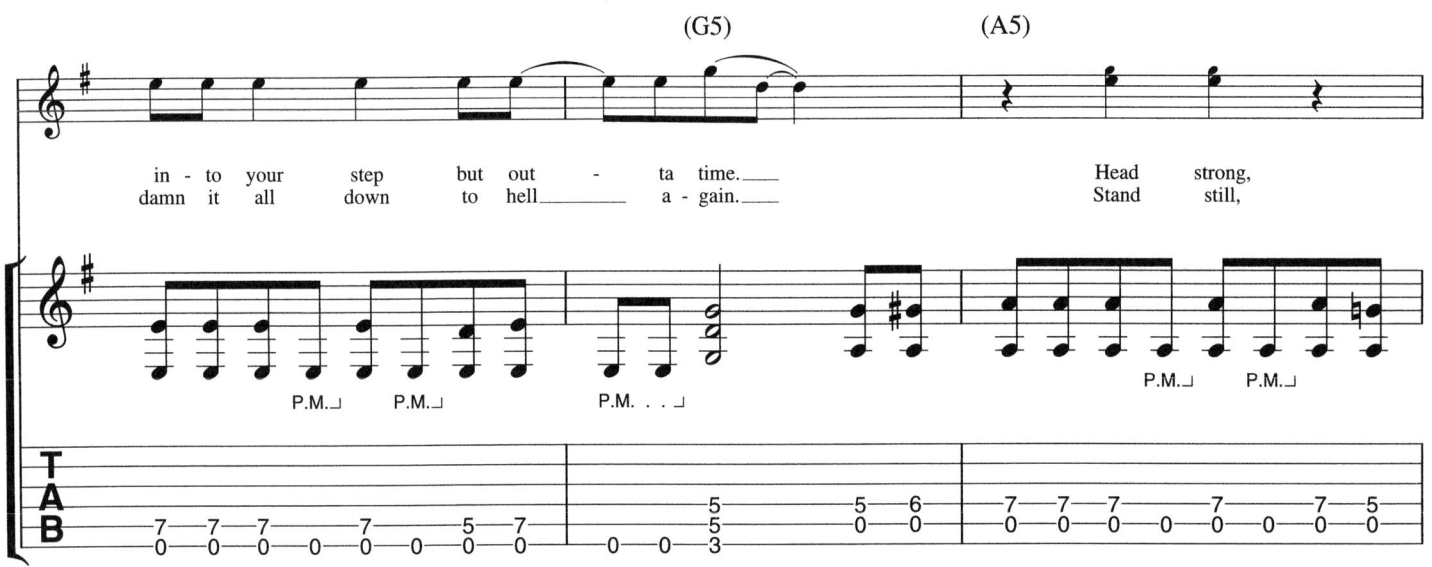
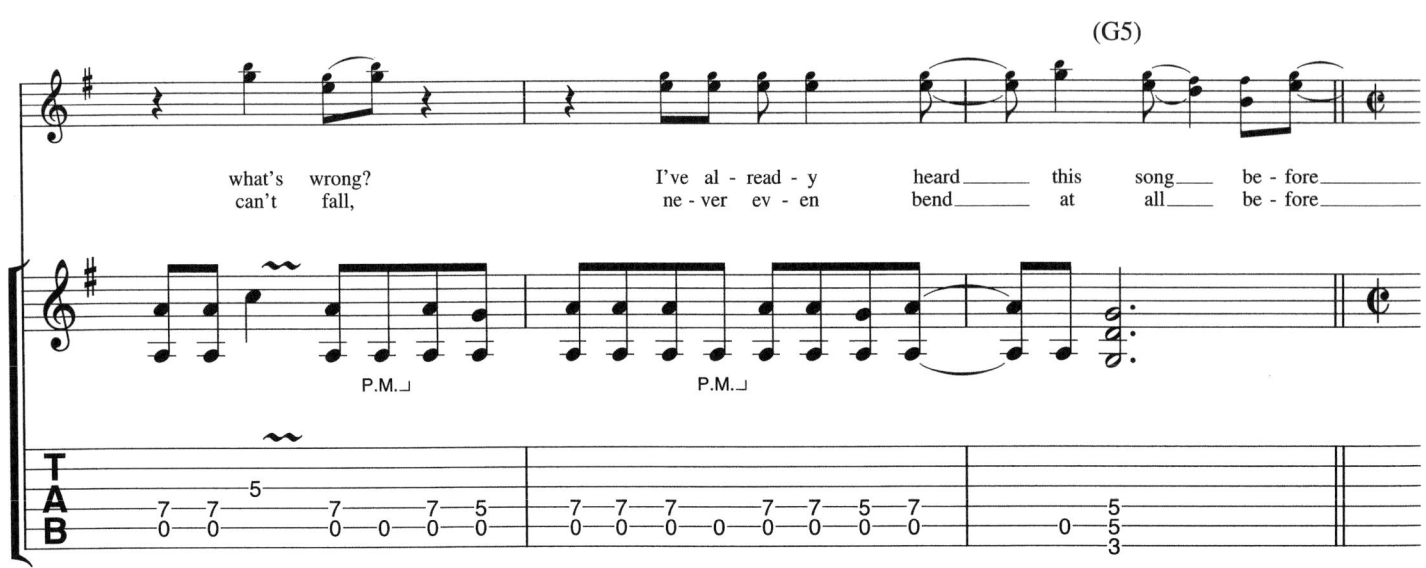

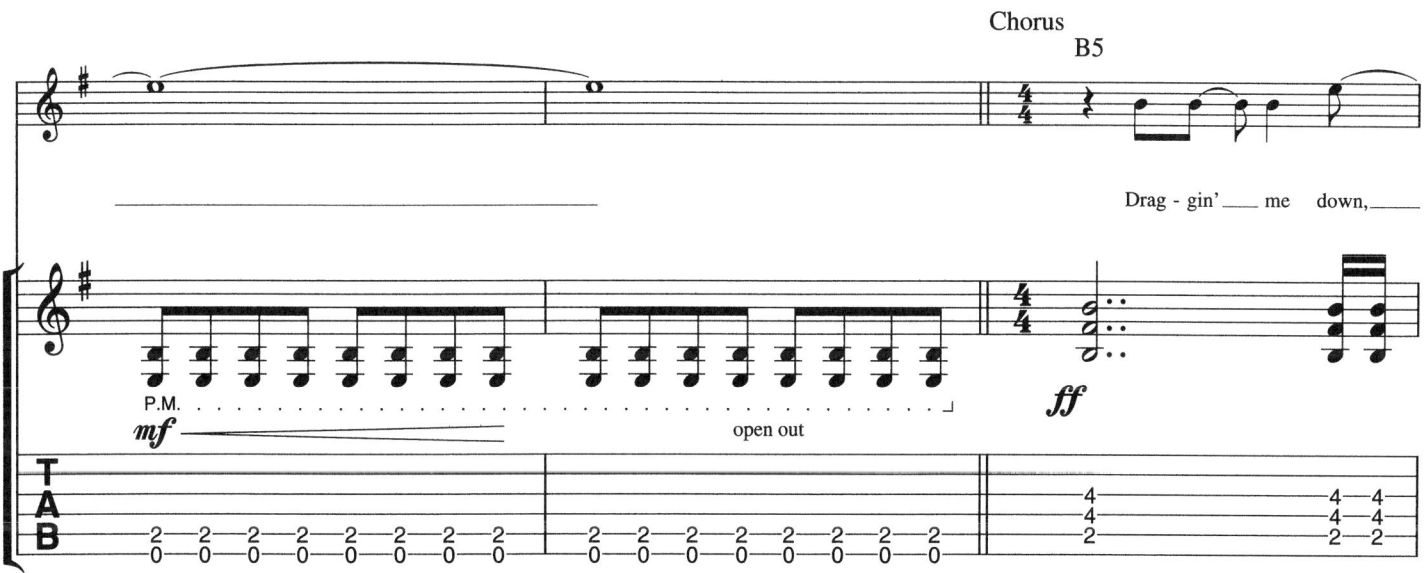
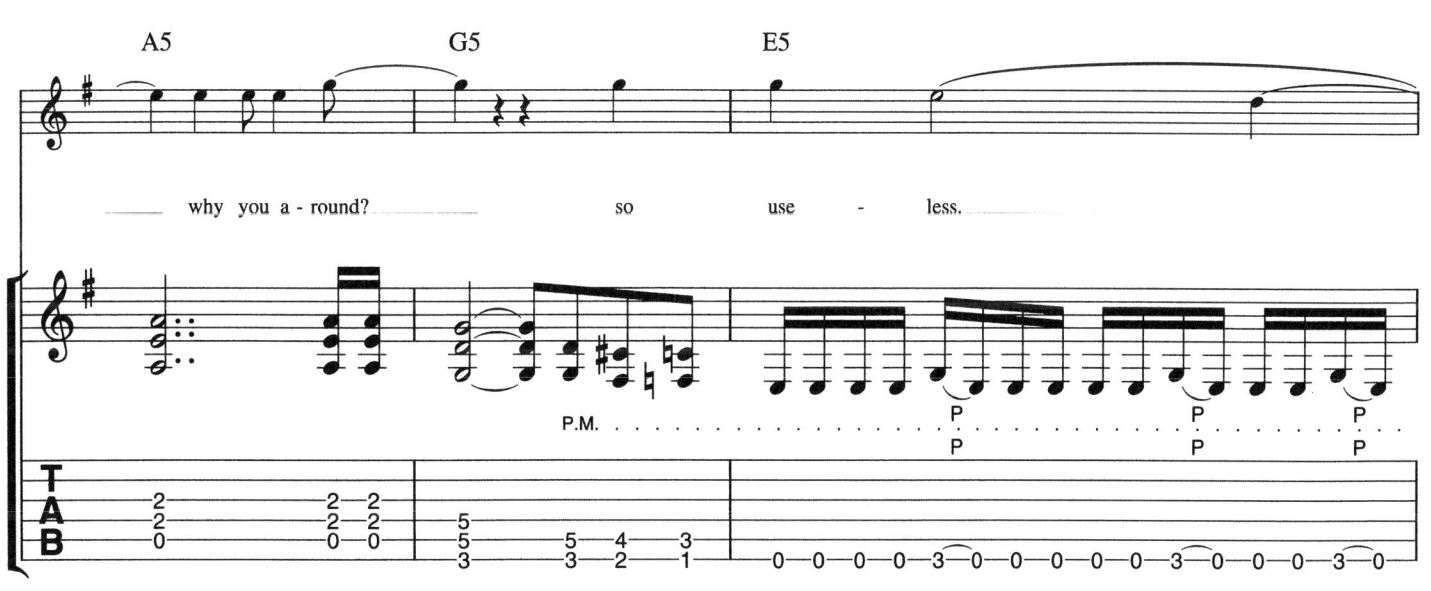

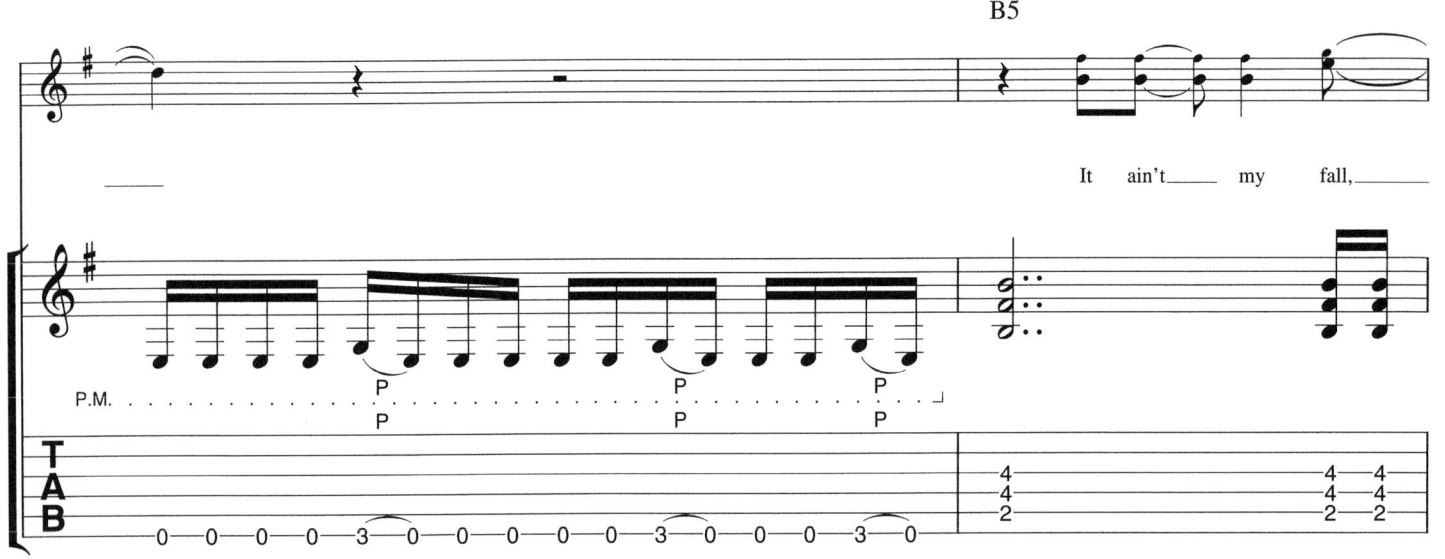
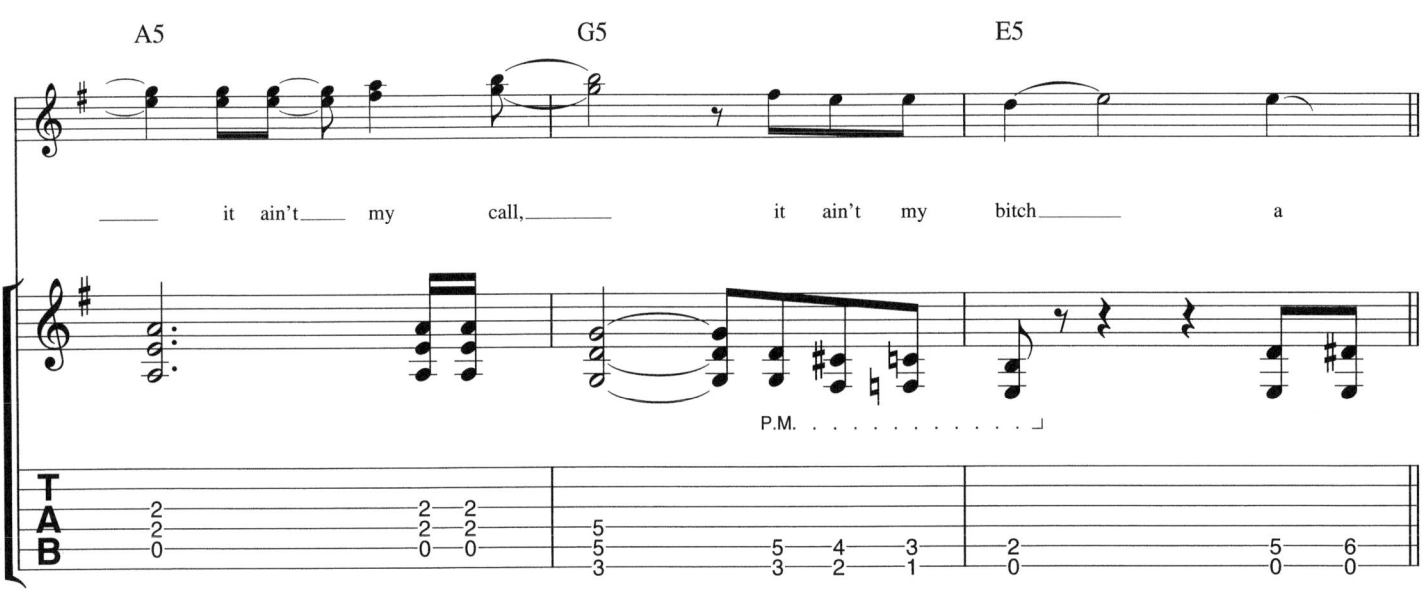

1.
G5
E5
it ain't my bitch.
1° only
Bend
2.
Full
1/2 Full
TAB

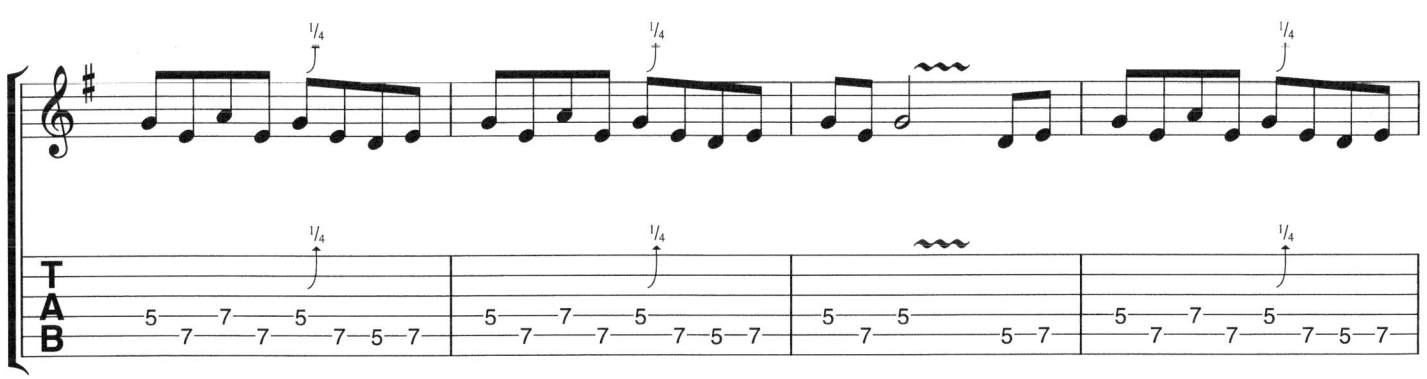

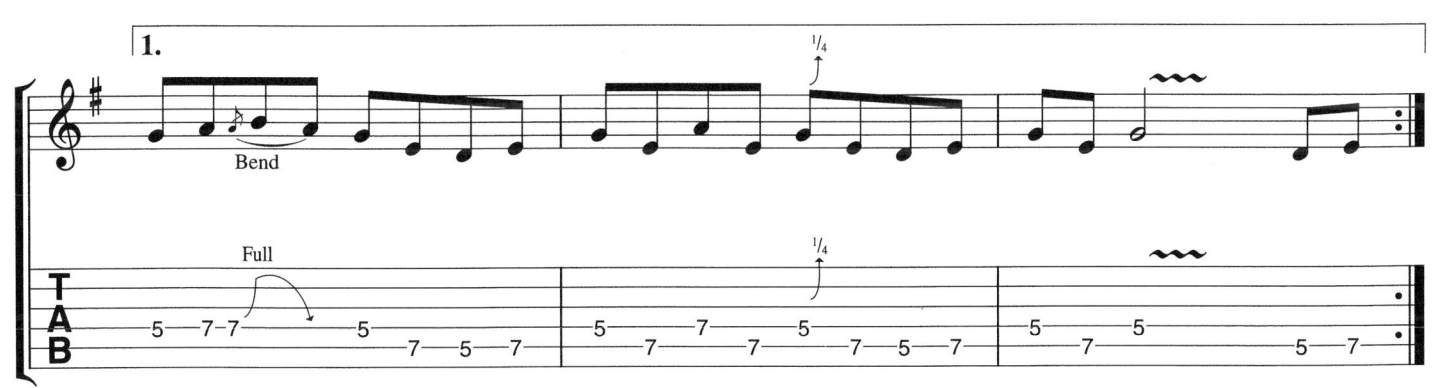

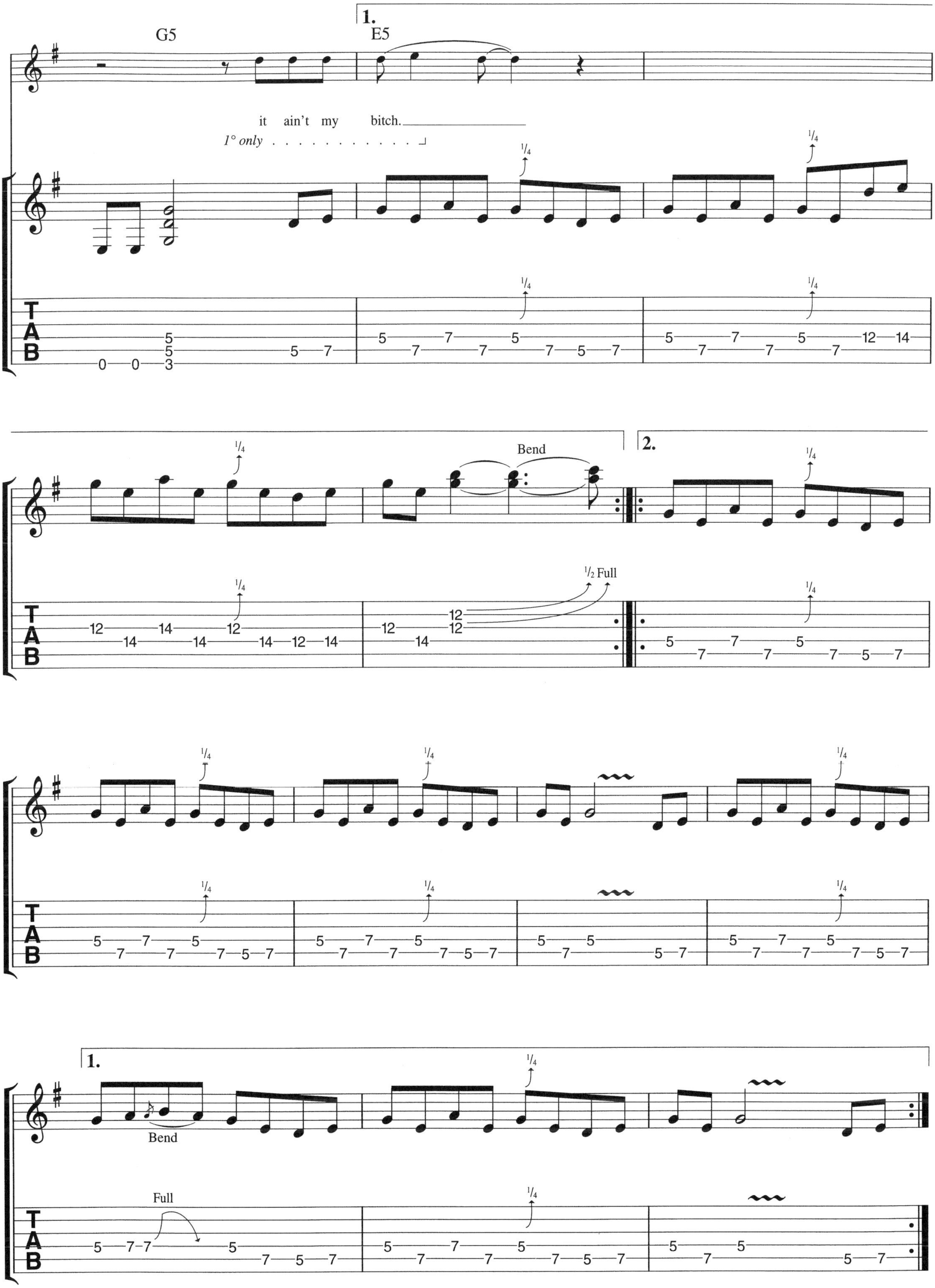

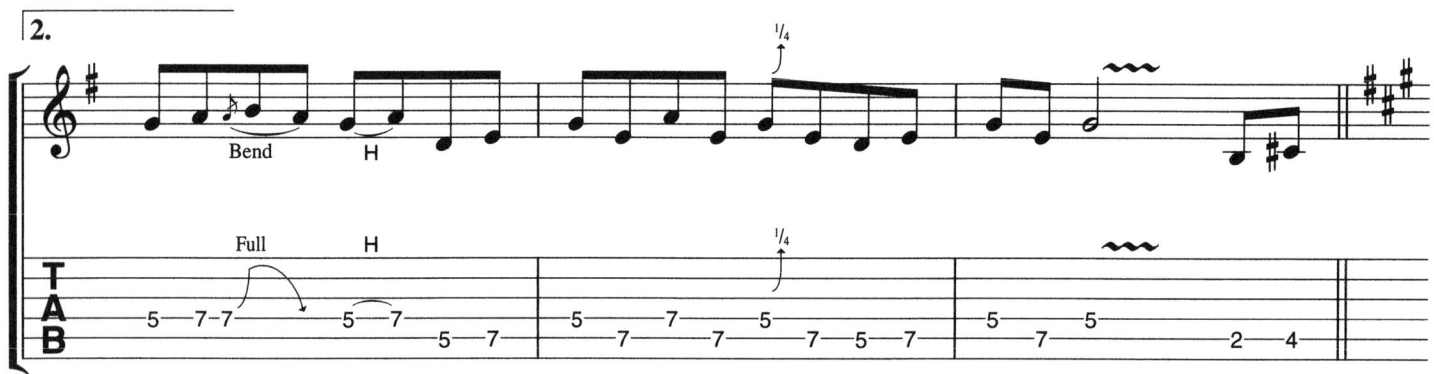

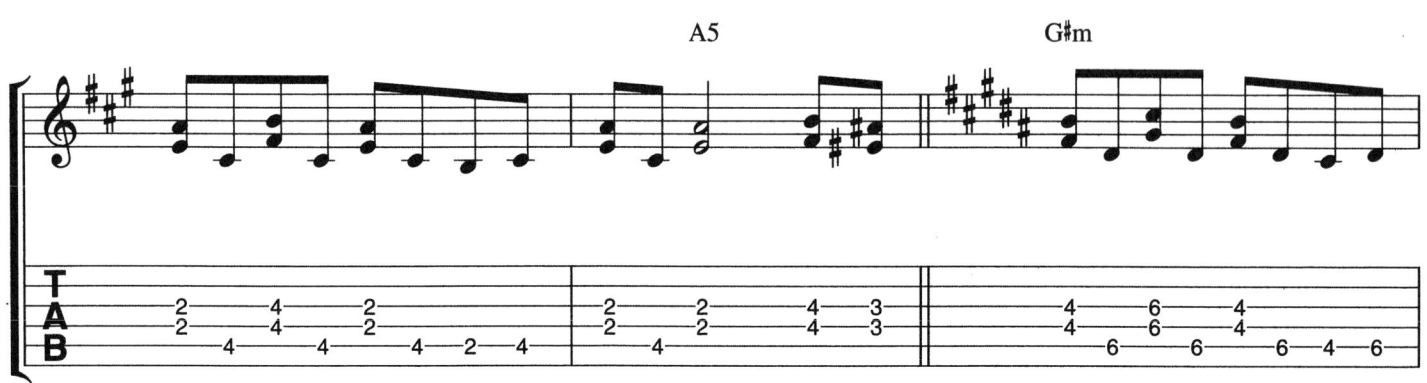

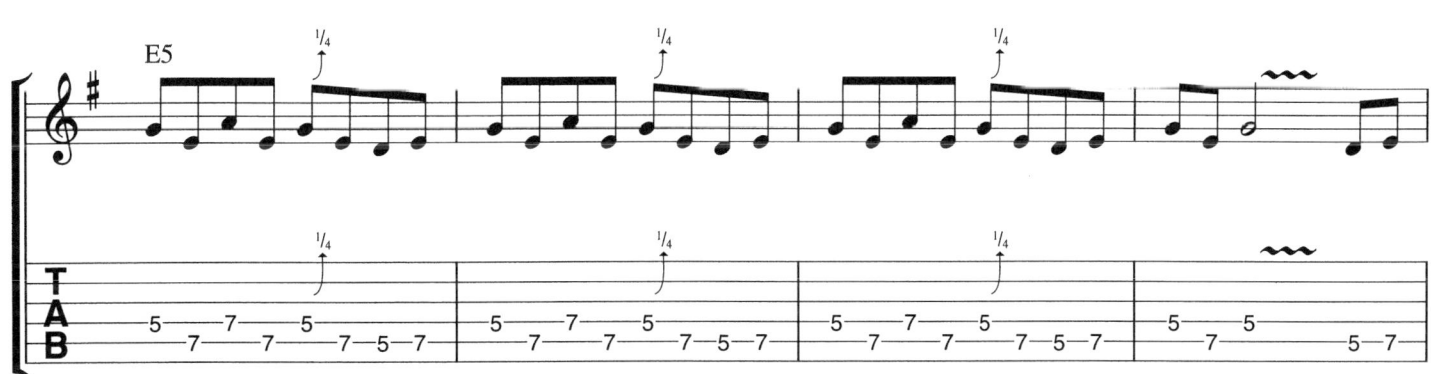
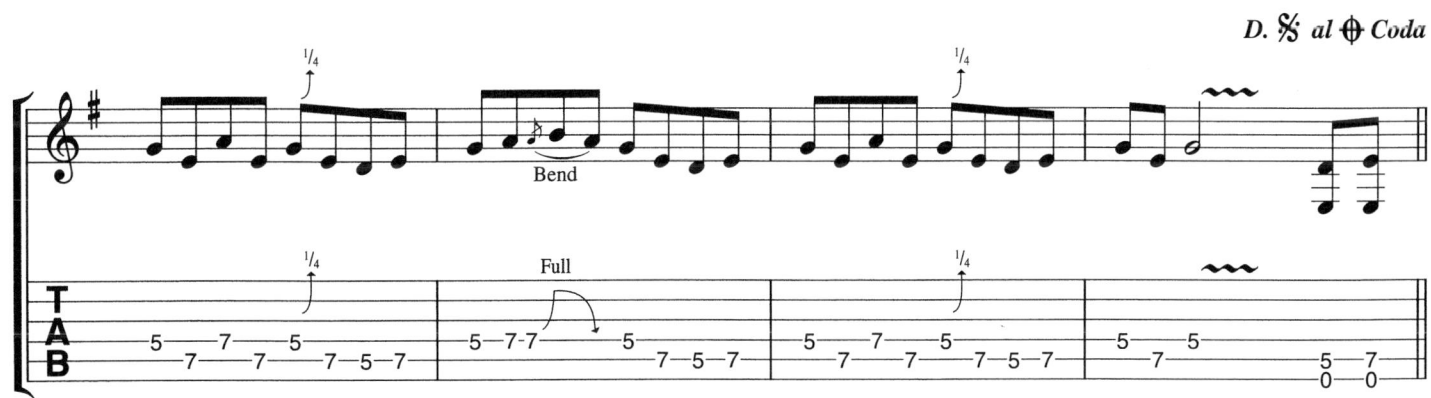

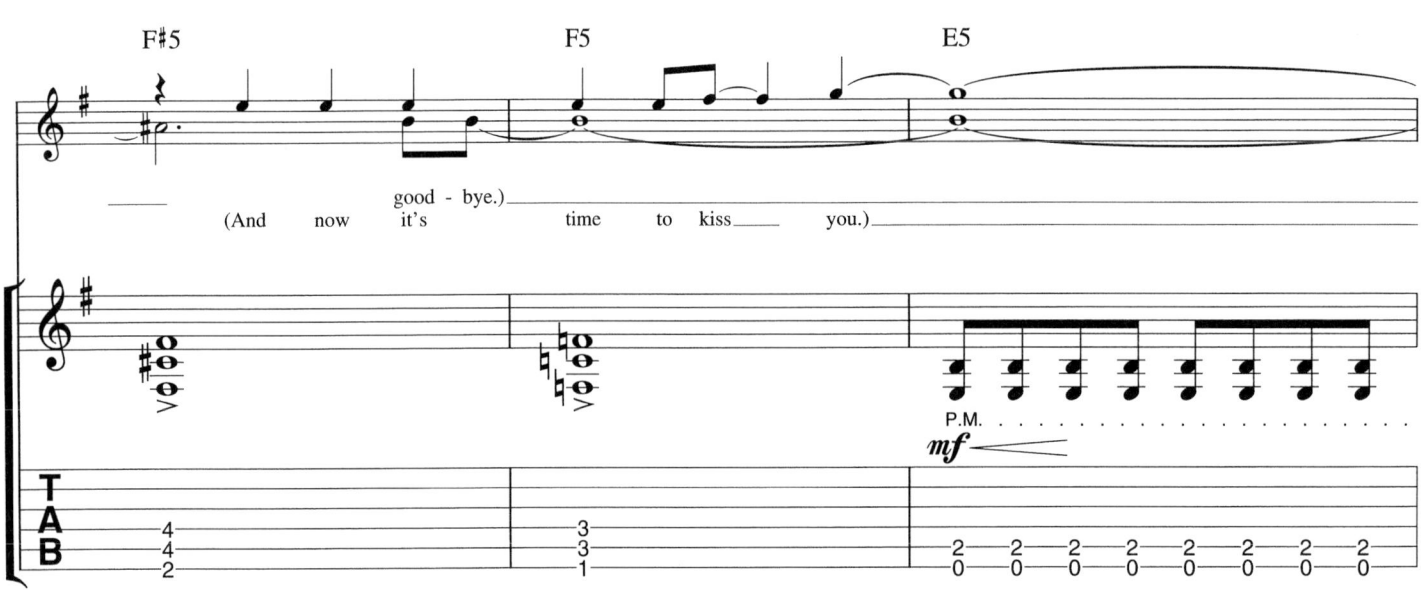
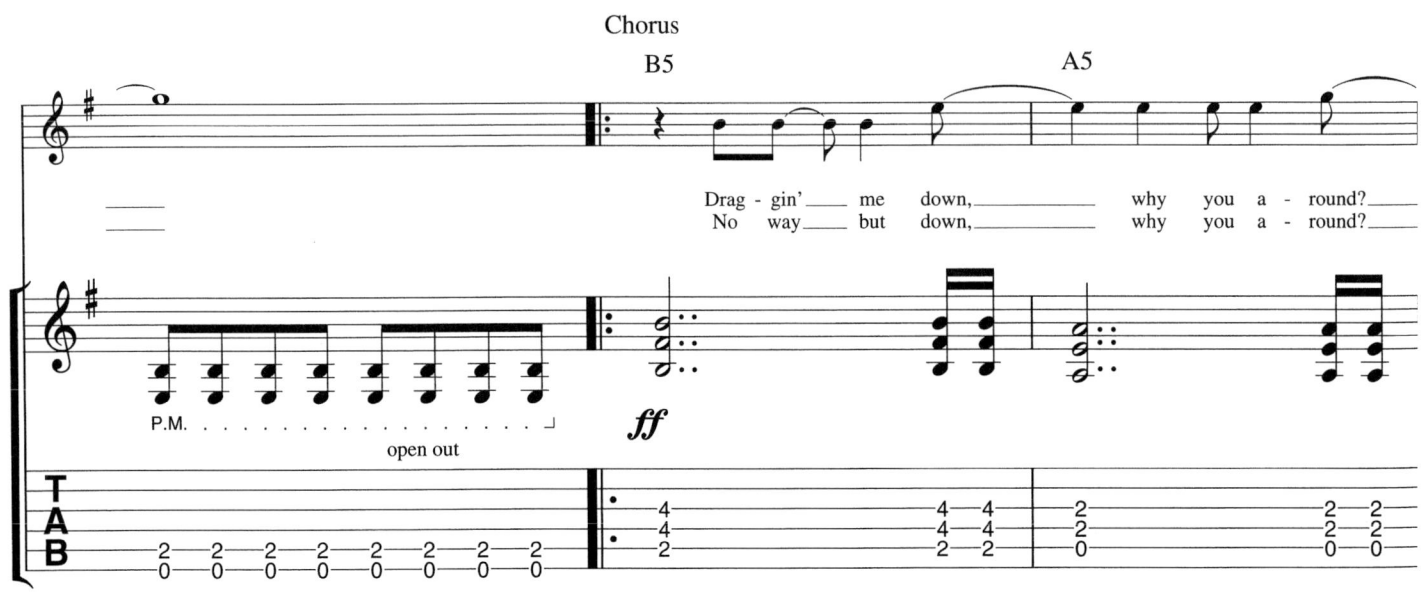

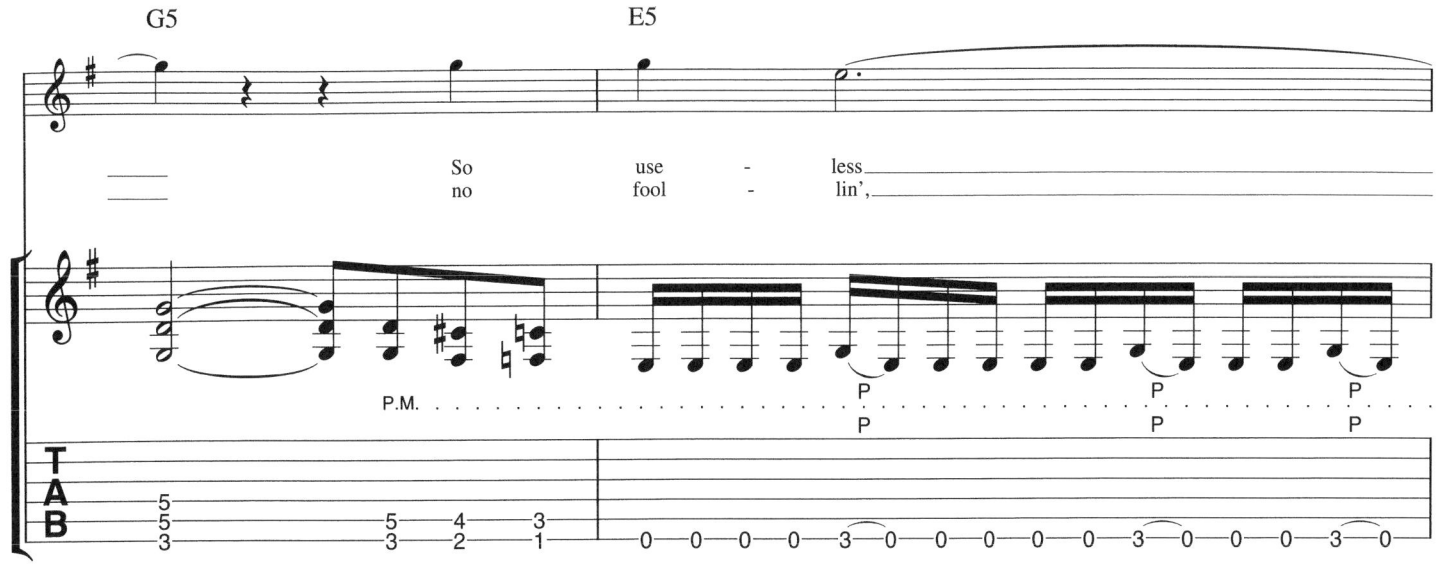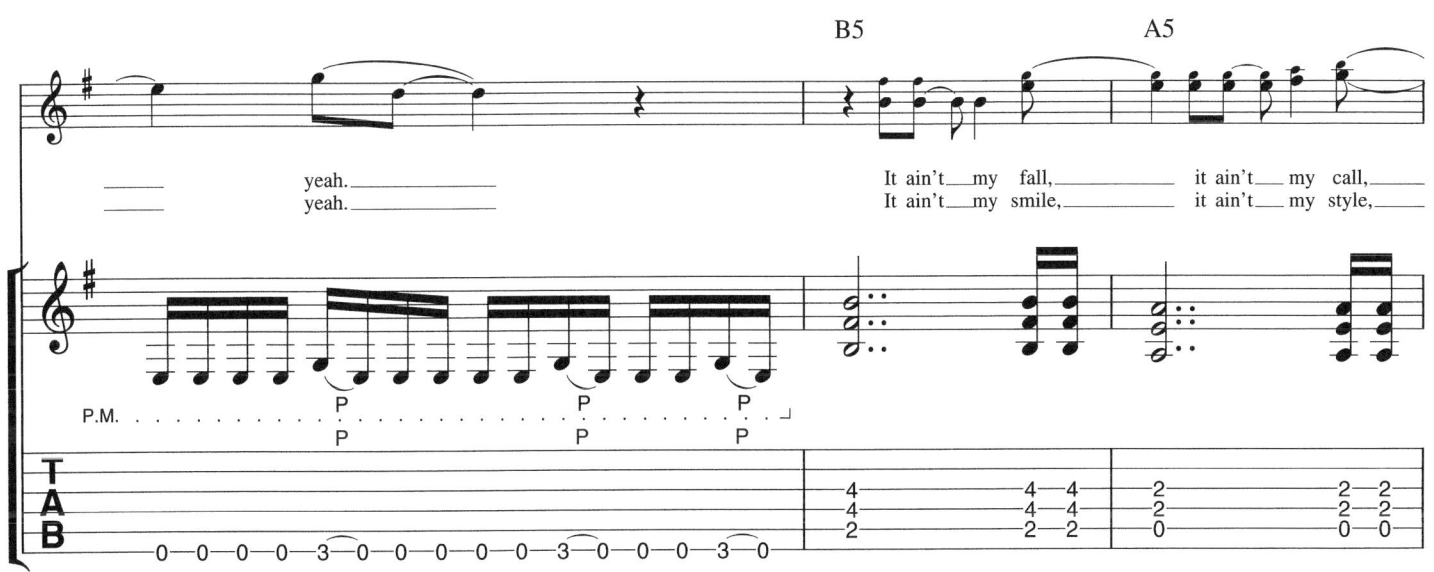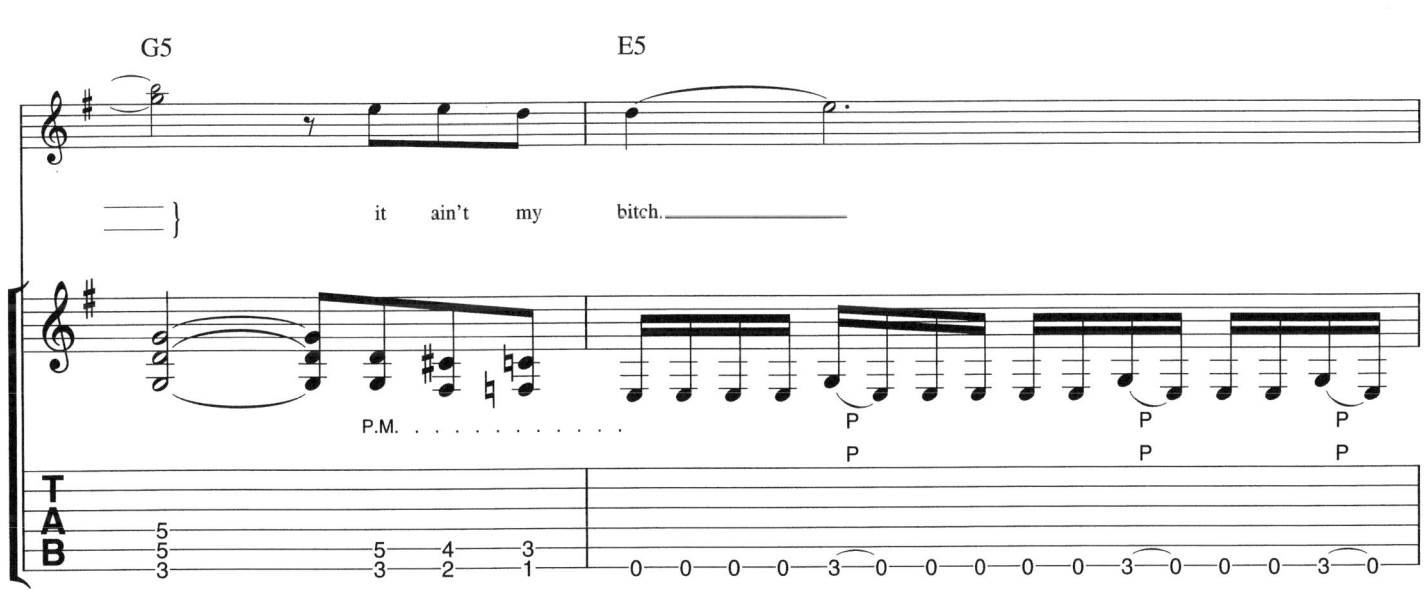

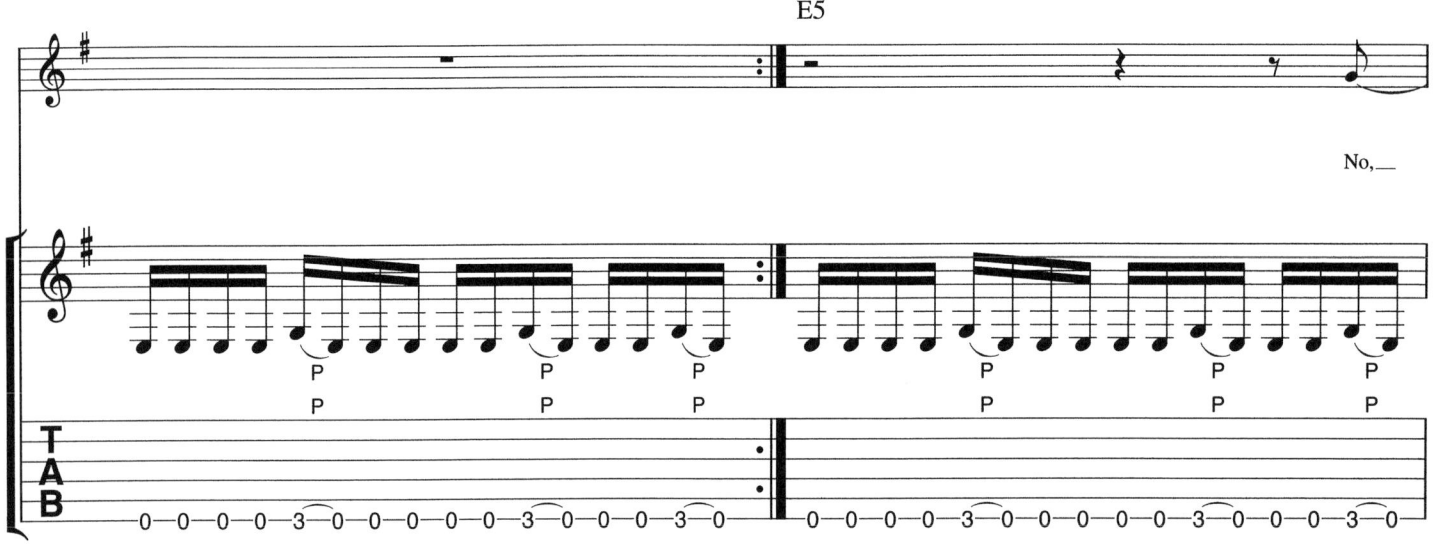
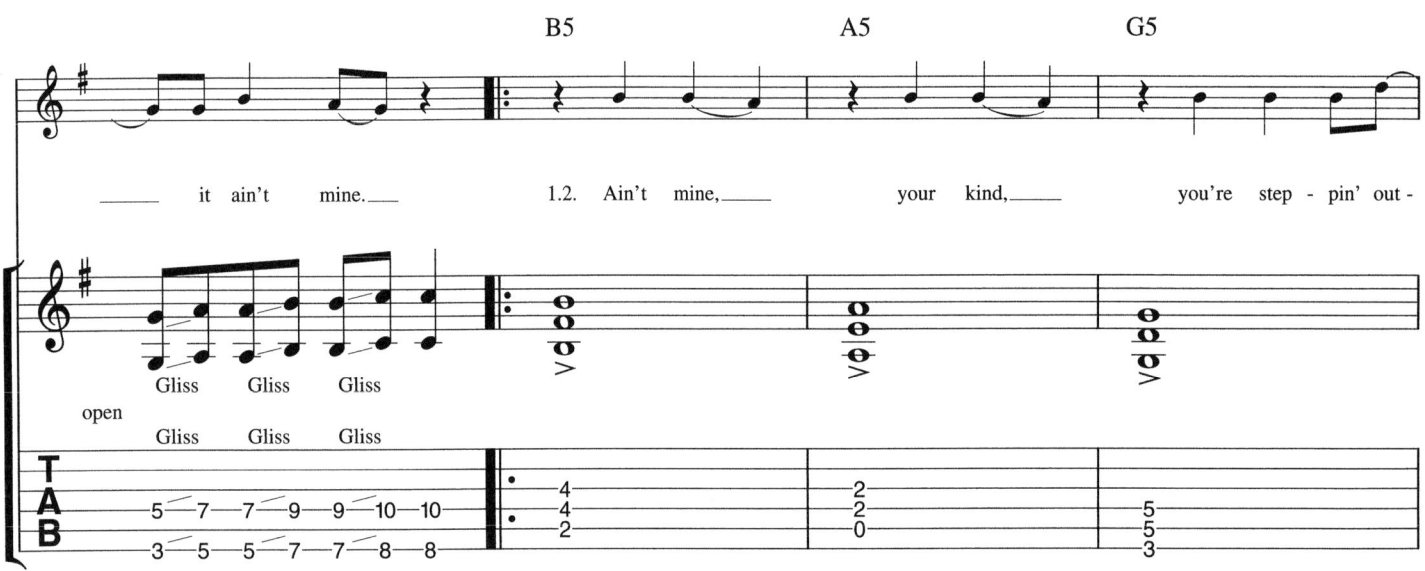
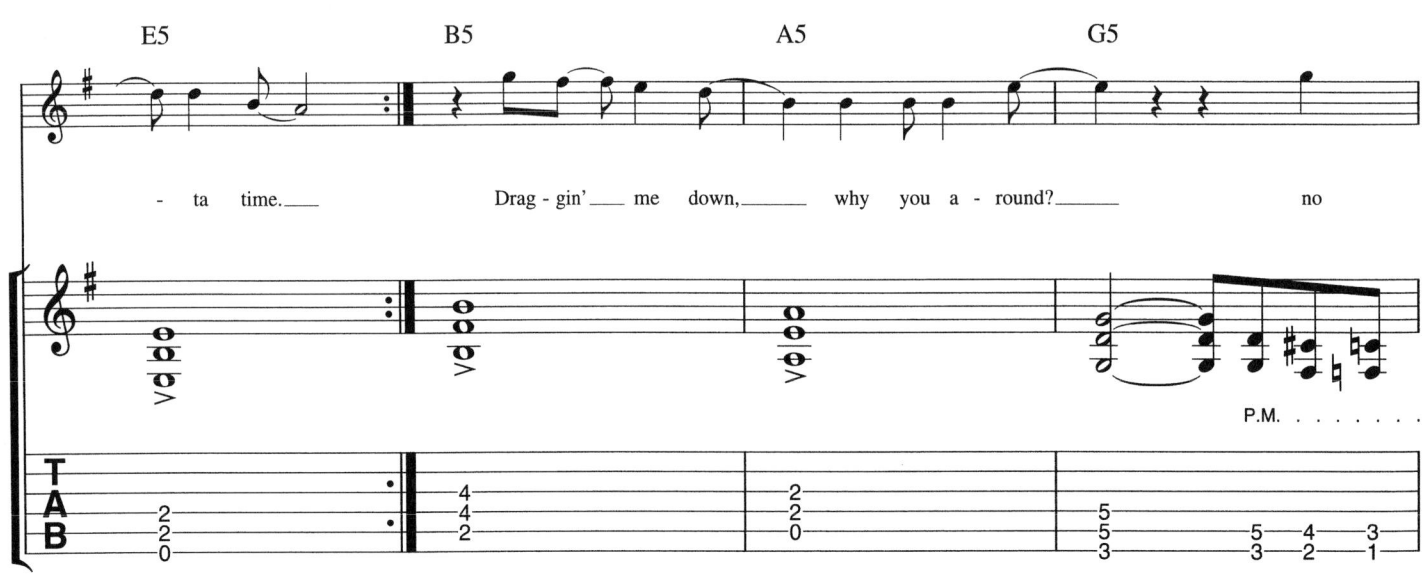

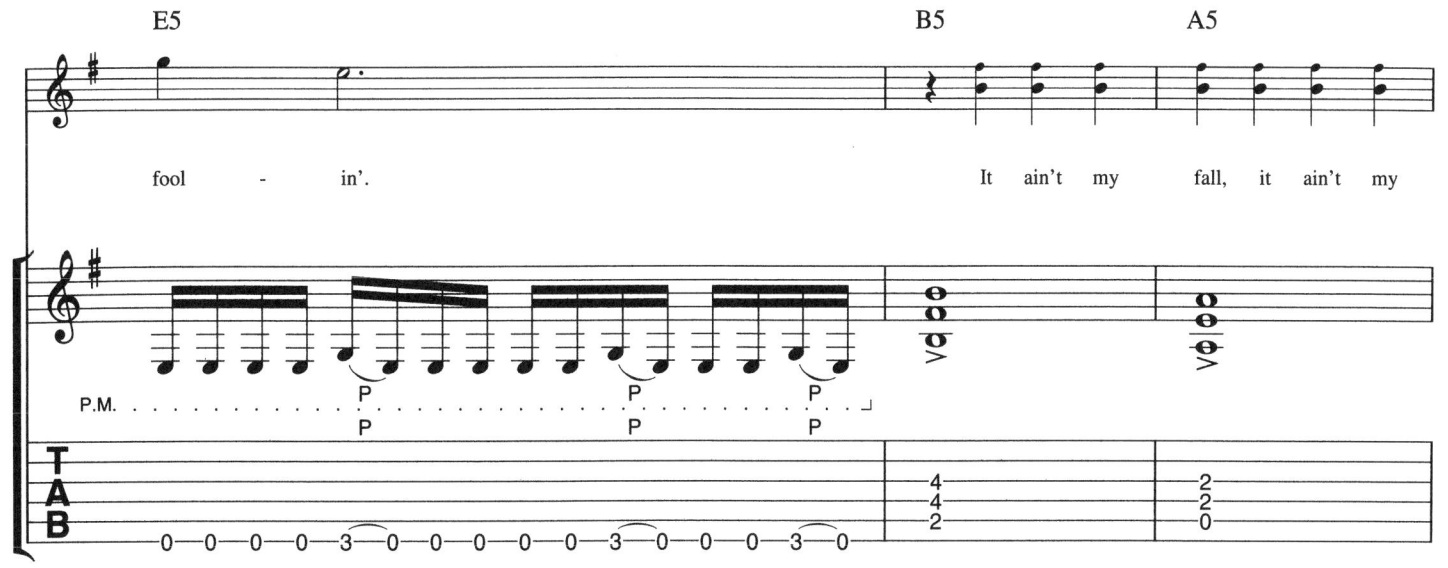
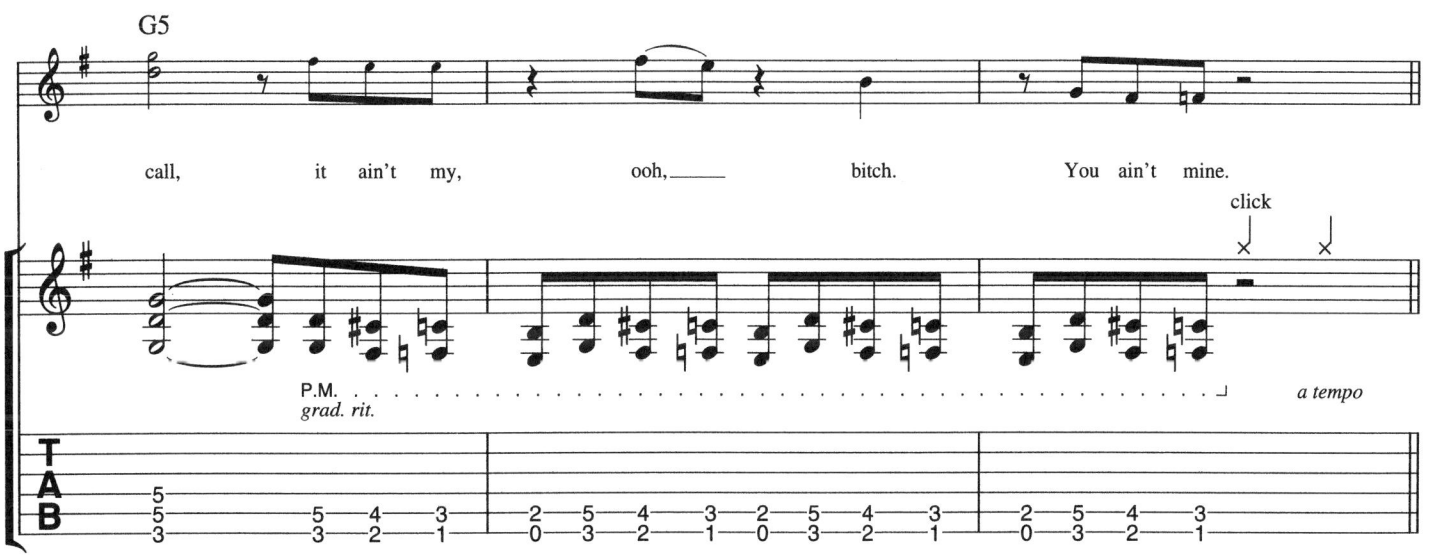

enter sandman

Words & Music by James Hetfield, Lars Ulrich & Kirk Hammett

© Copyright 1991 Creeping Death Music, USA.
PolyGram Music Publishing Limited, 47 British Grove, London W4.
All Rights Reserved. International Copyright Secured.

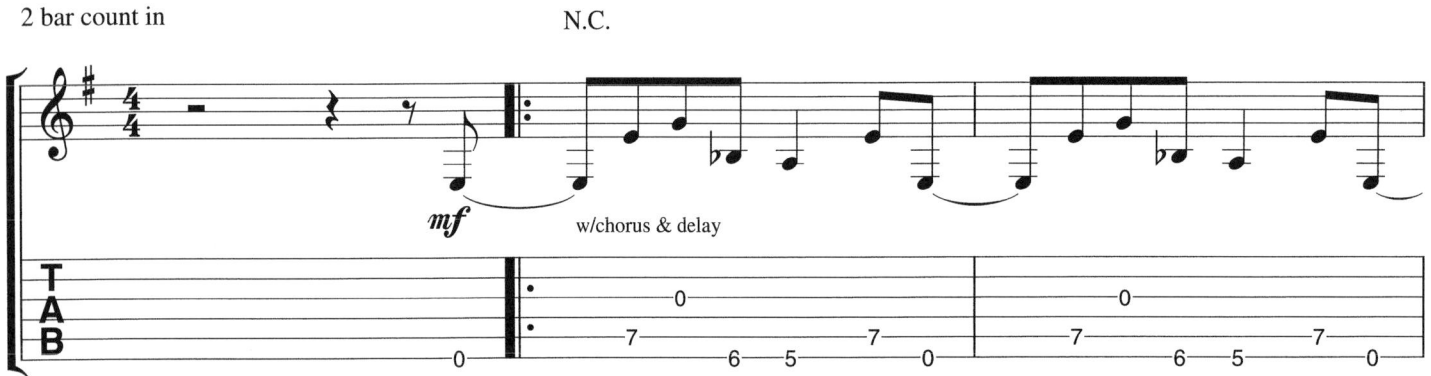

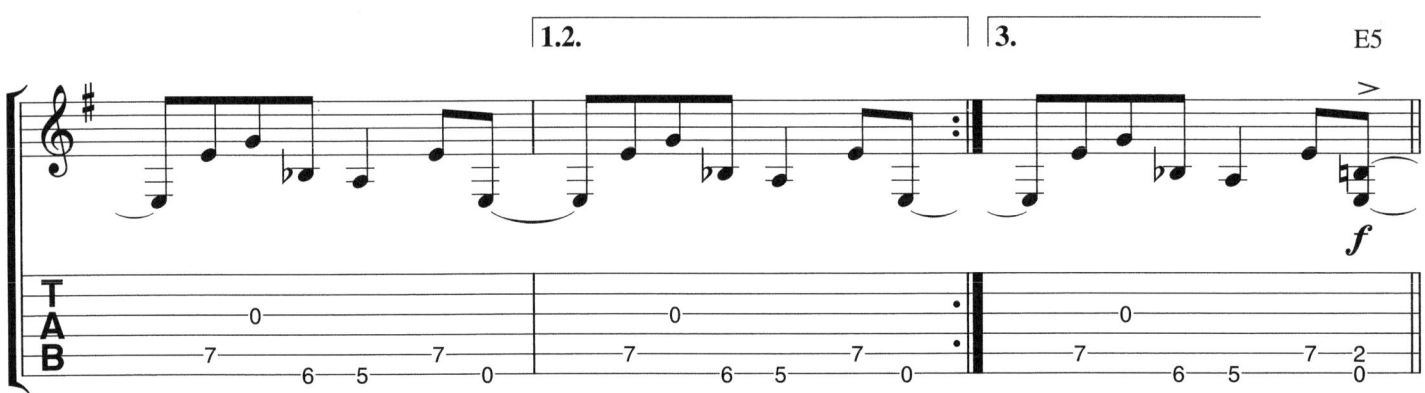

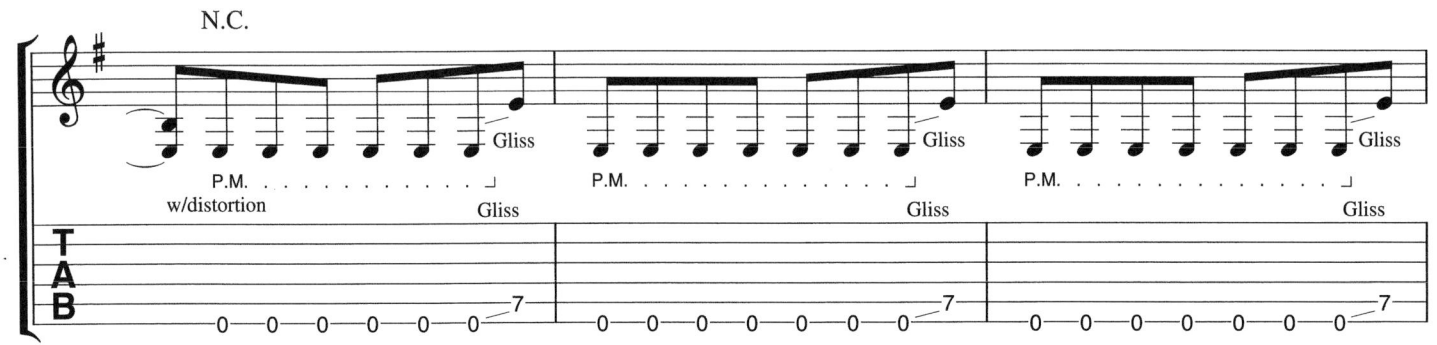

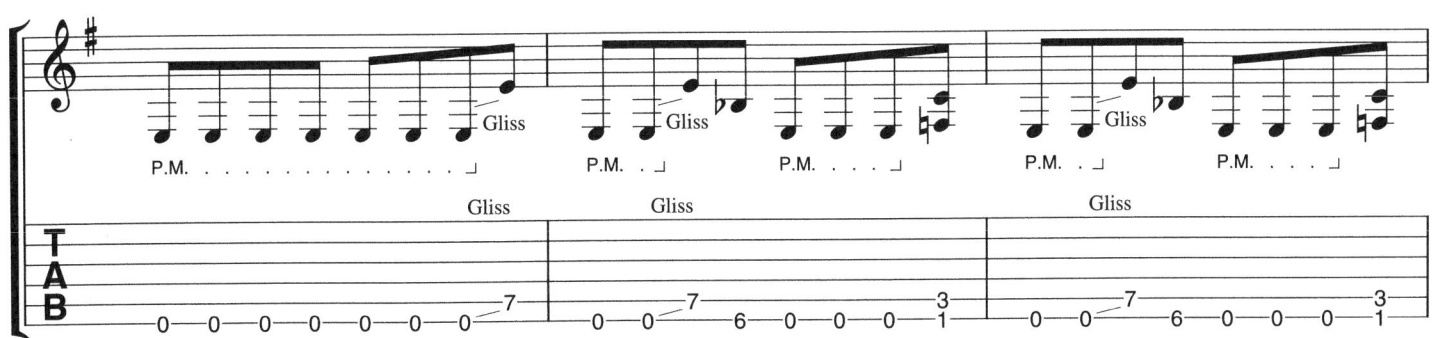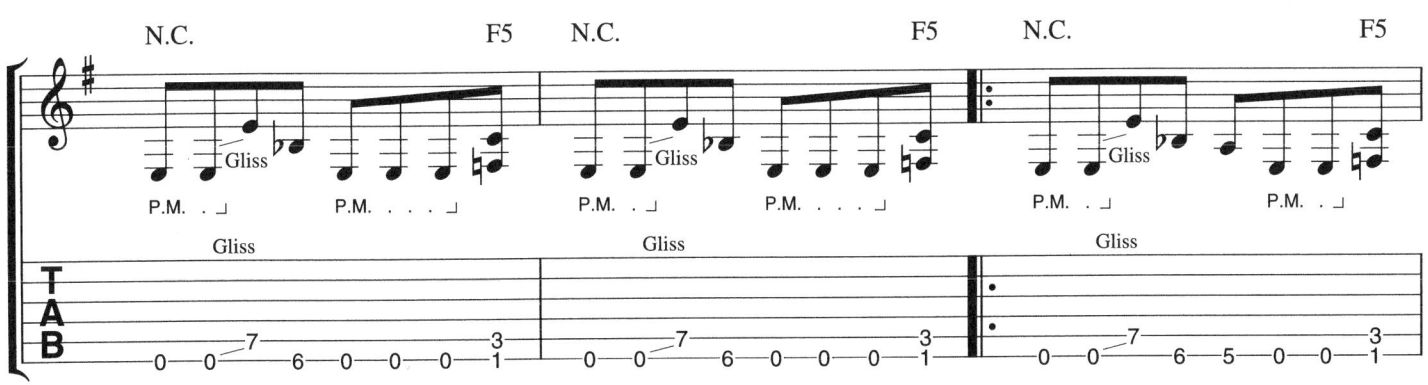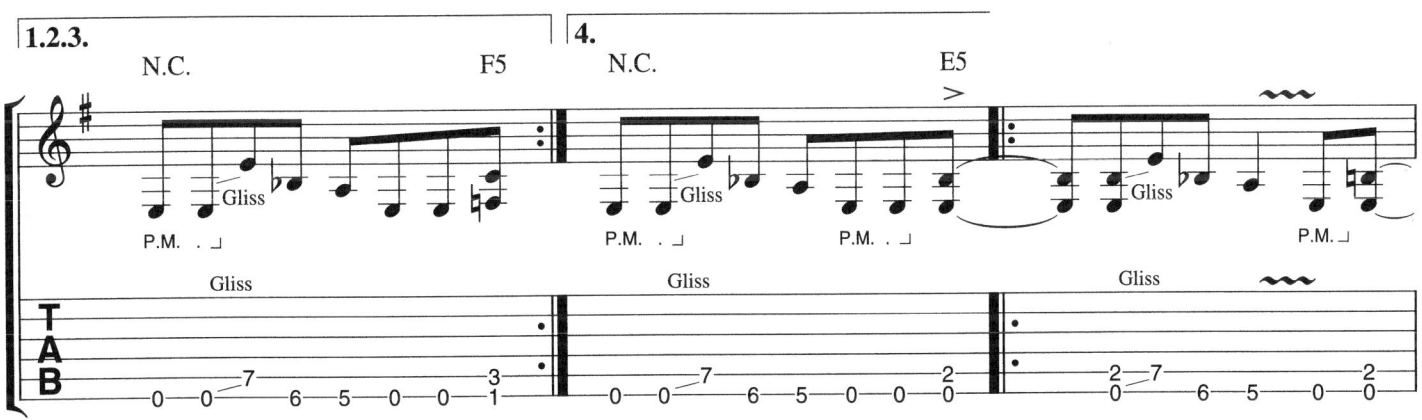

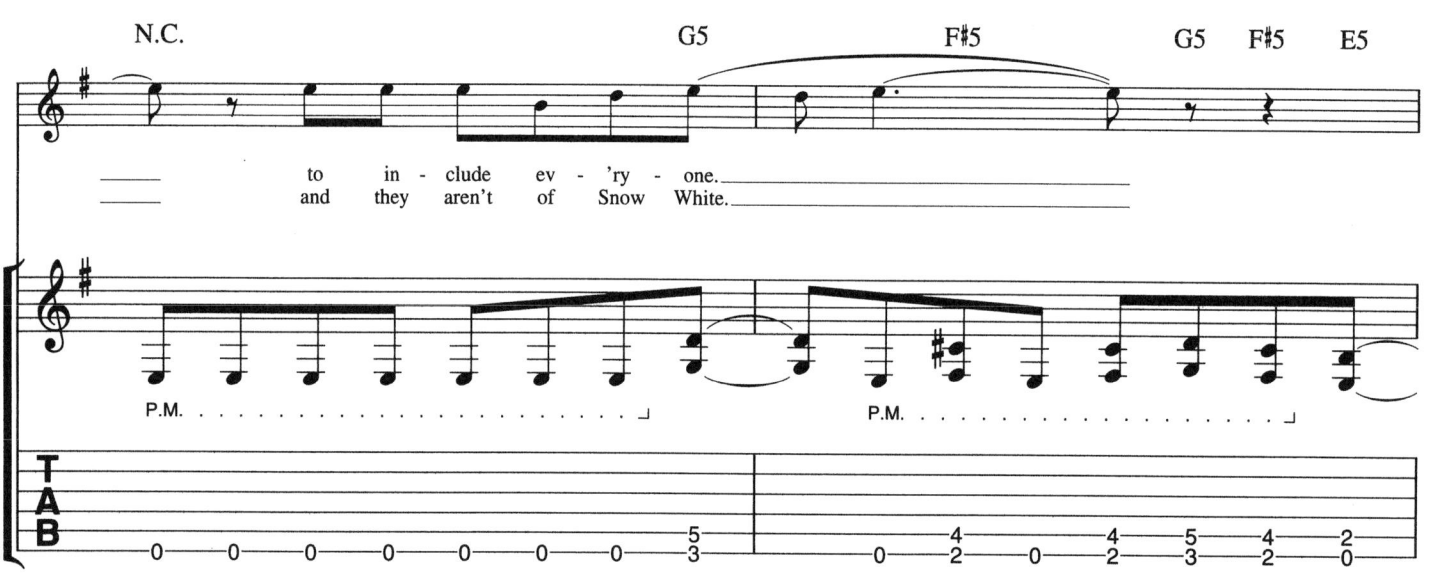

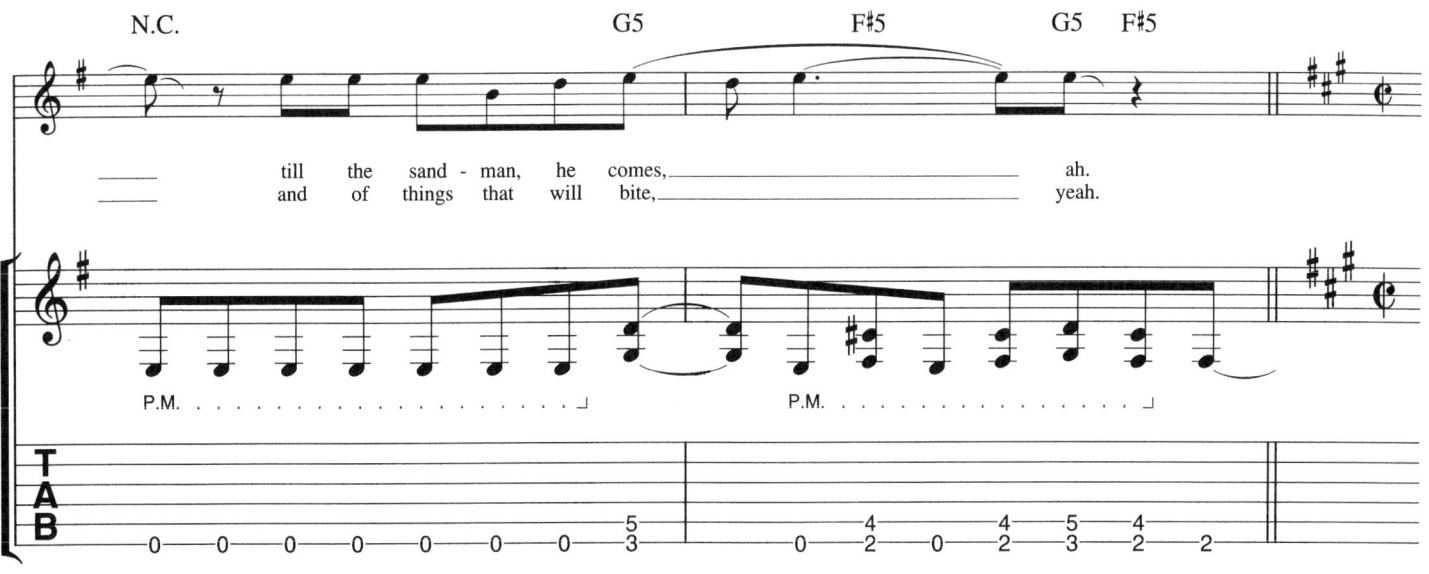
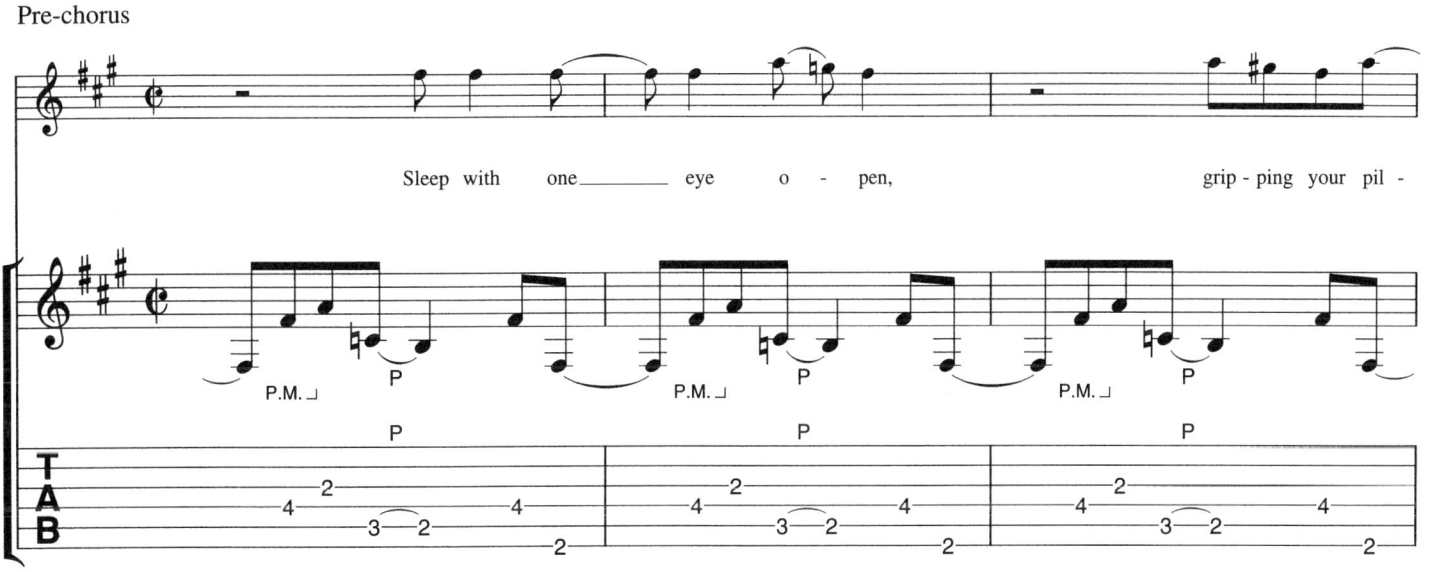
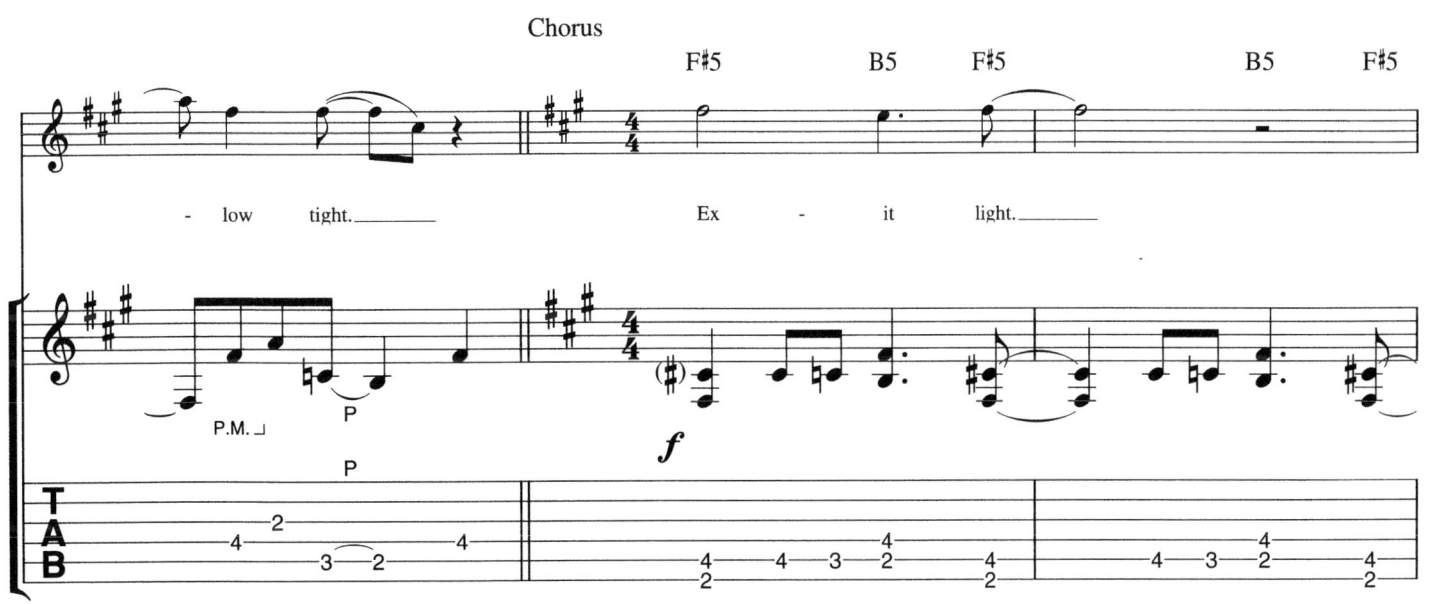

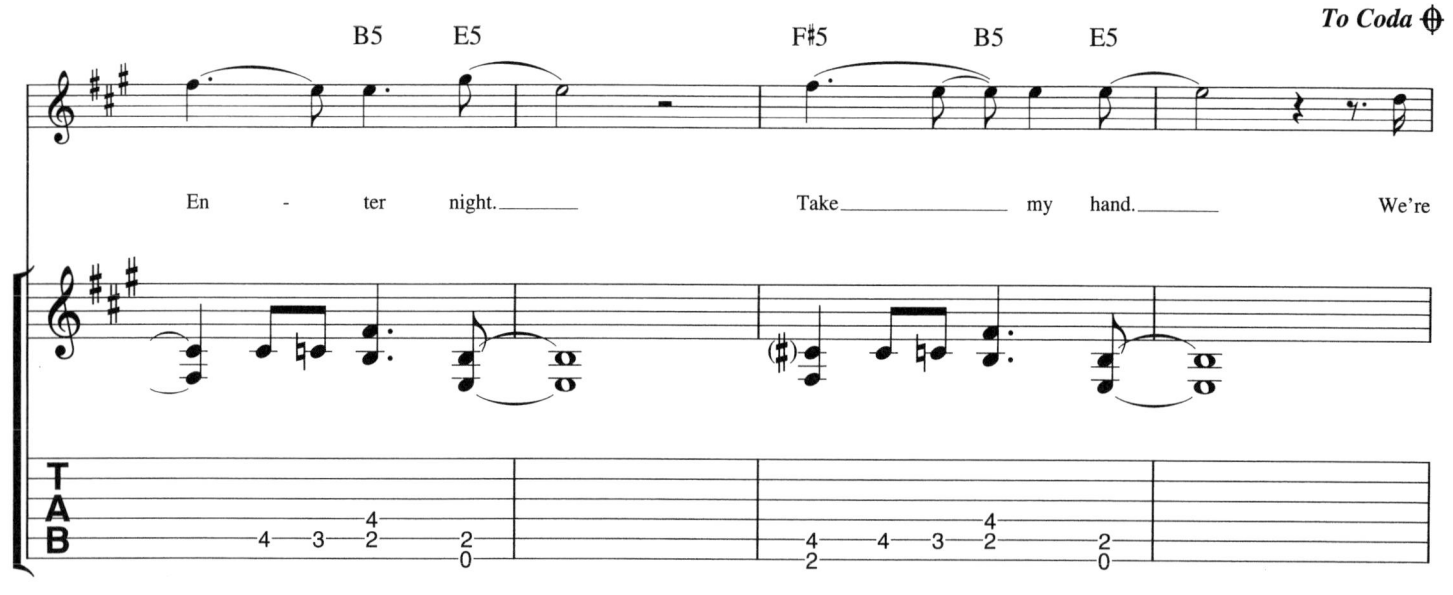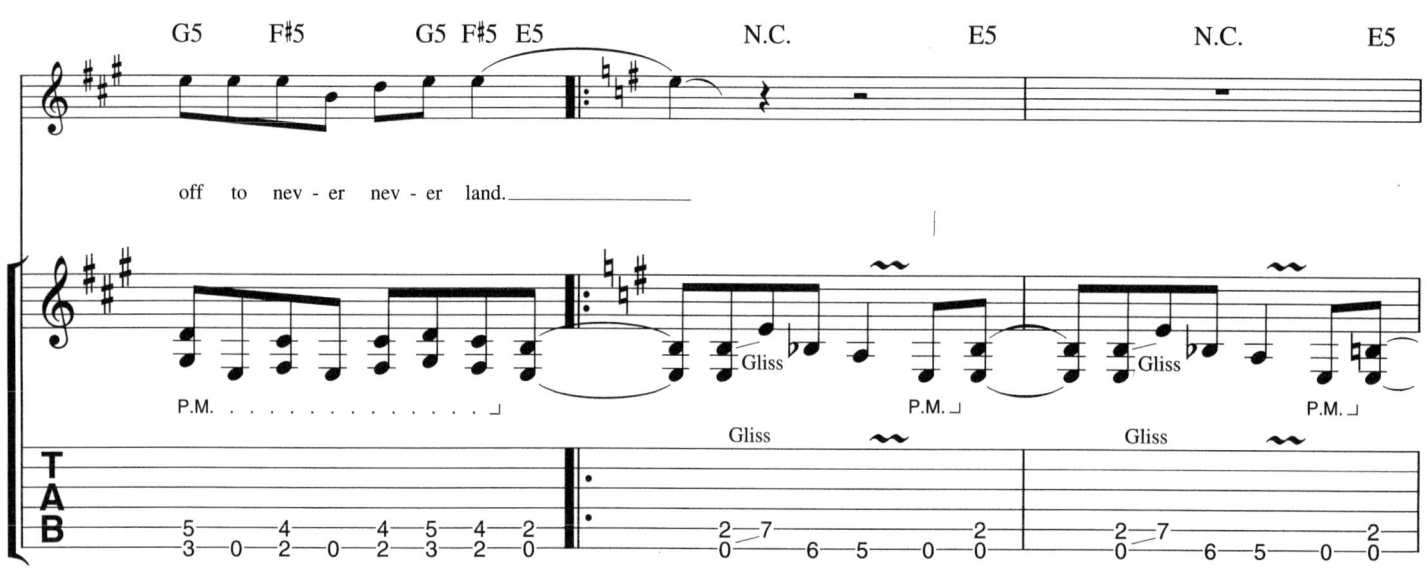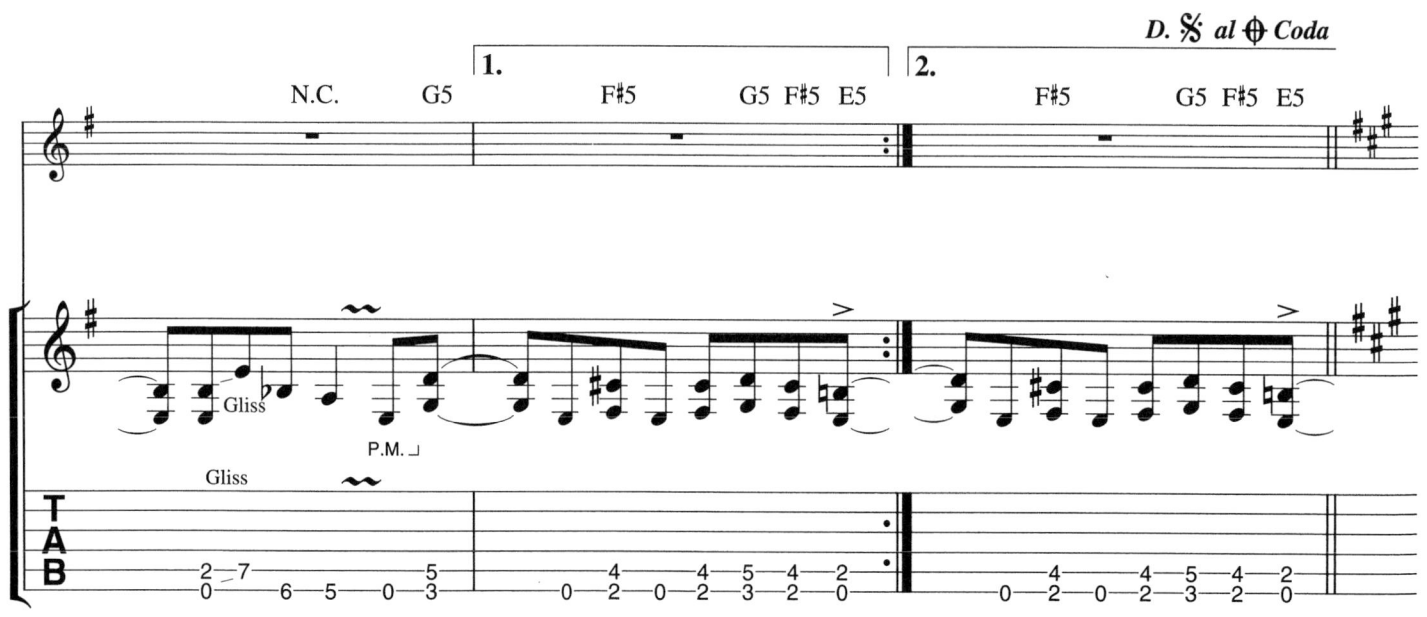

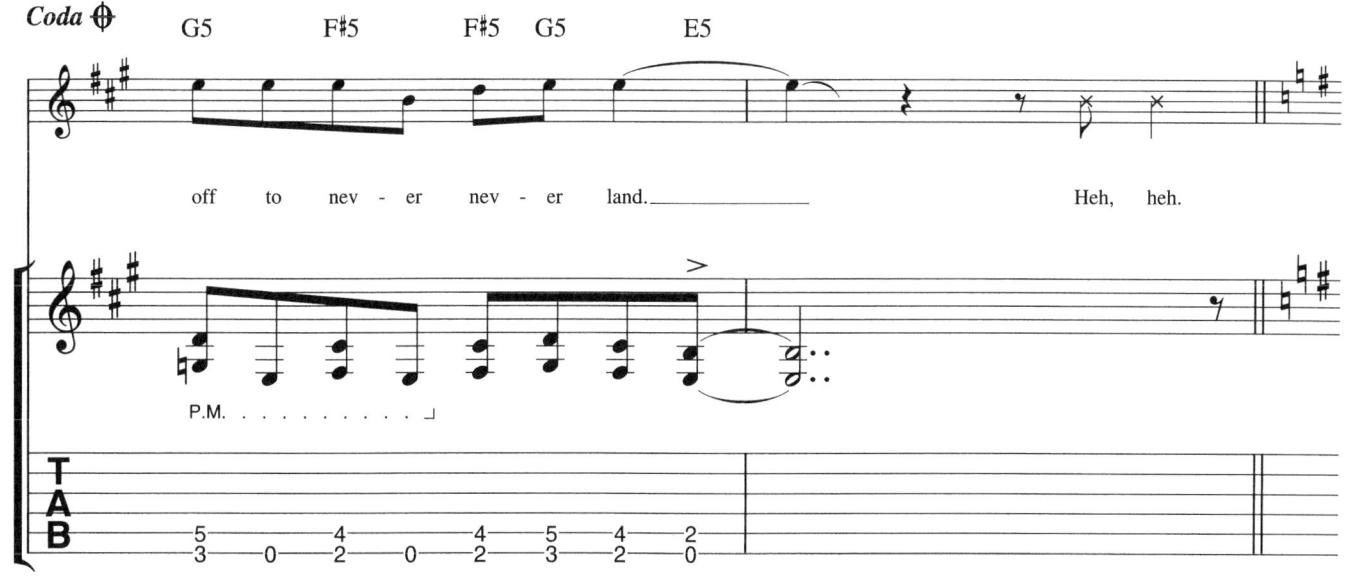
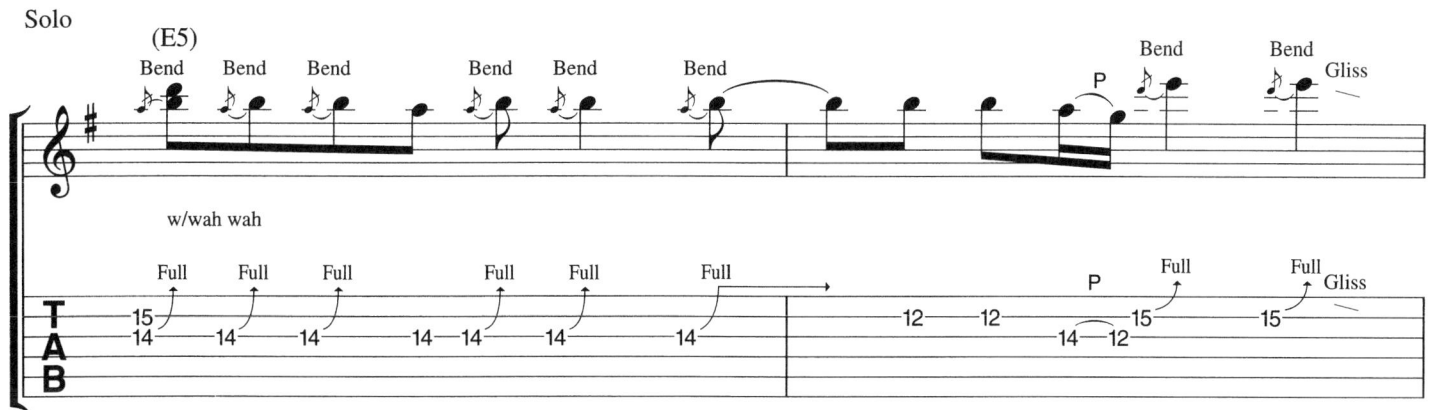
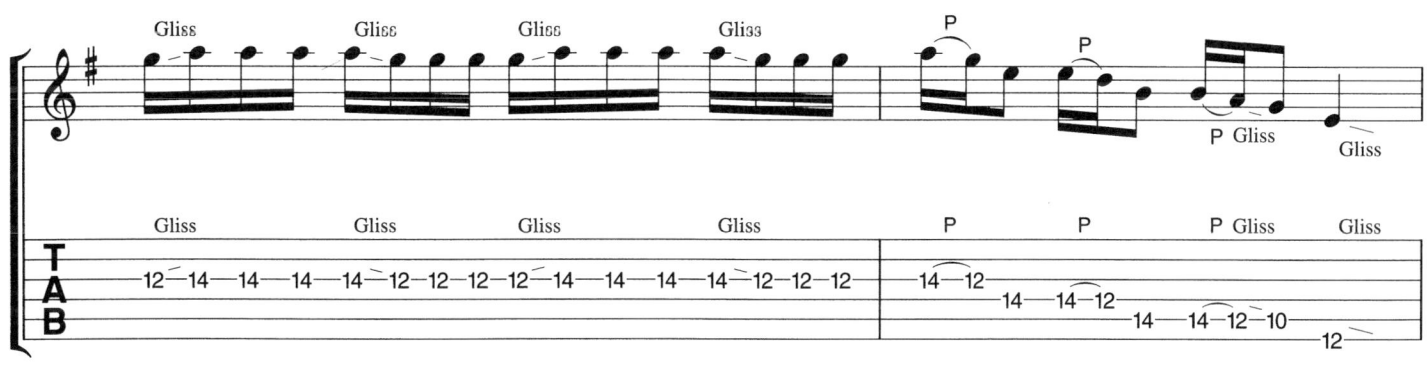
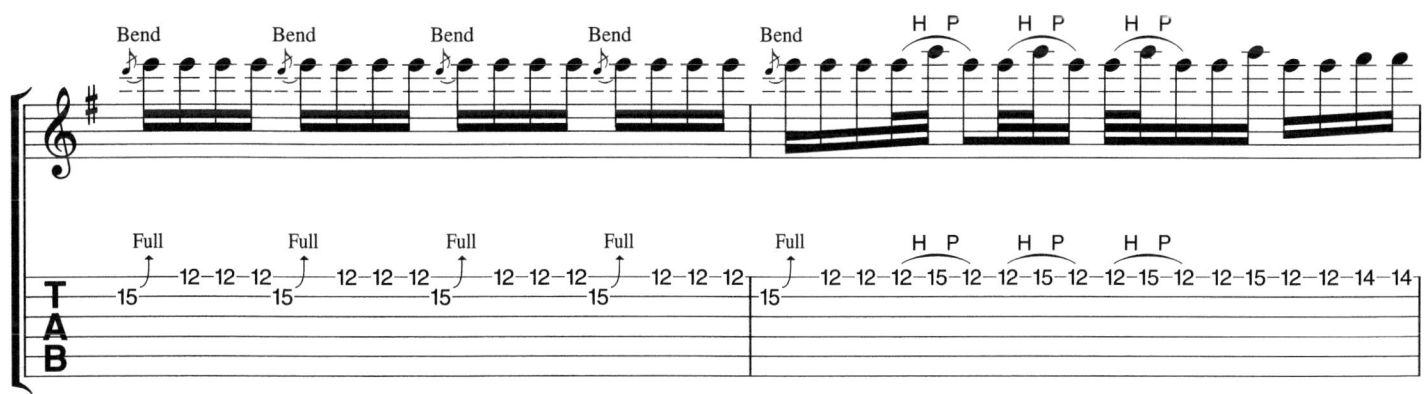

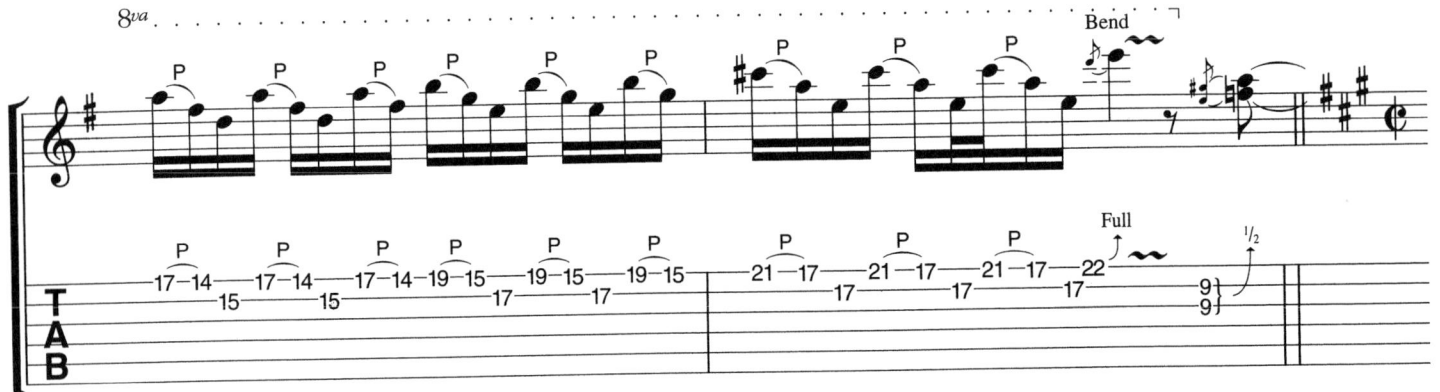
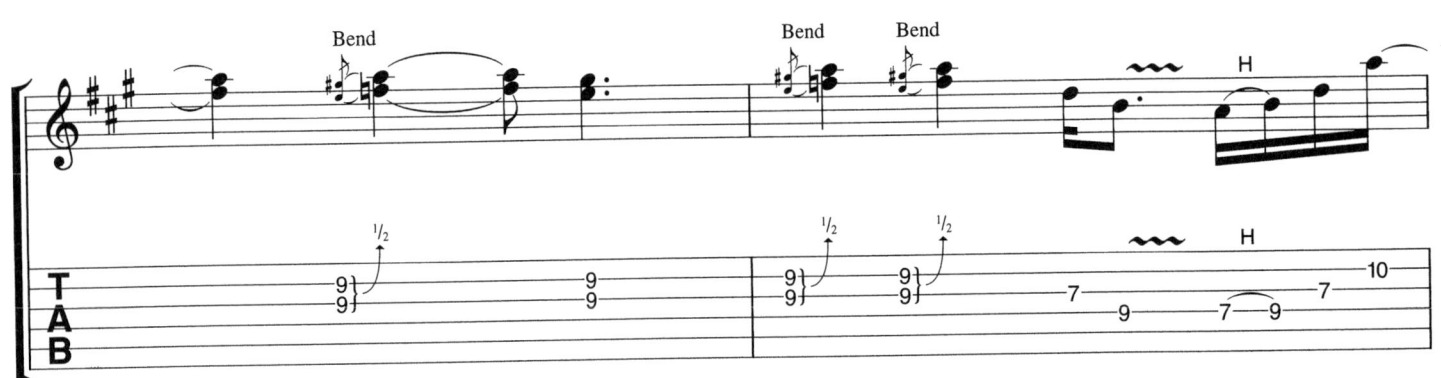
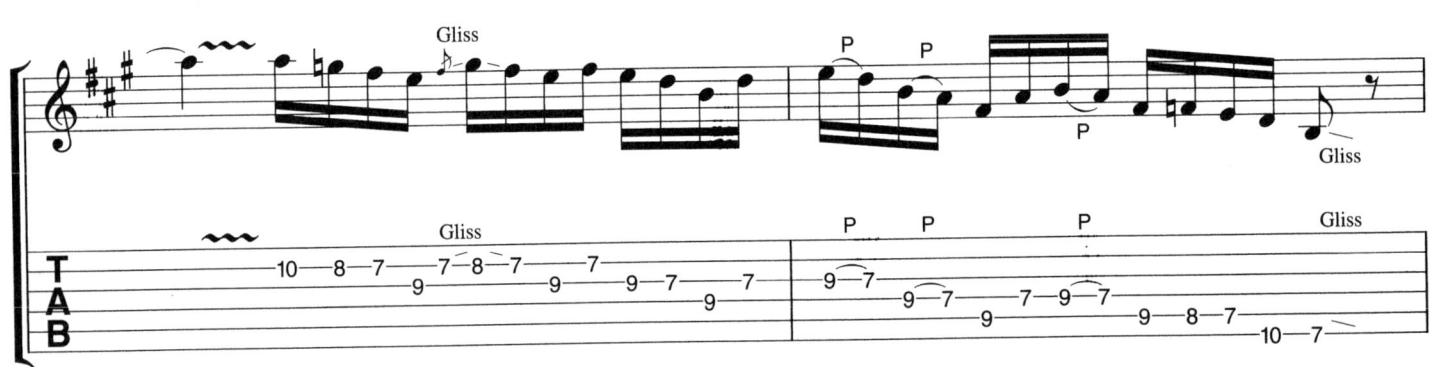
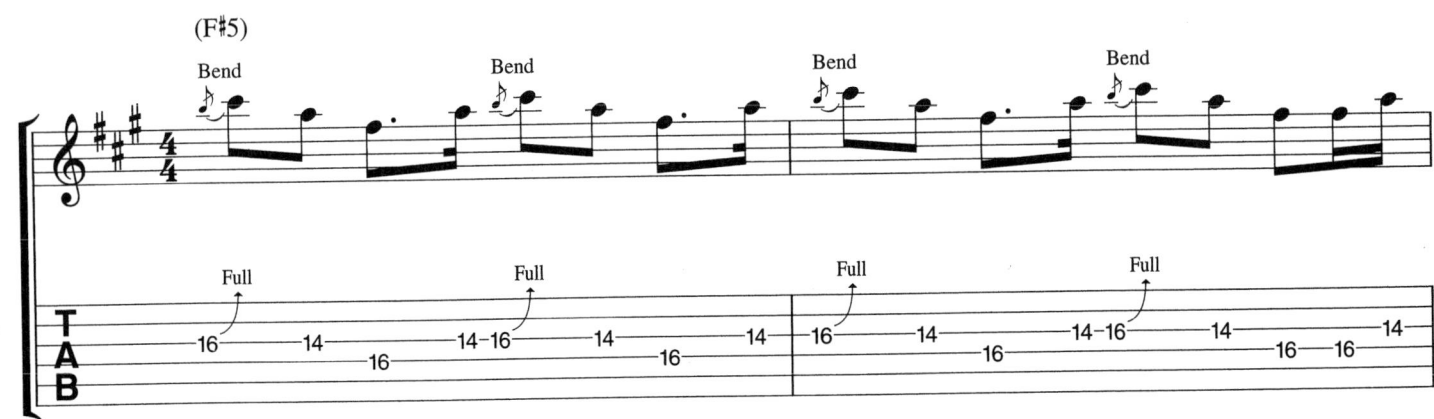

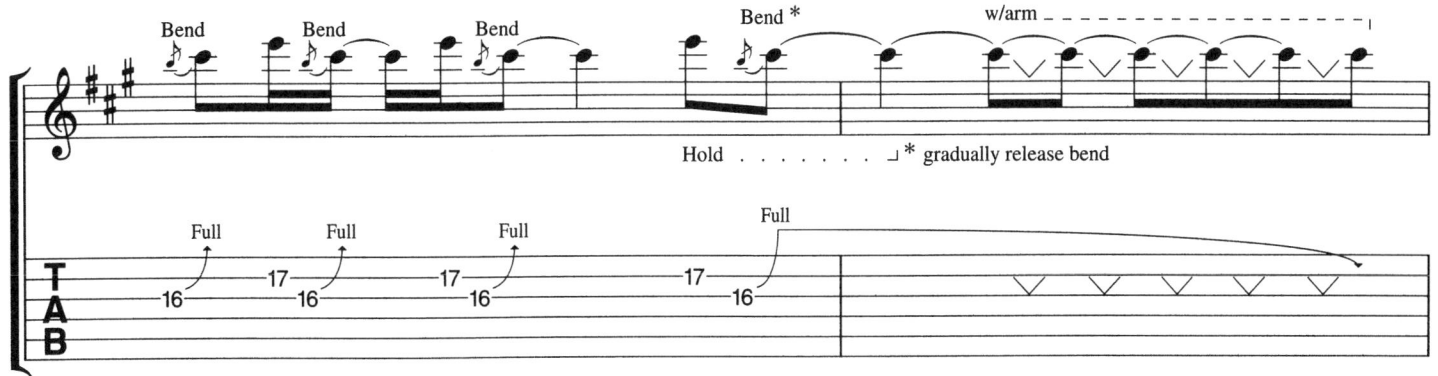
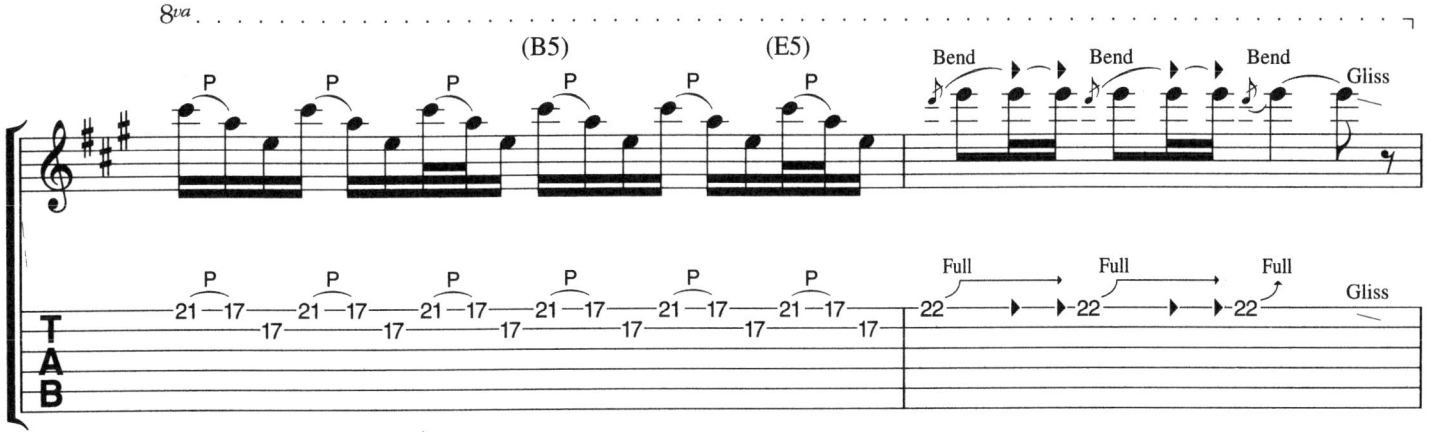
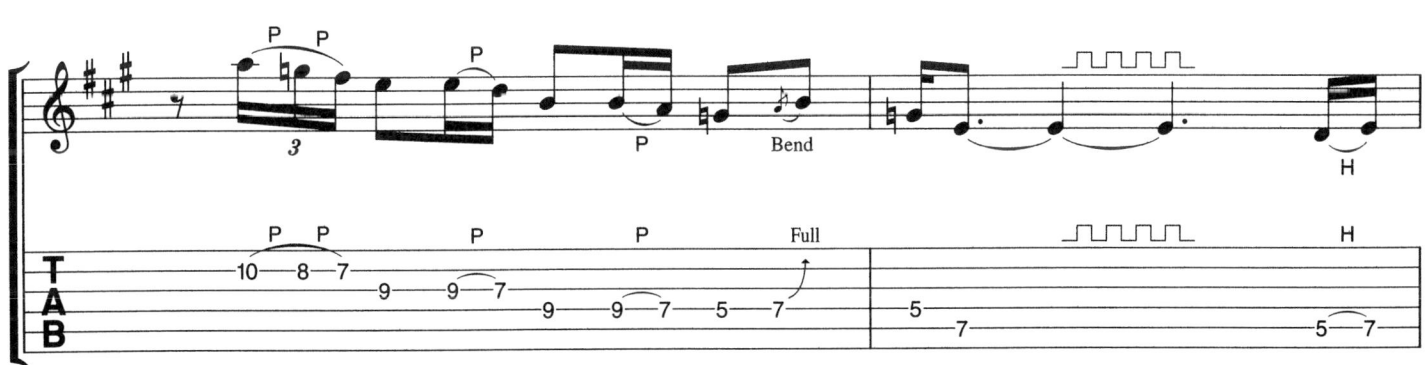

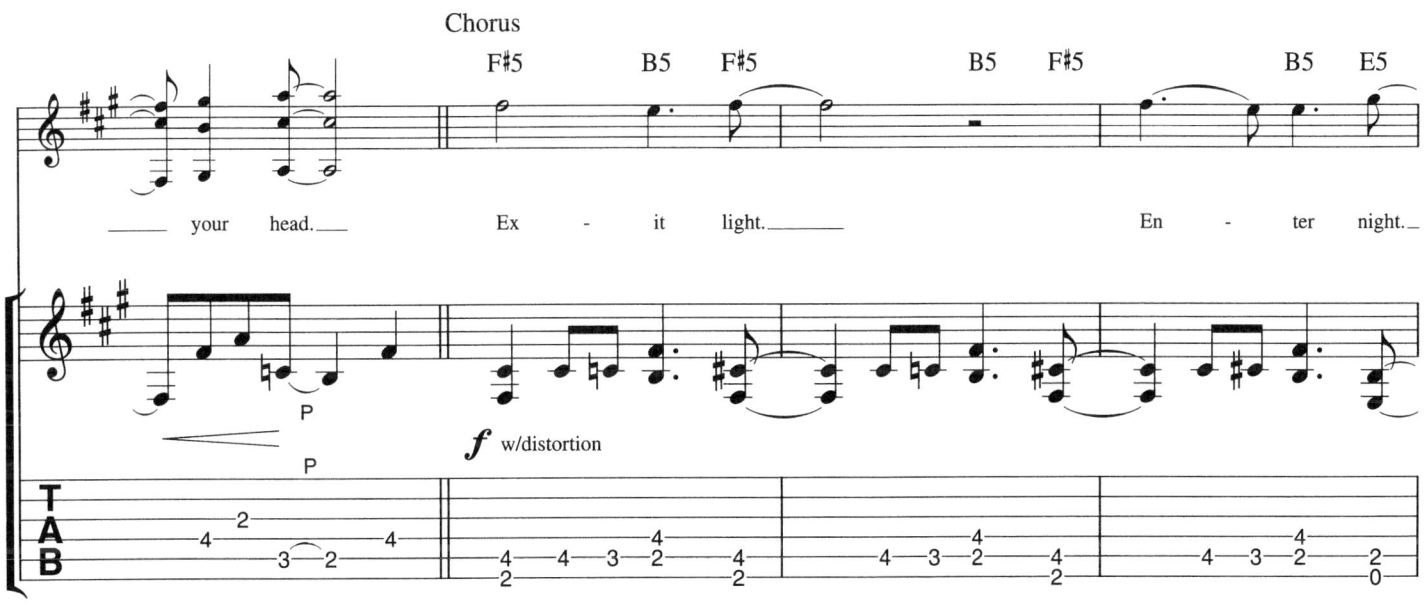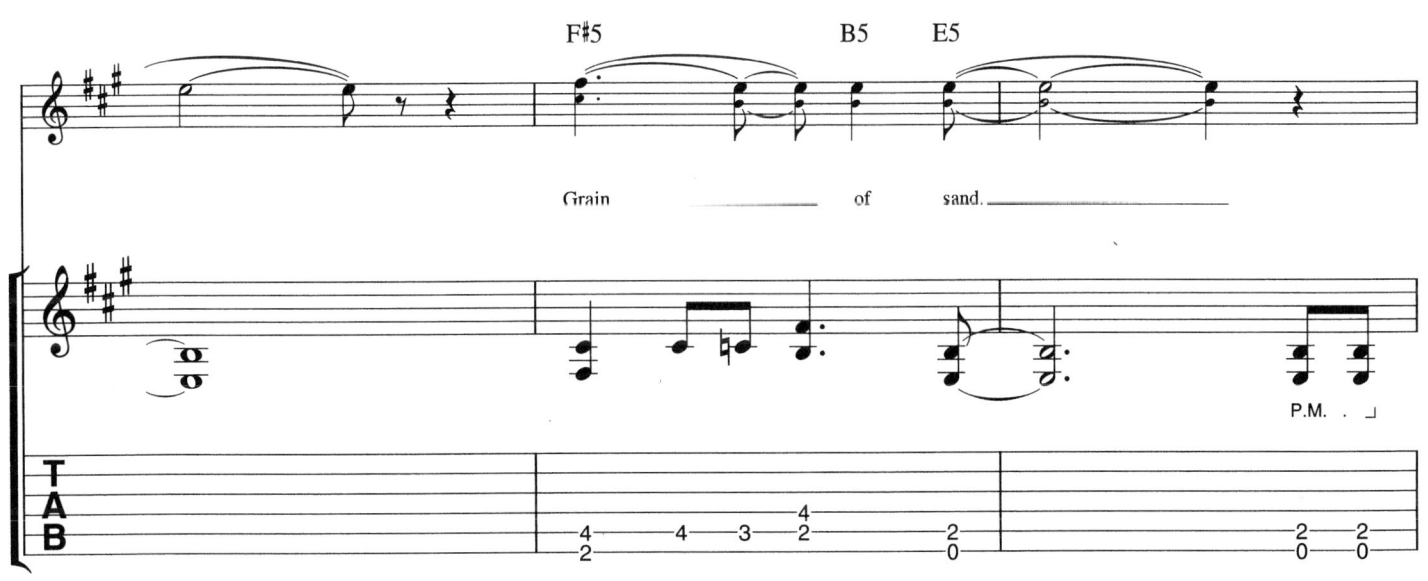

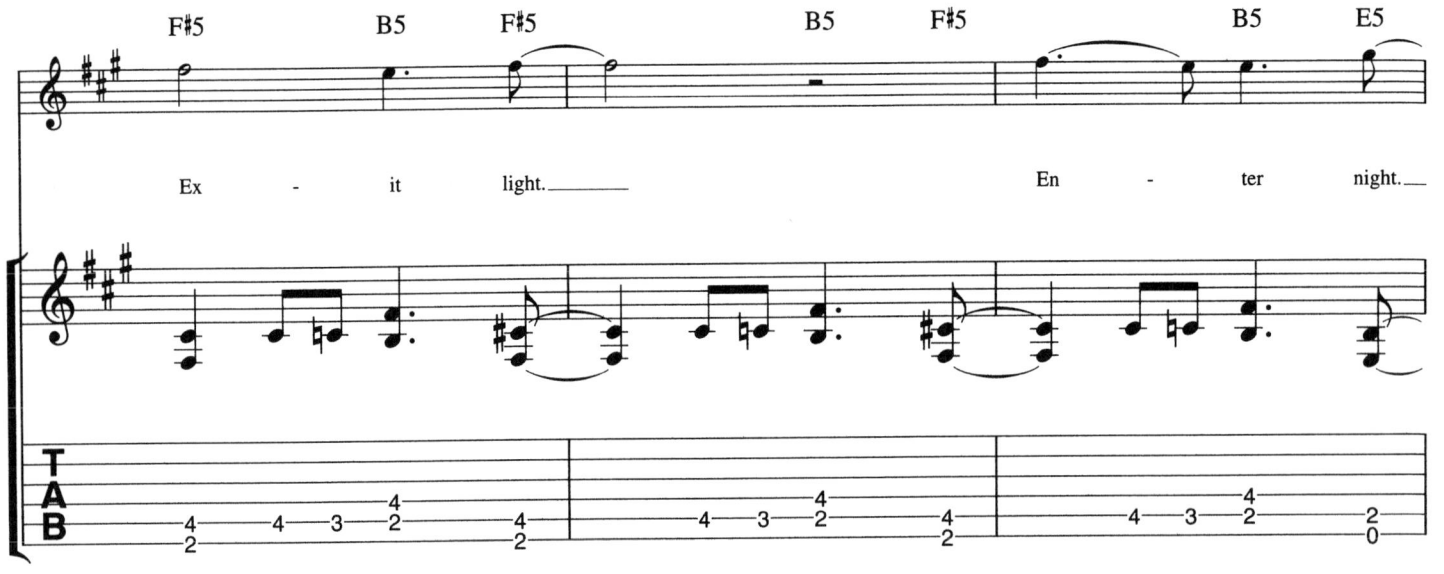
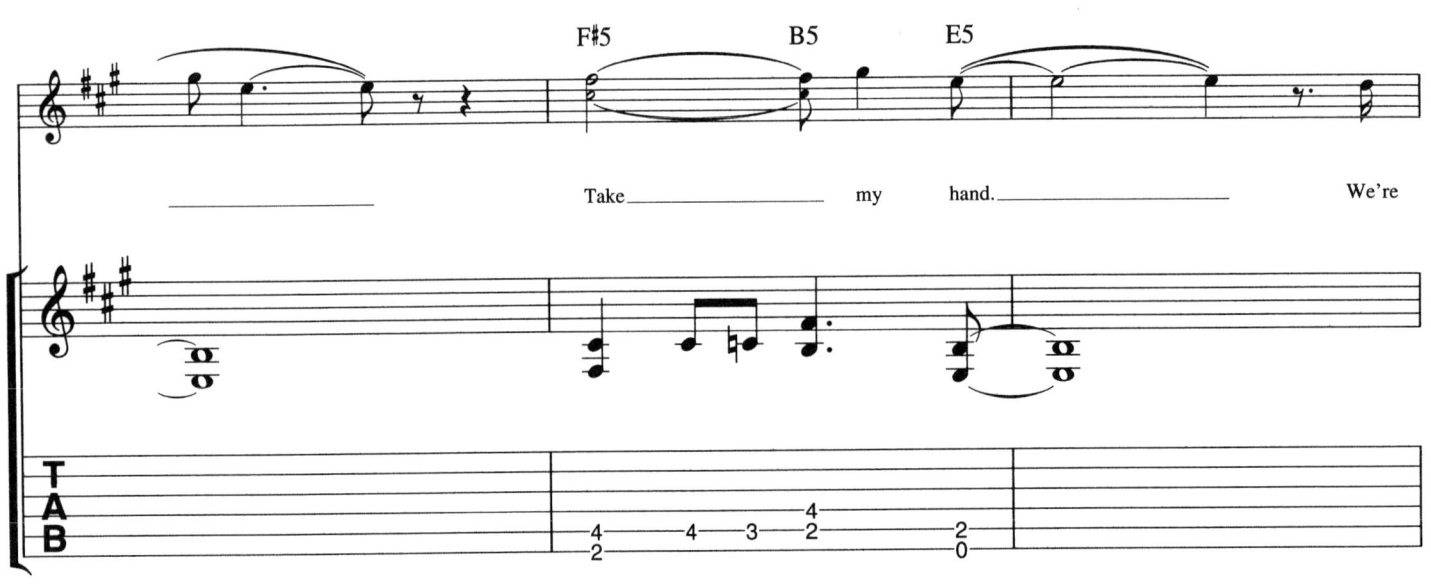
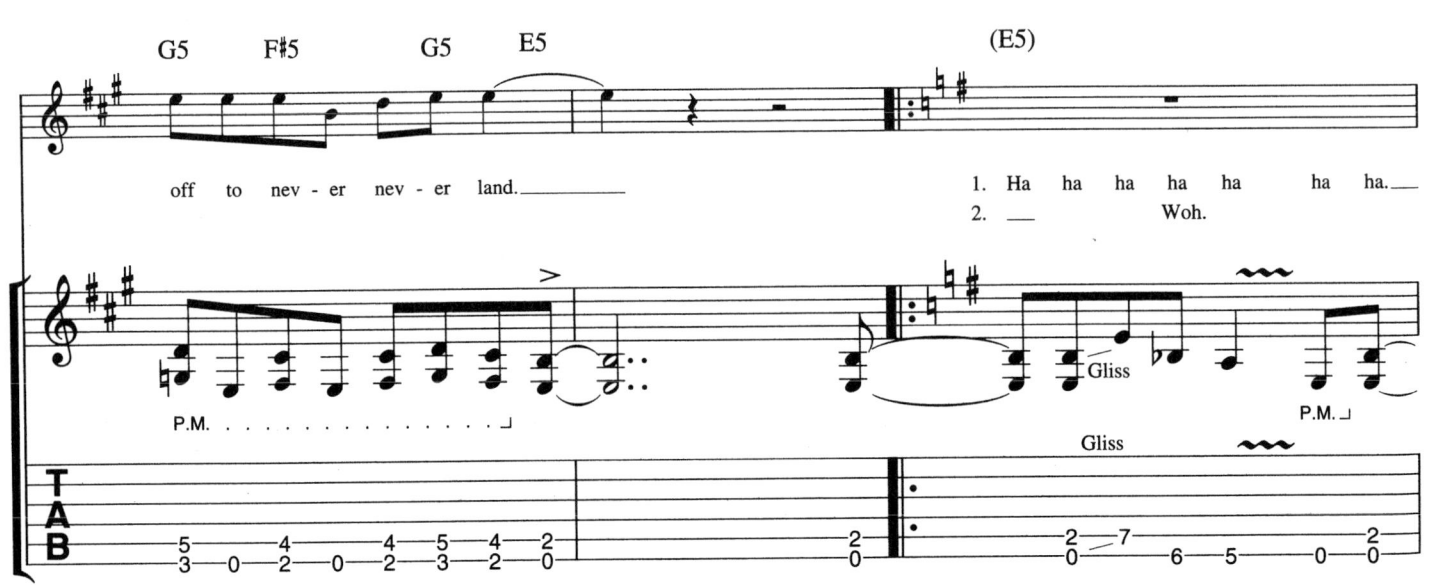

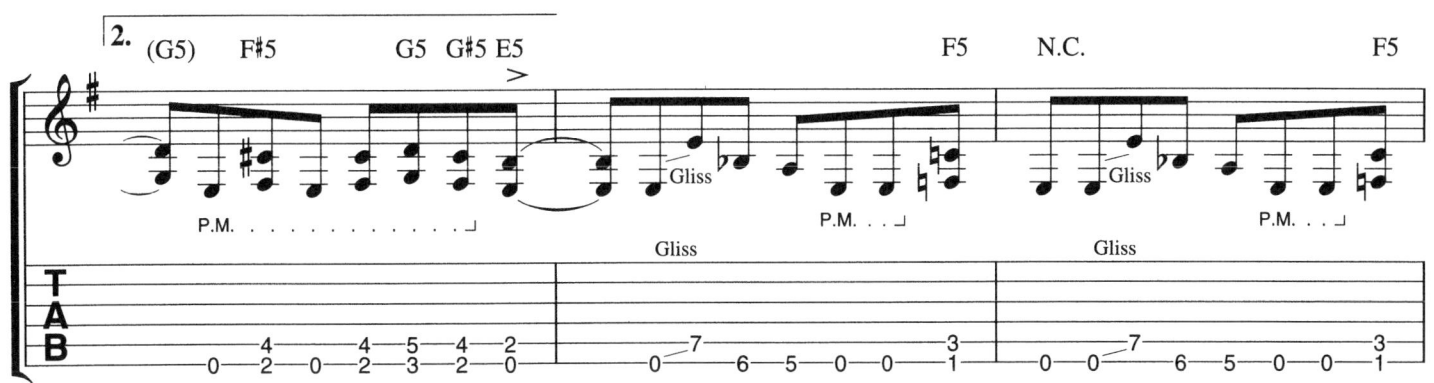
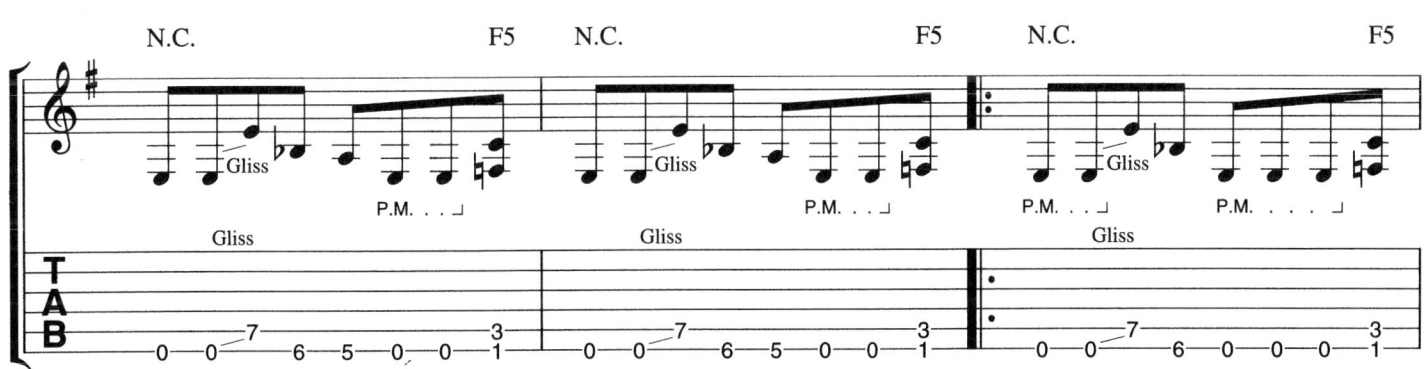
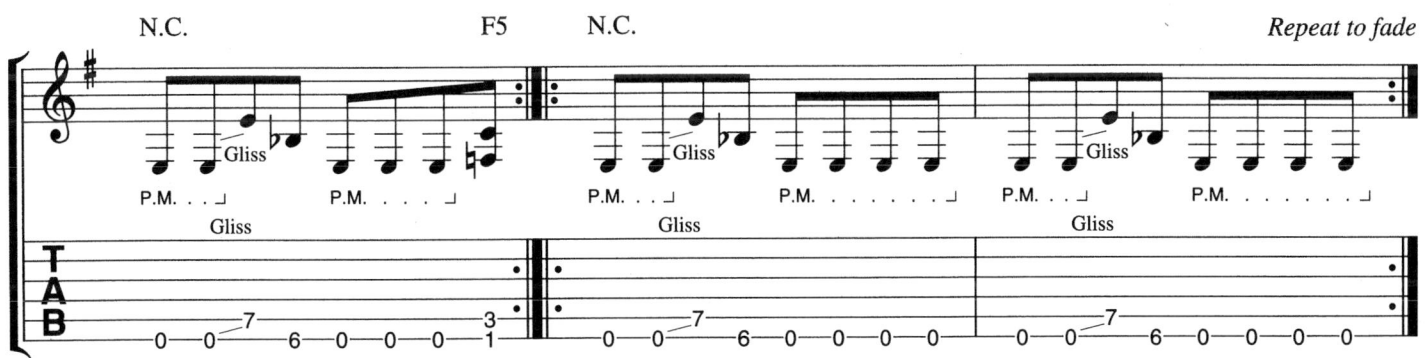

fade to black

Words & Music by James Hetfield, Lars Ulrich, Cliff Burton & Kirk Hammett

© Copyright 1984 Creeping Death Music, USA.
PolyGram Music Publishing Limited, 47 British Grove, London W4.
All Rights Reserved. International Copyright Secured.

2 bar count in

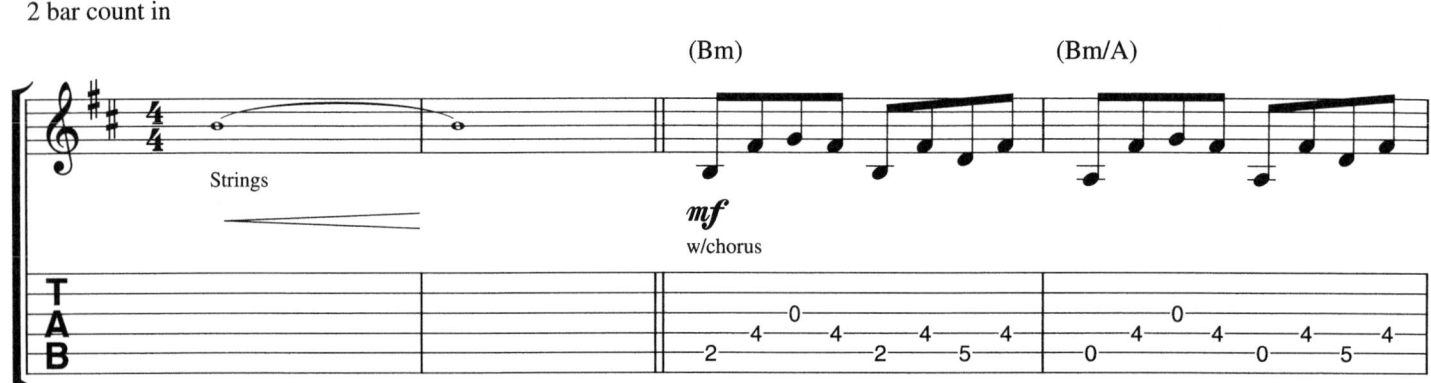

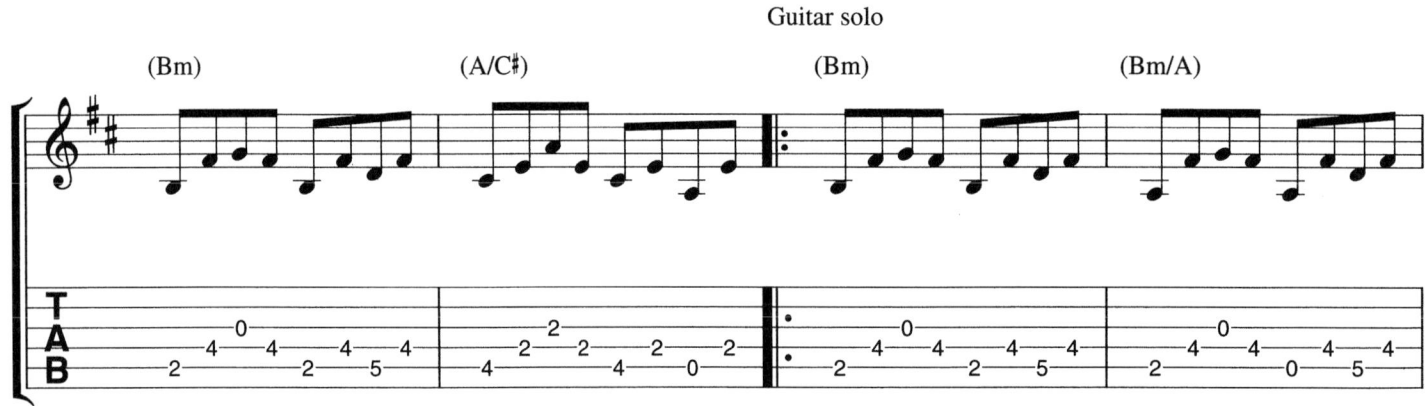

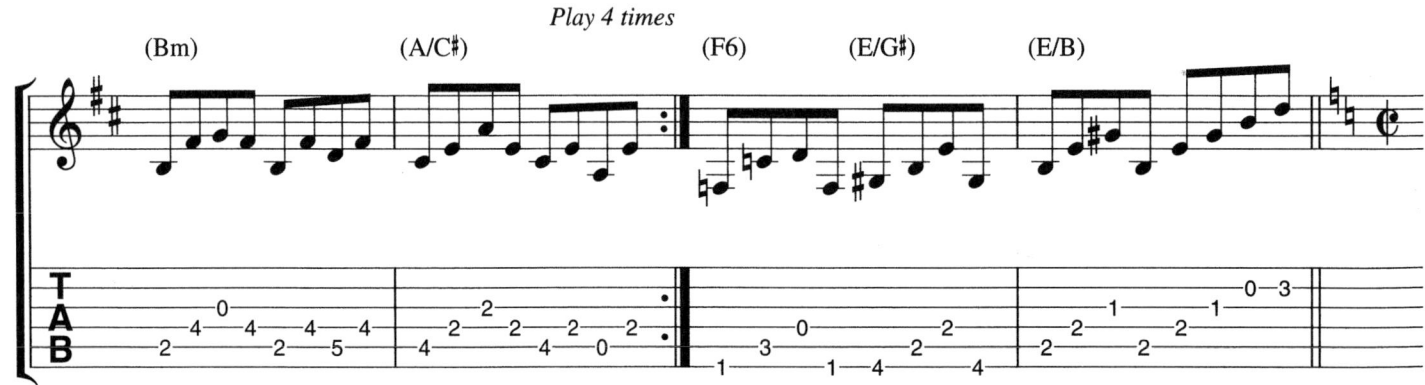

36

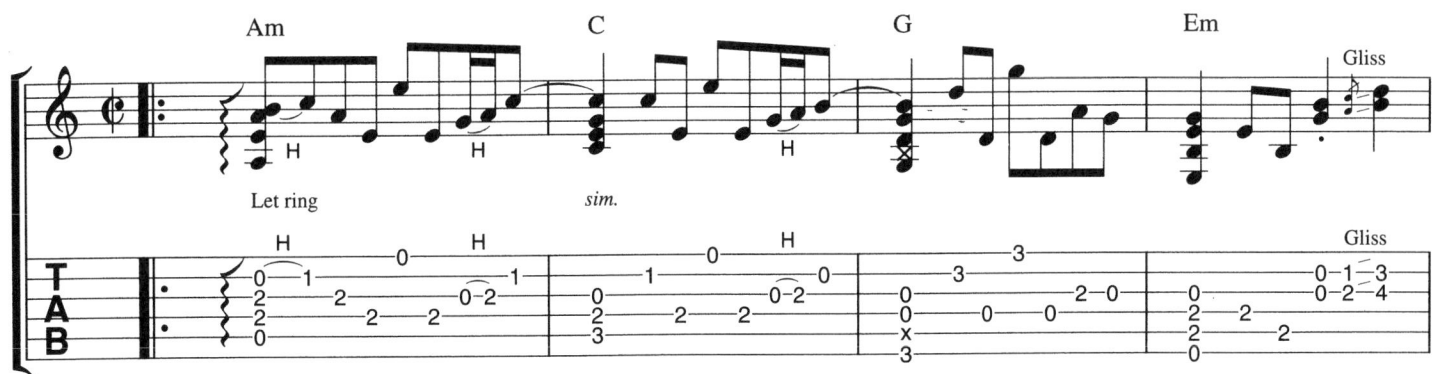

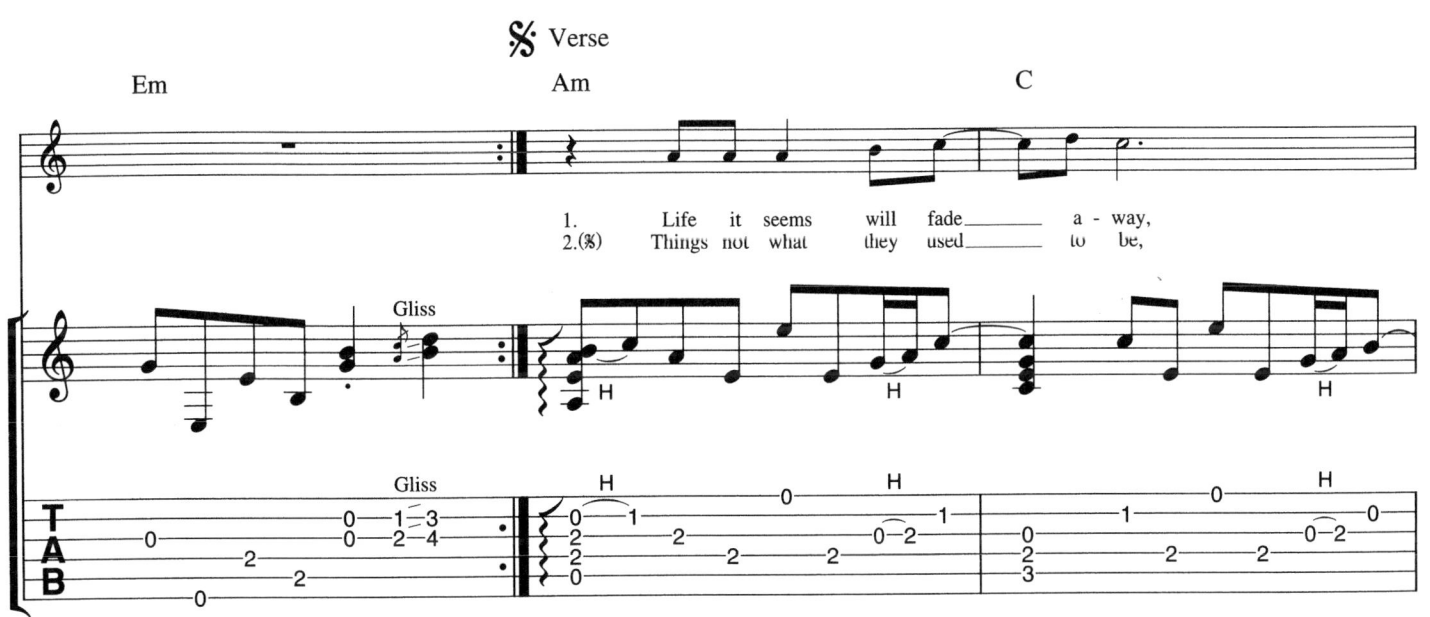

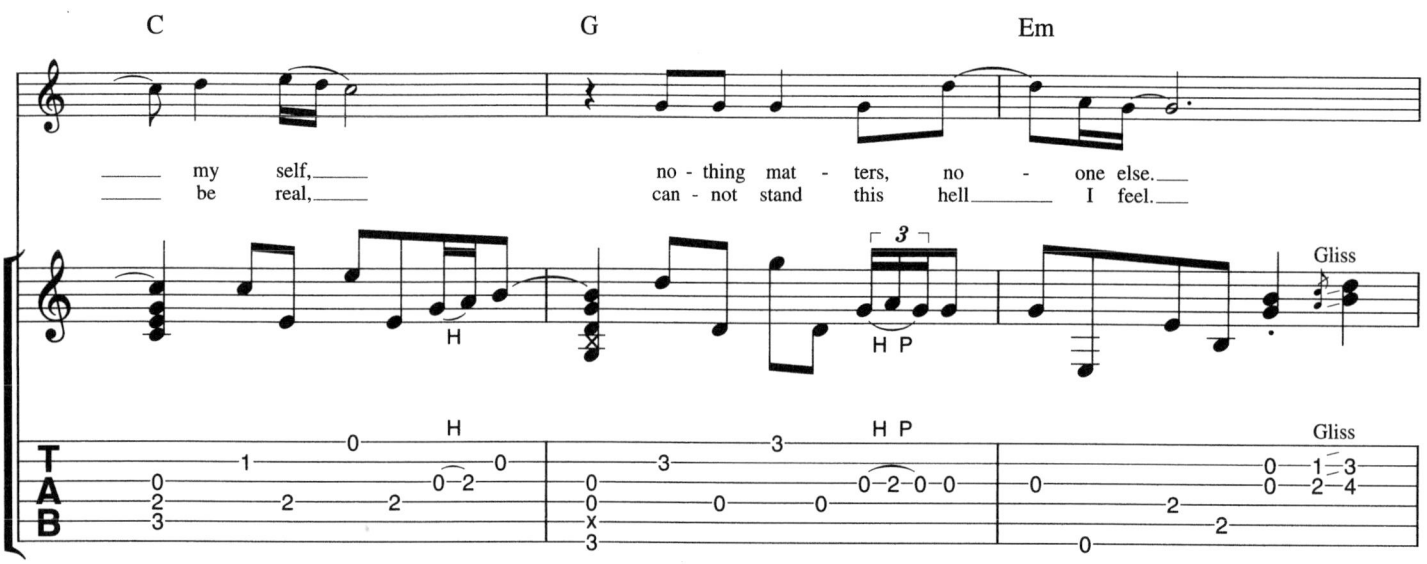
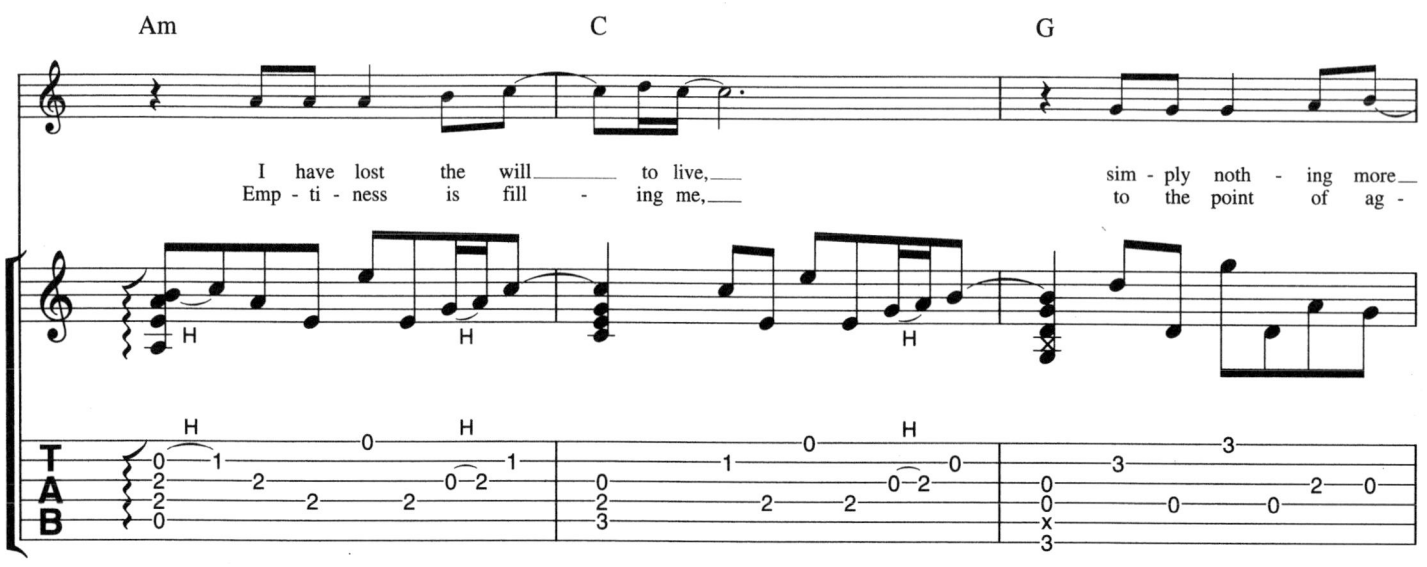

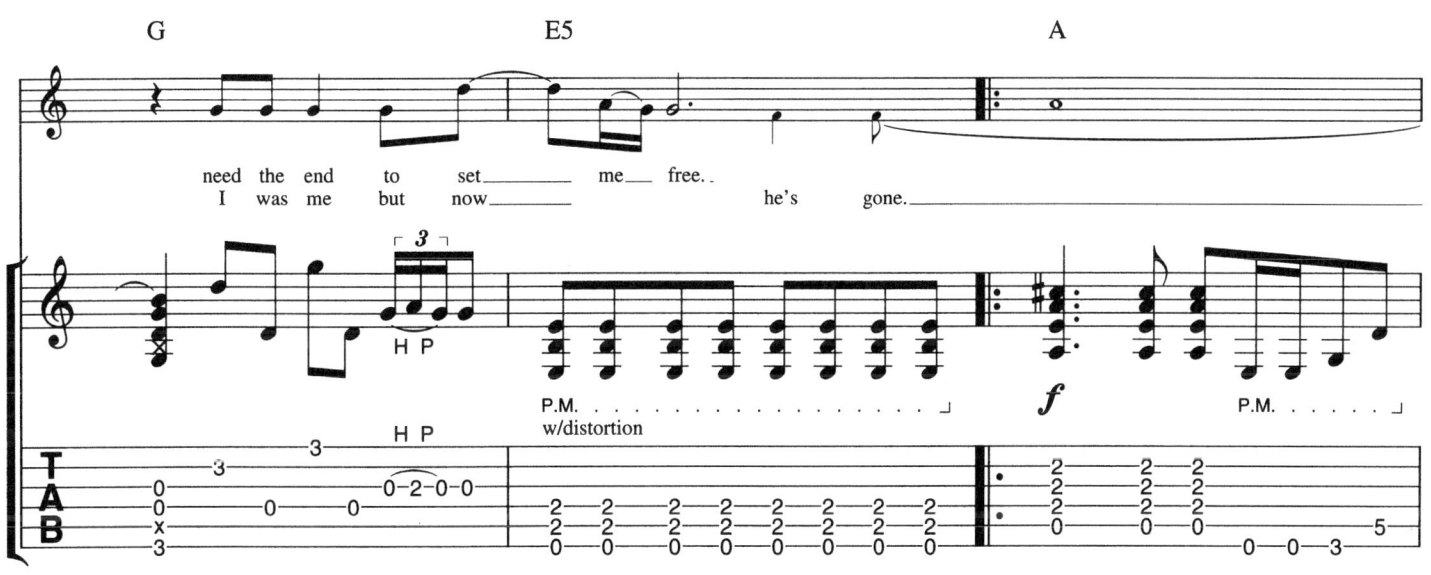
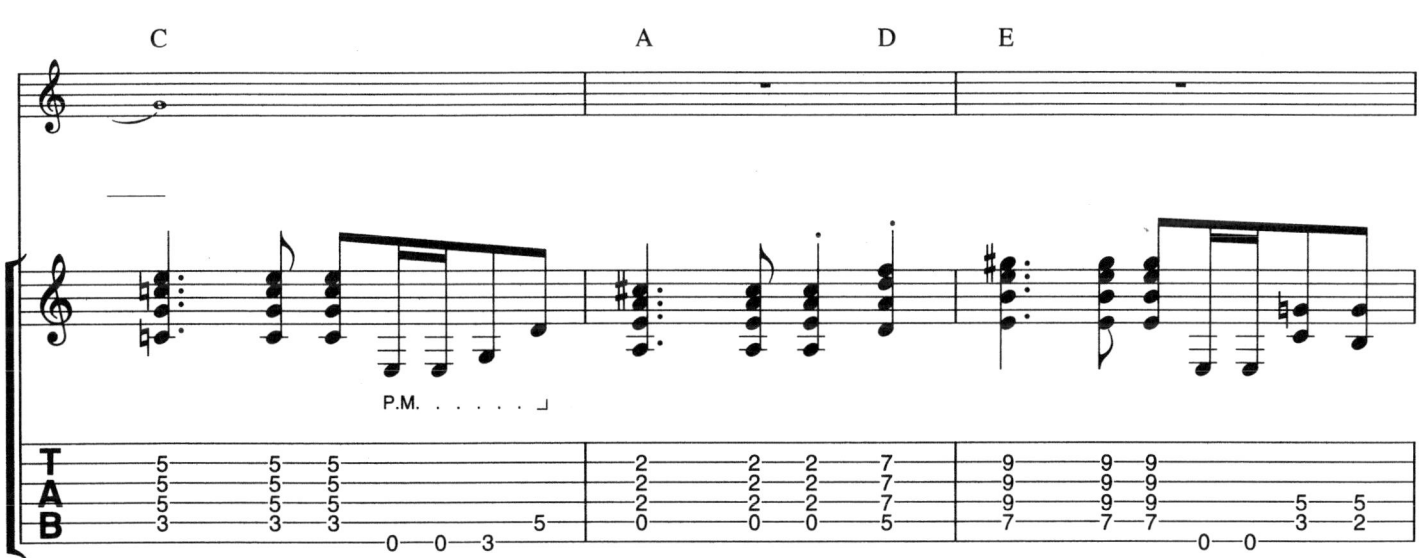

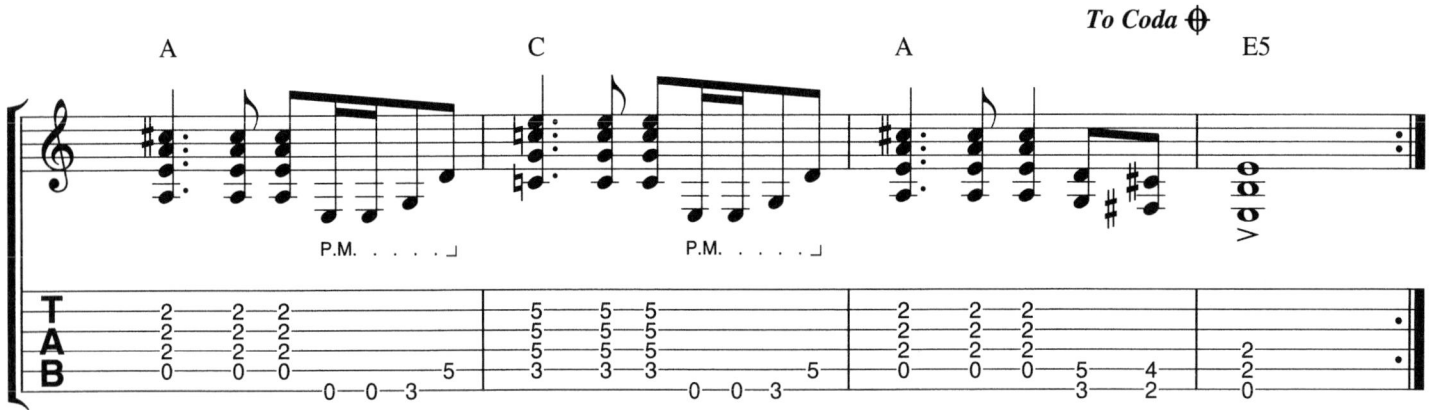
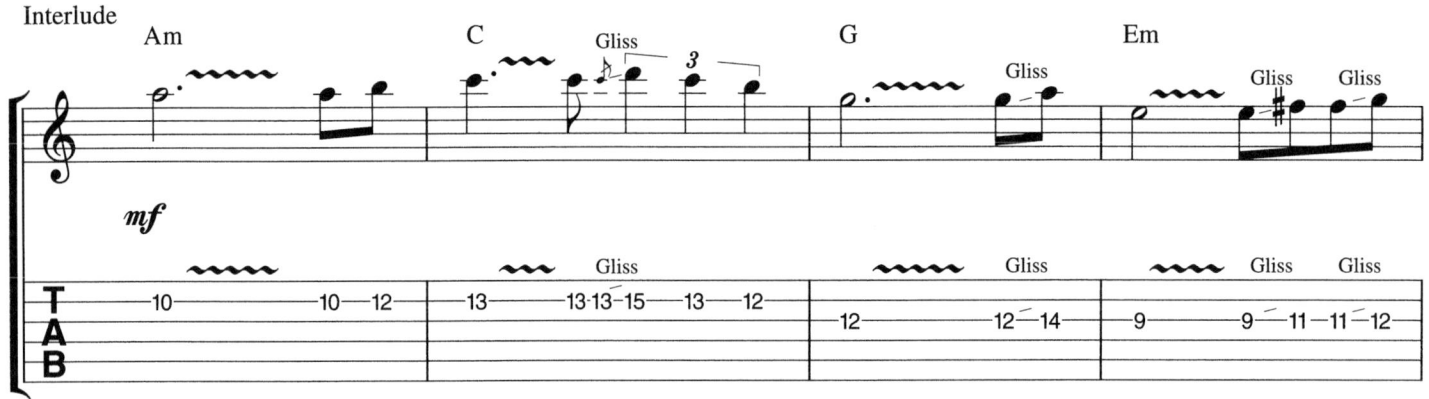
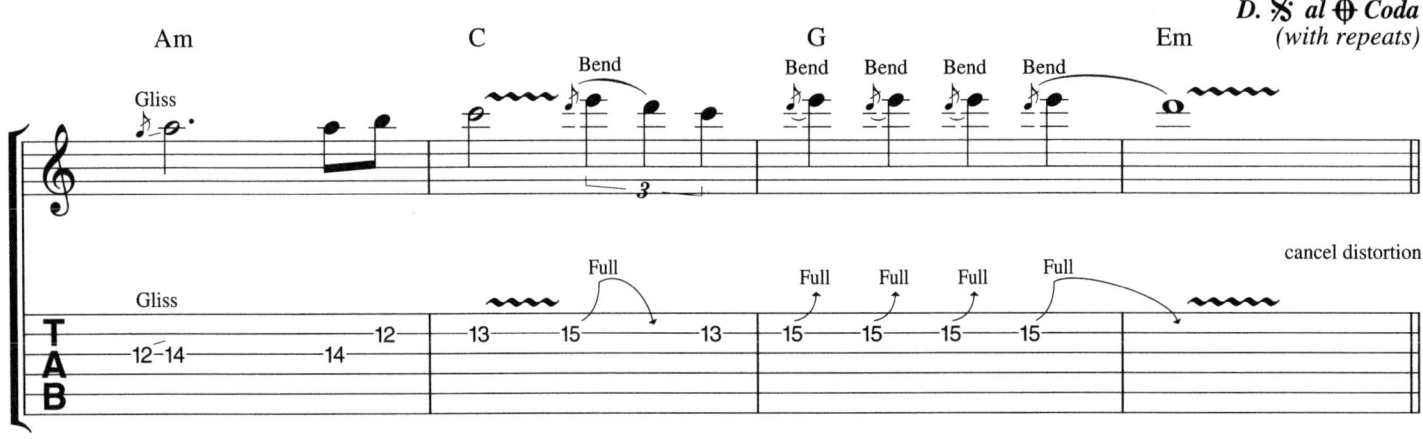

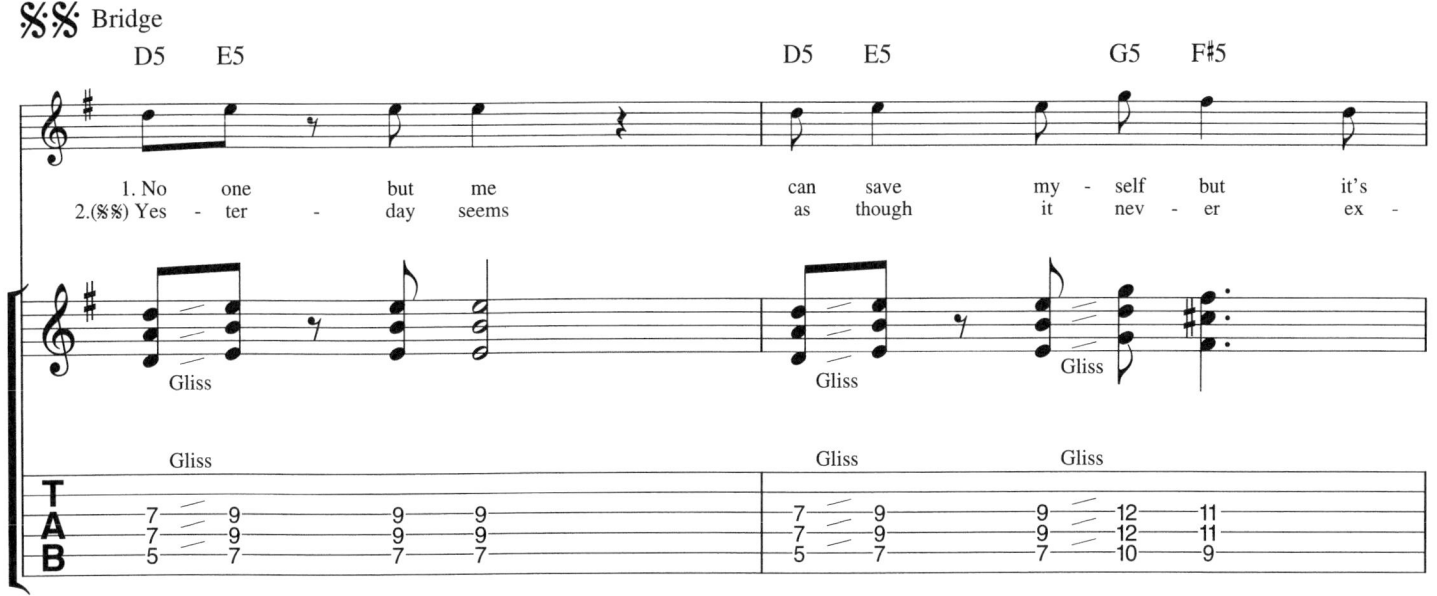

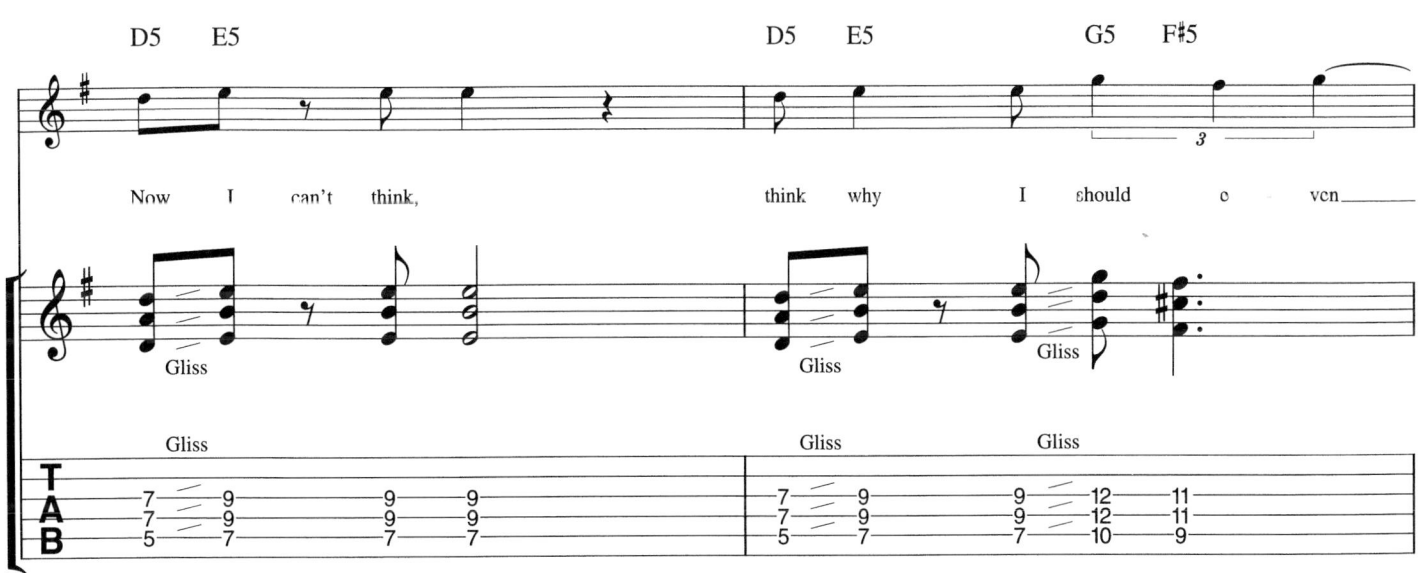

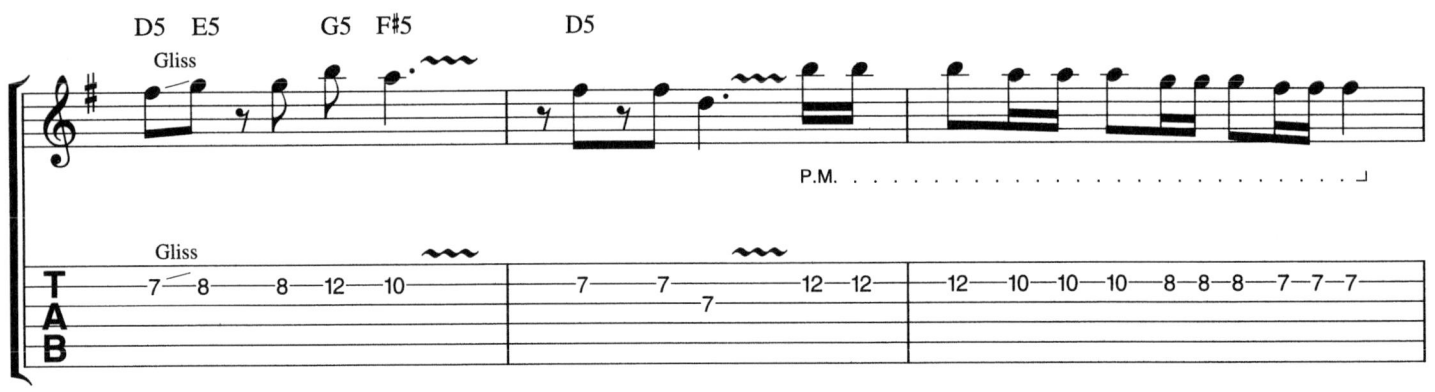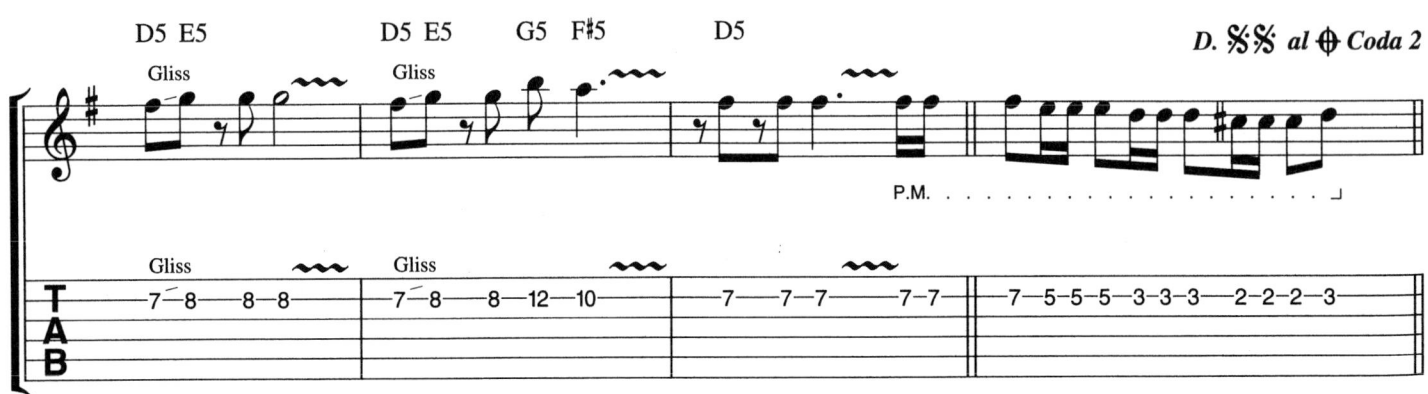

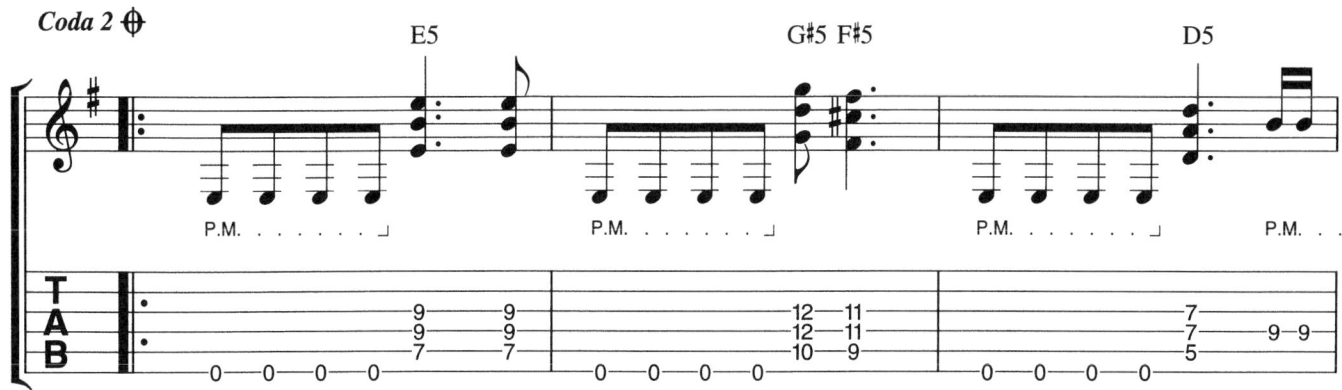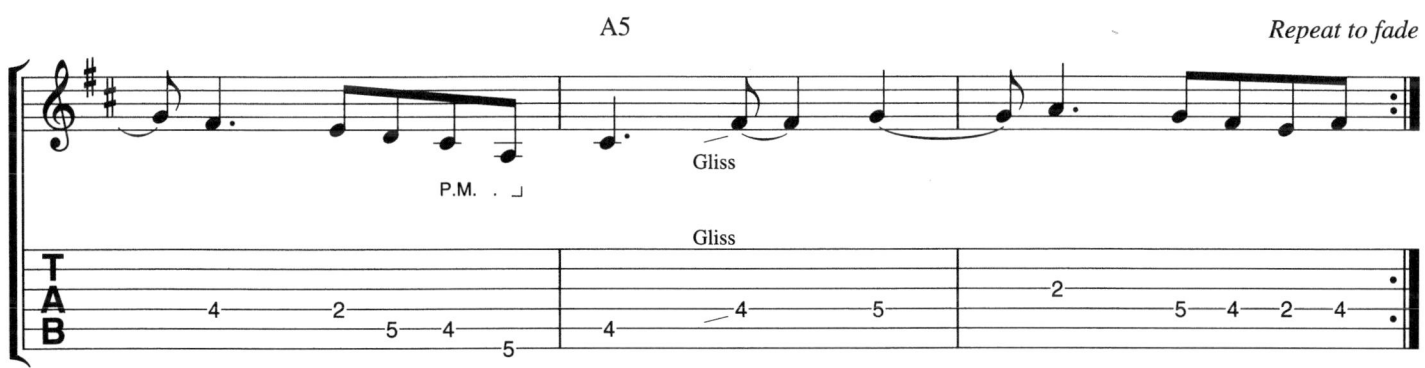

welcome home (sanitarium)

Words & Music by James Hetfield, Lars Ulrich & Kirk Hammett

© Copyright 1986 Creeping Death Music, USA.
PolyGram Music Publishing Limited, 47 British Grove, London W4.
All Rights Reserved. International Copyright Secured.

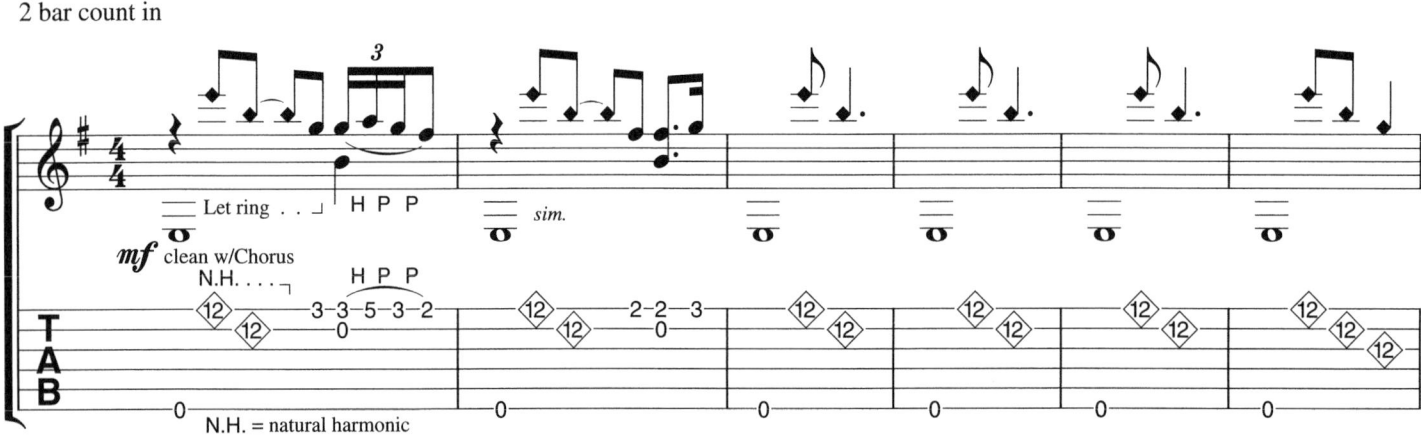

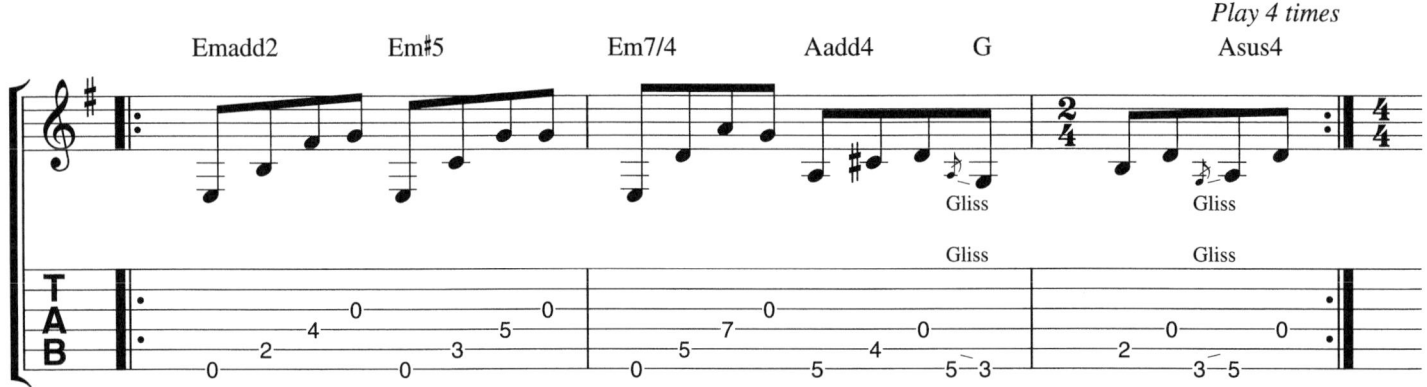

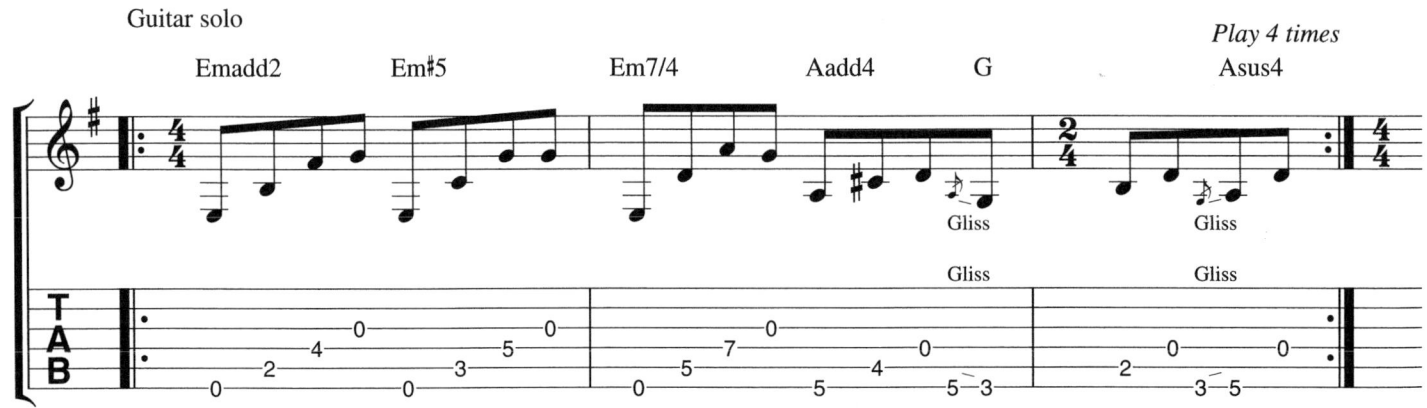

44

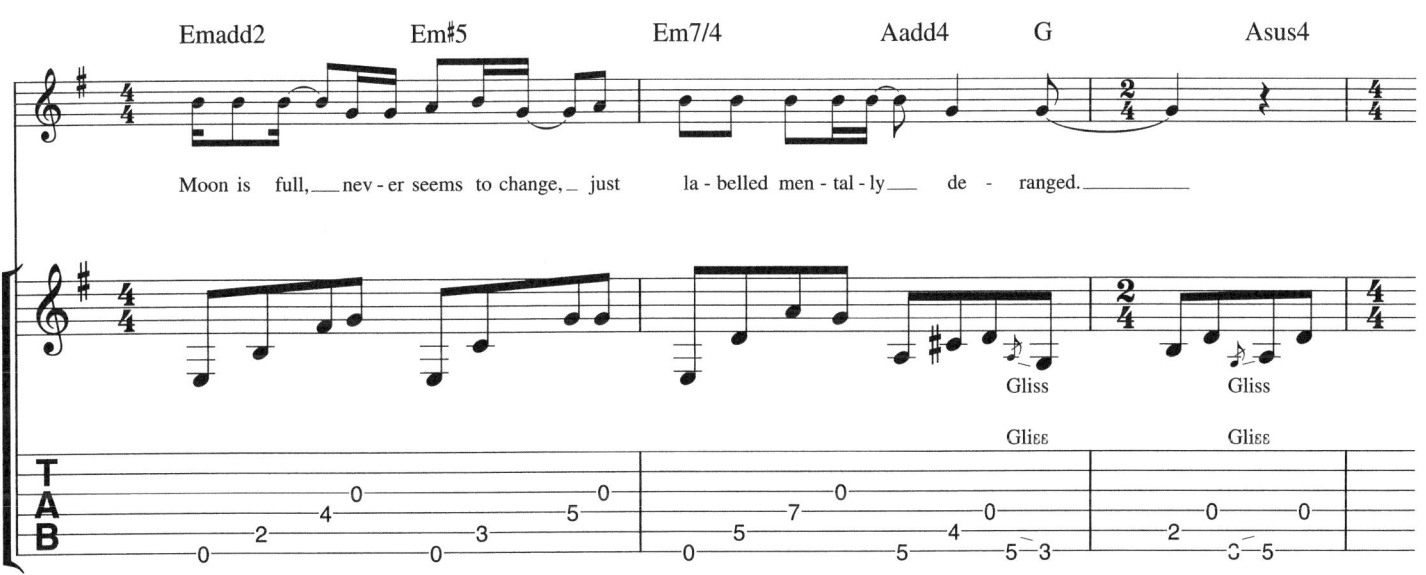
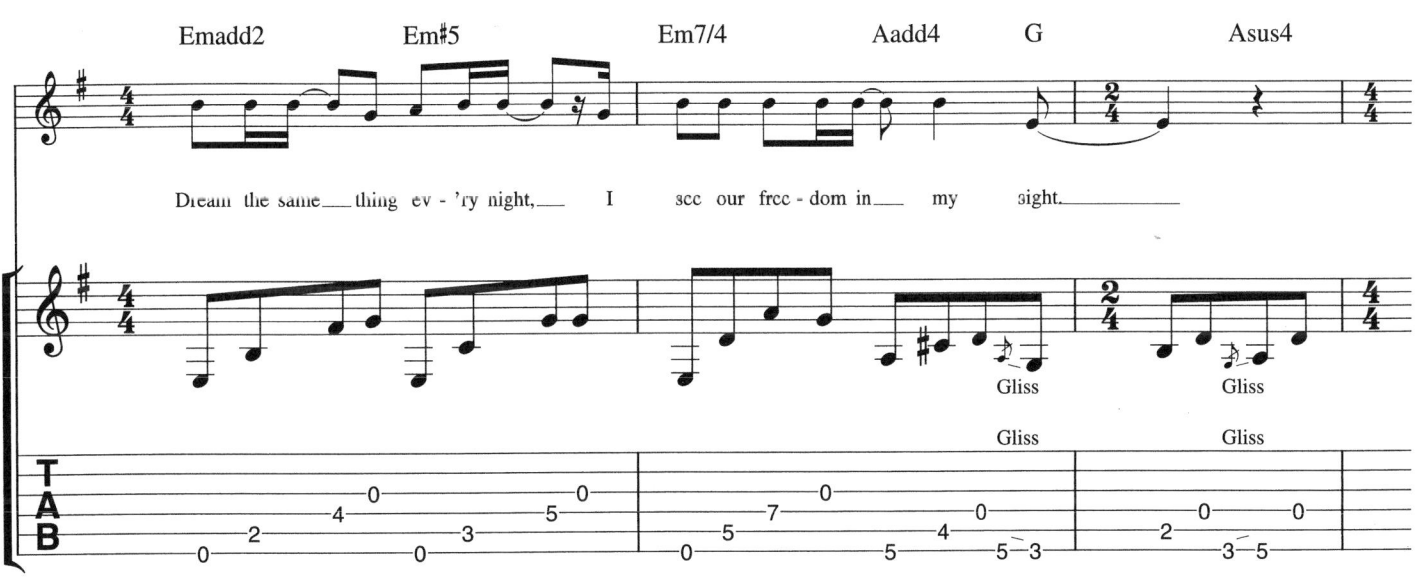

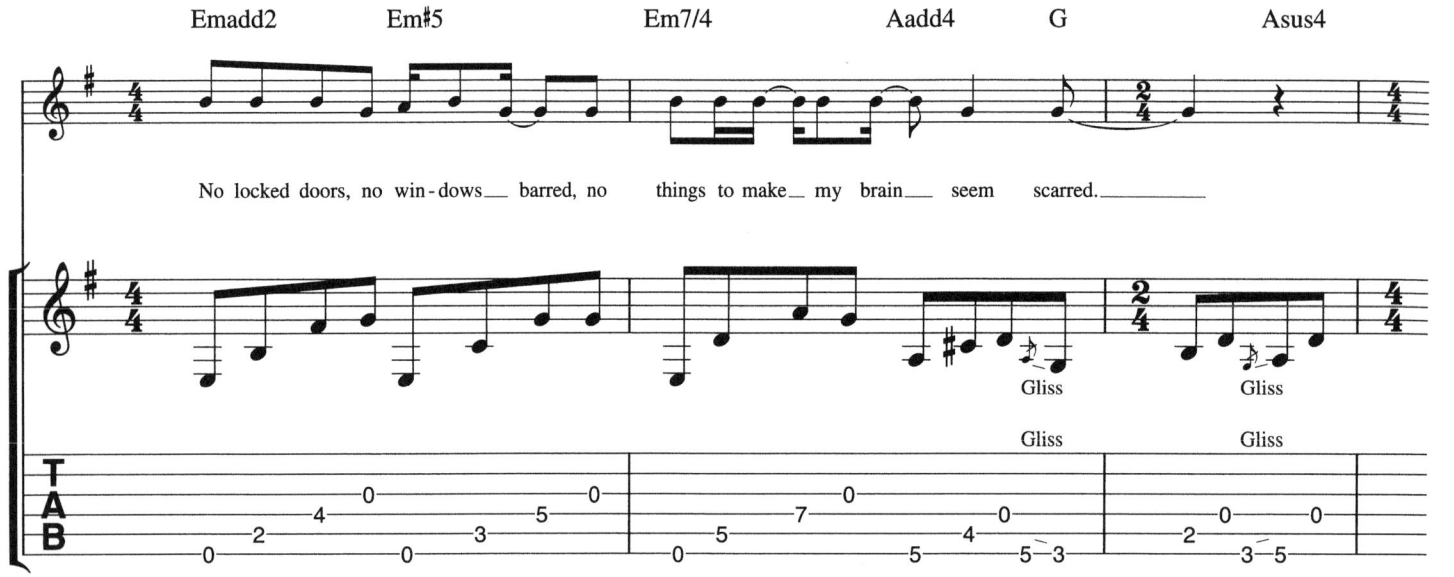
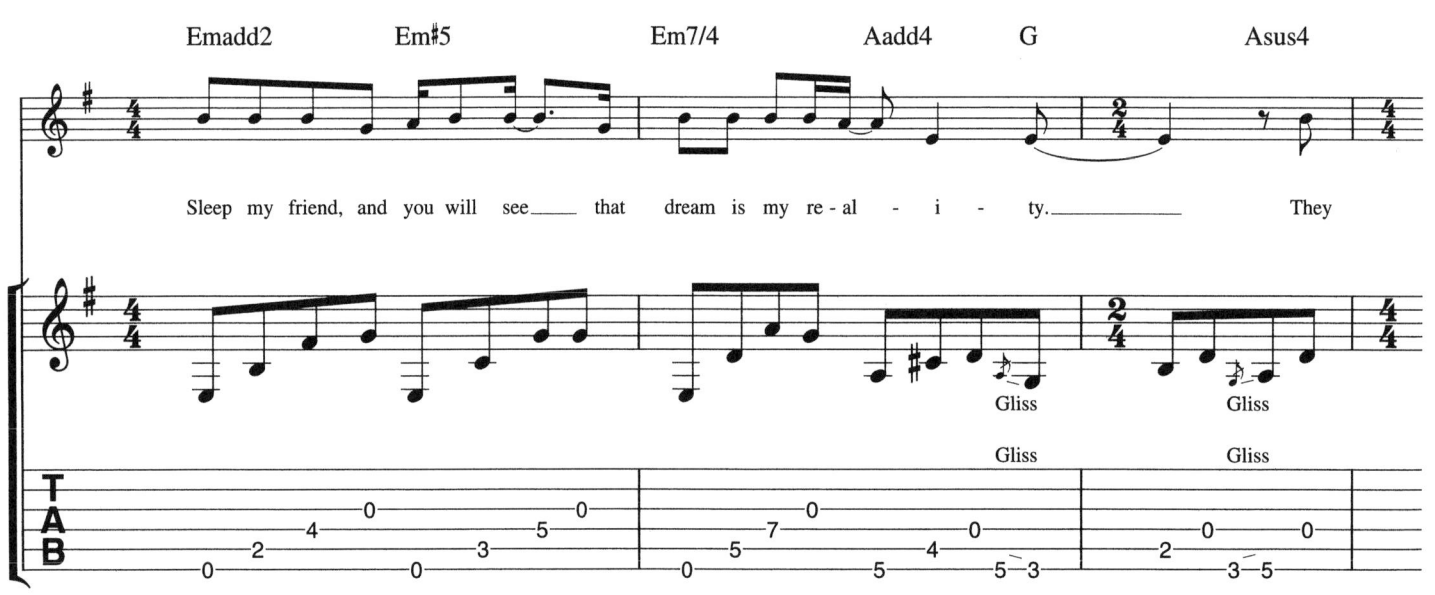
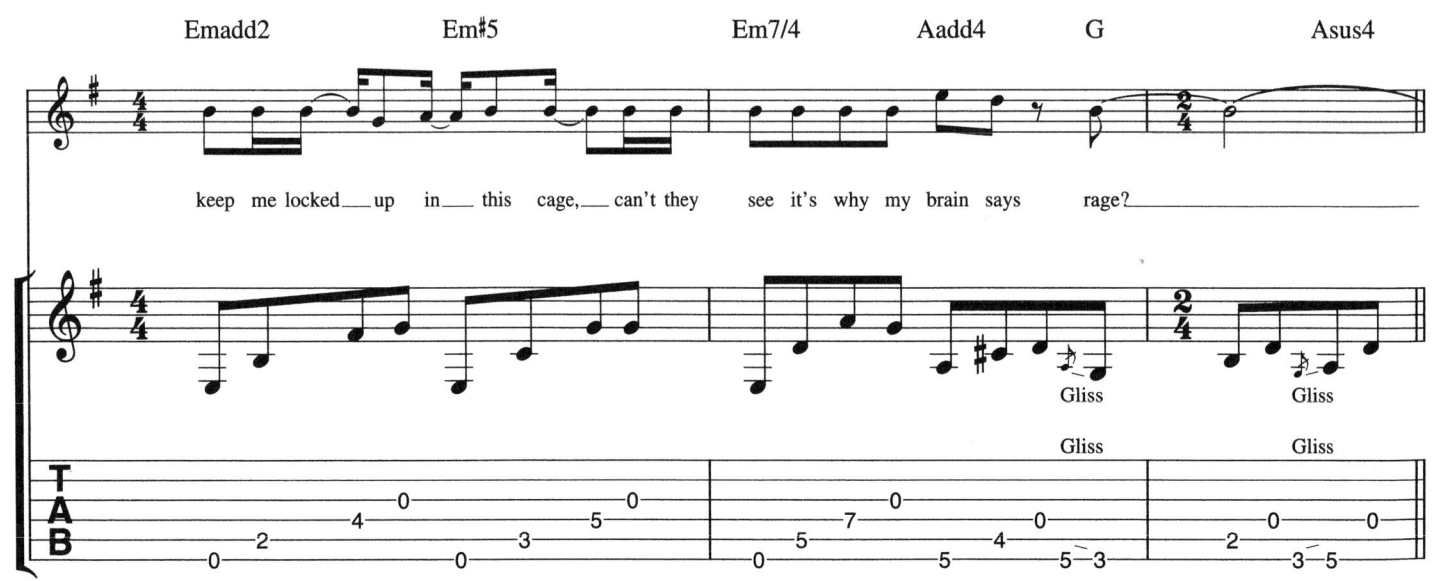

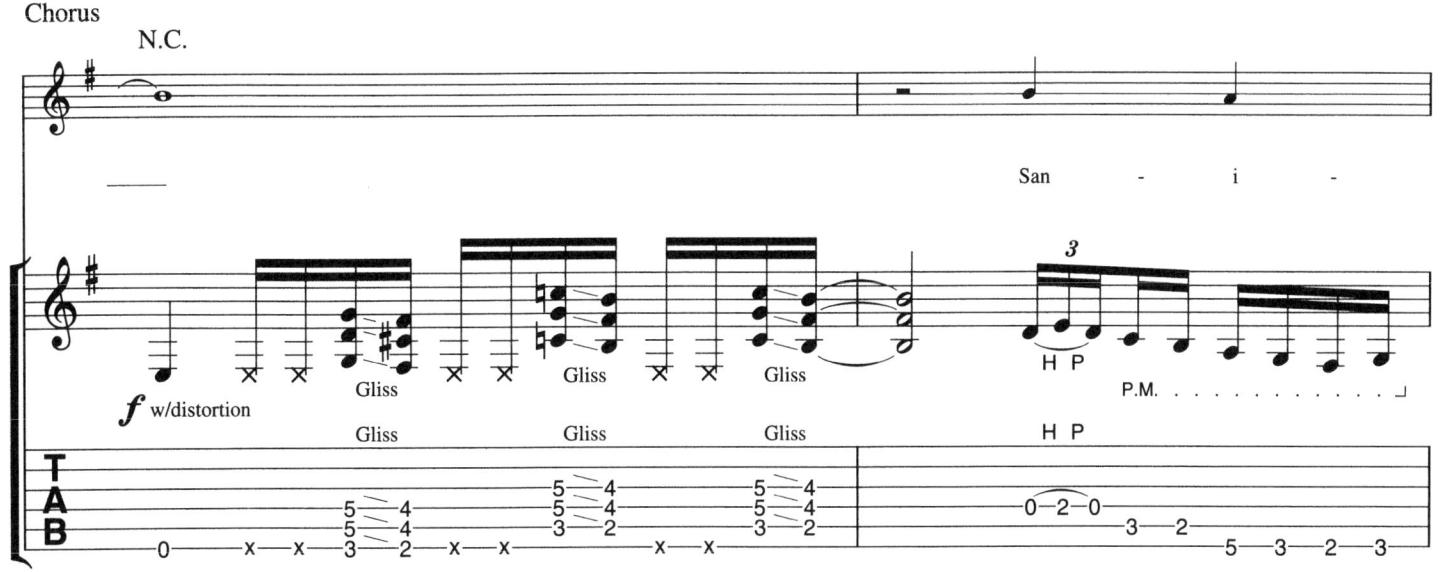
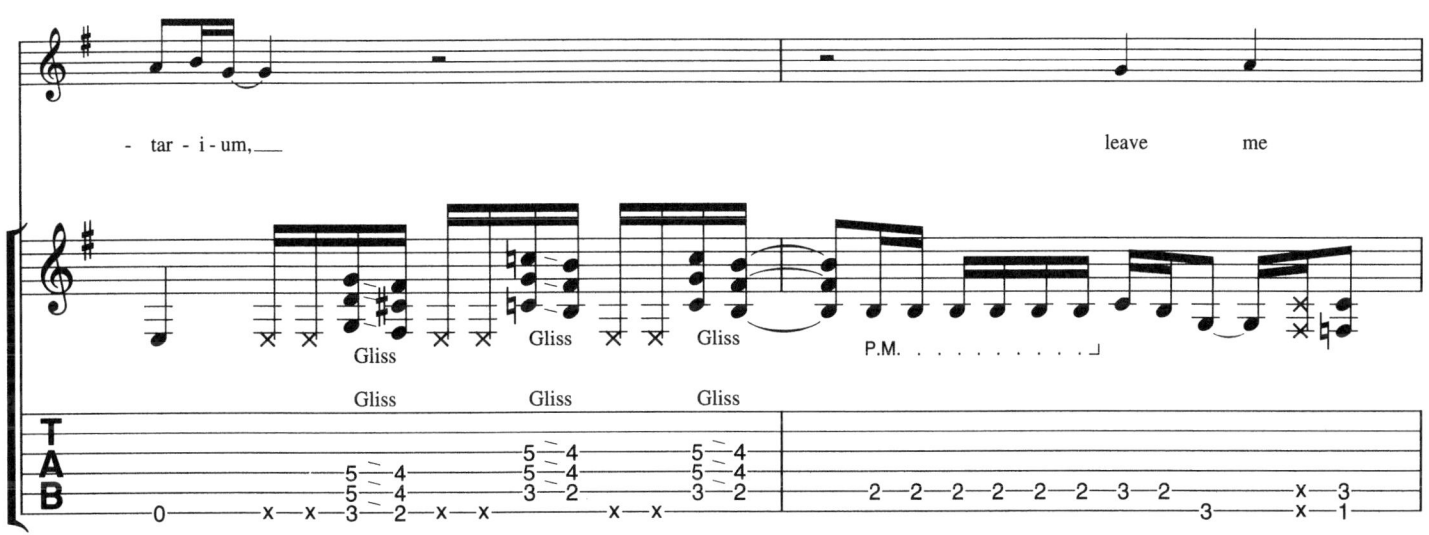
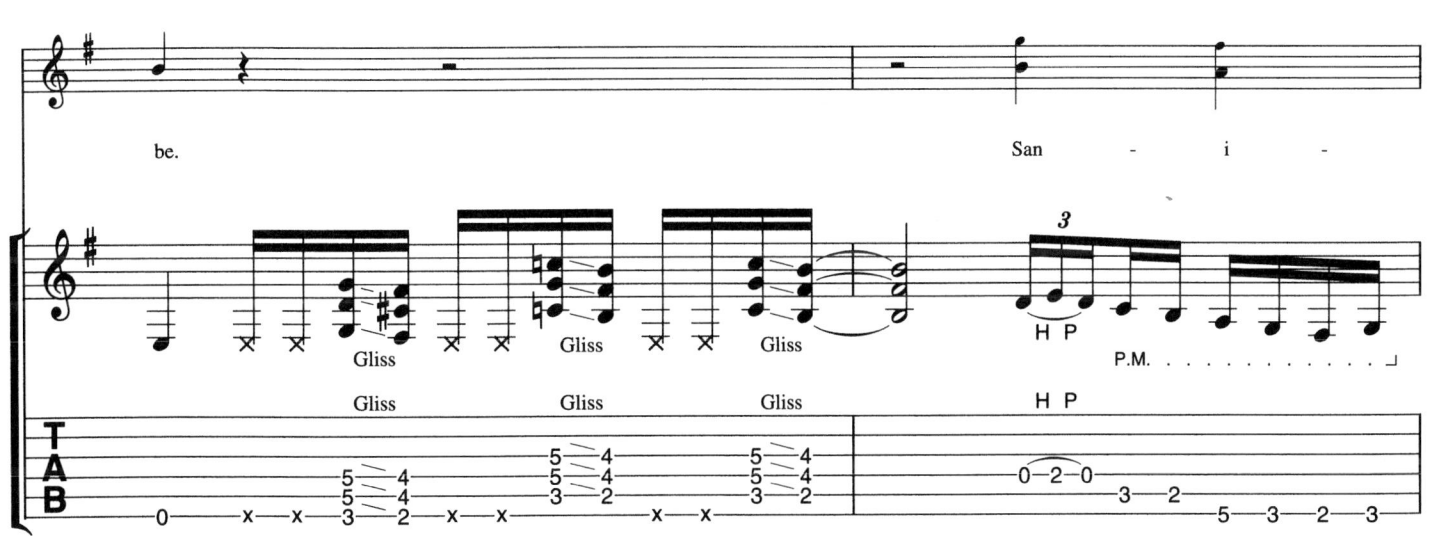

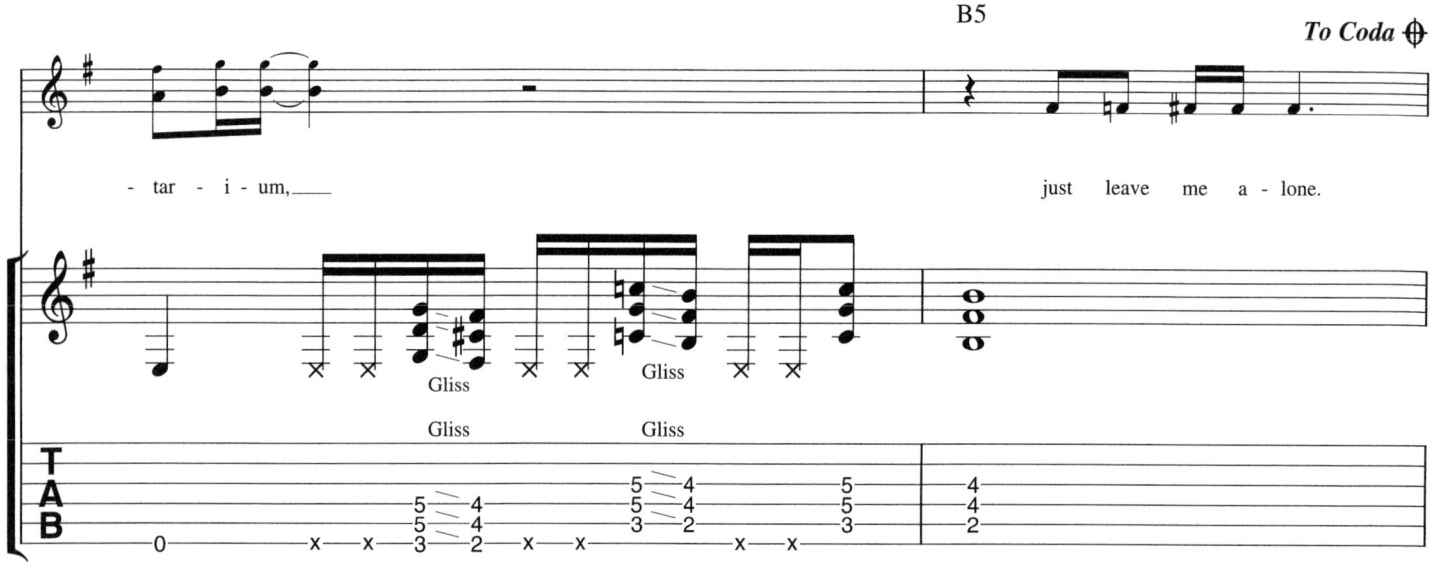
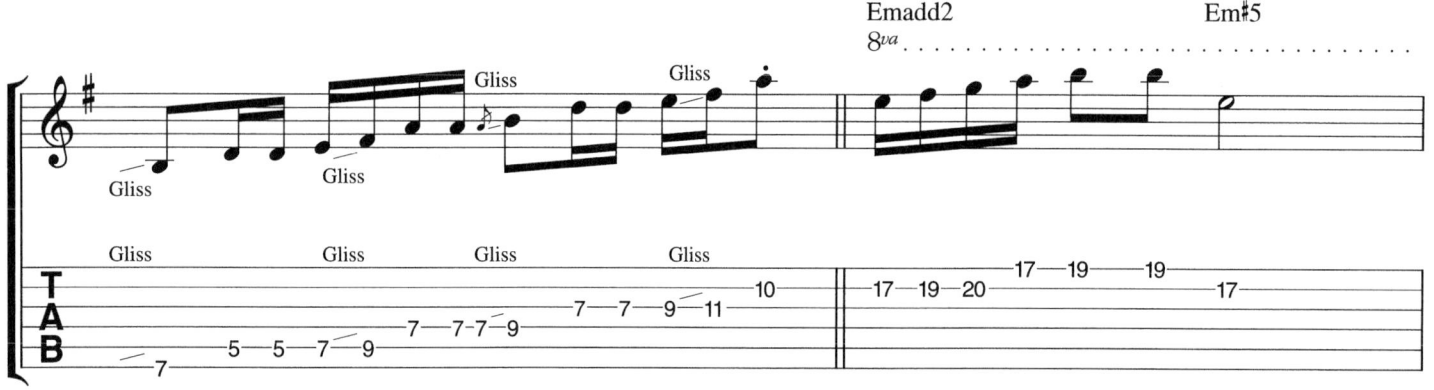
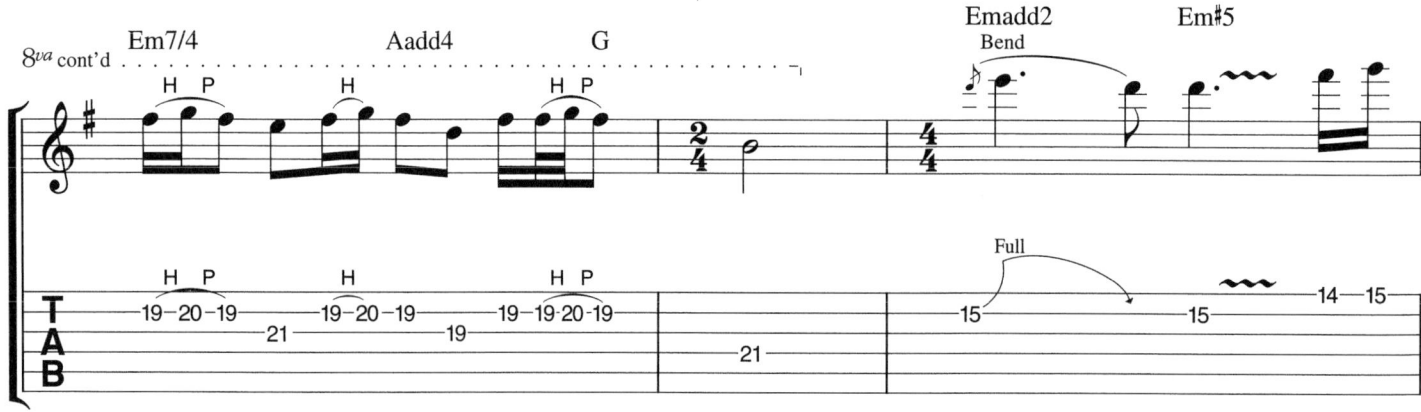
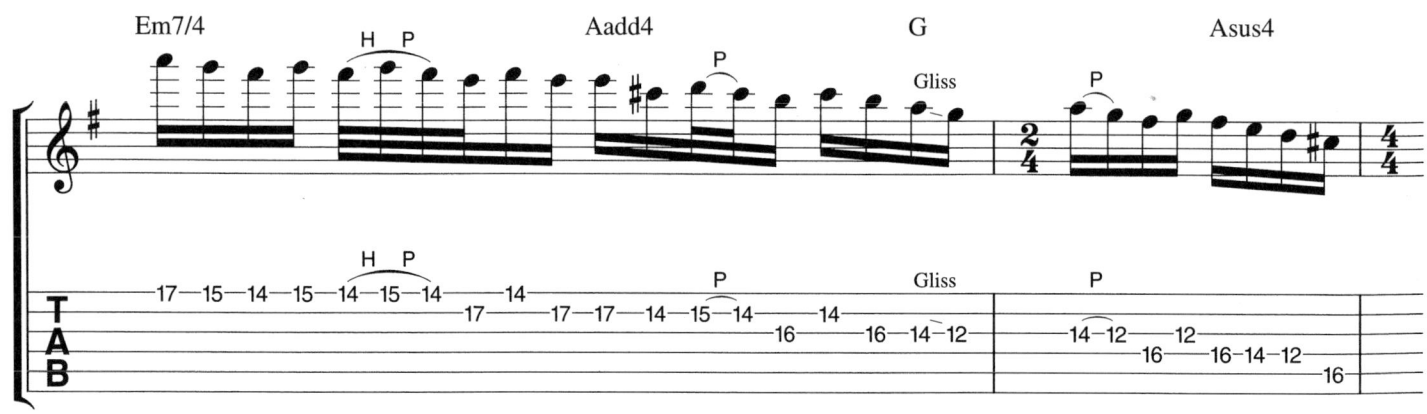

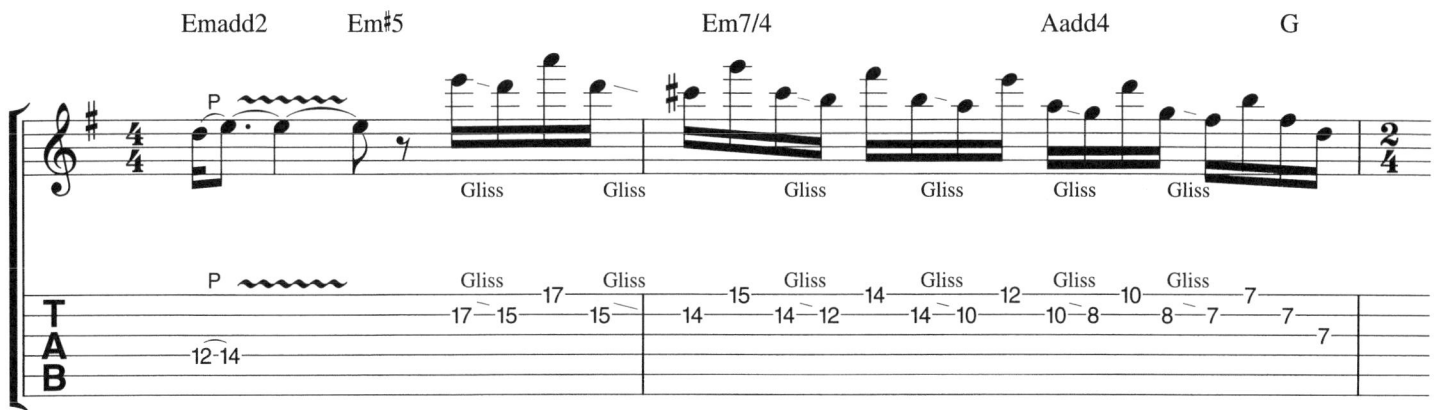
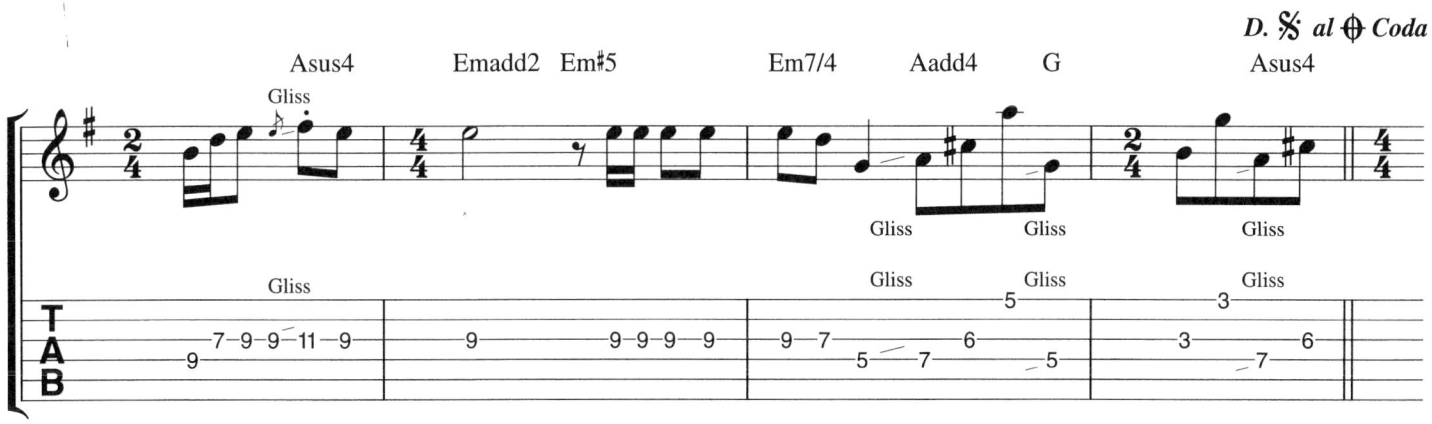
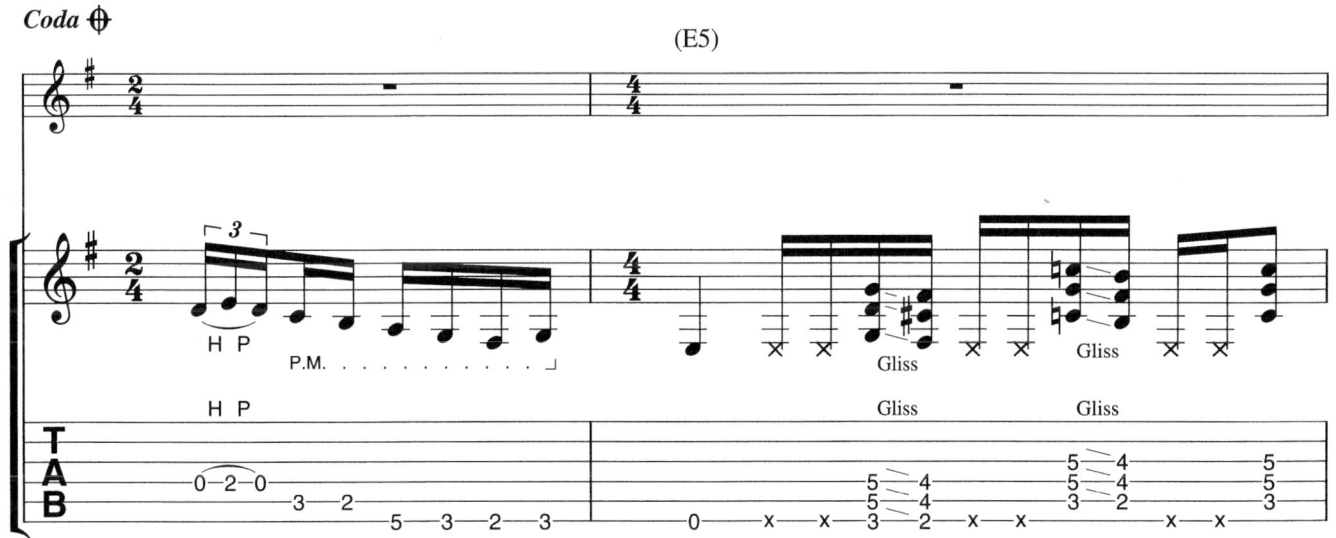

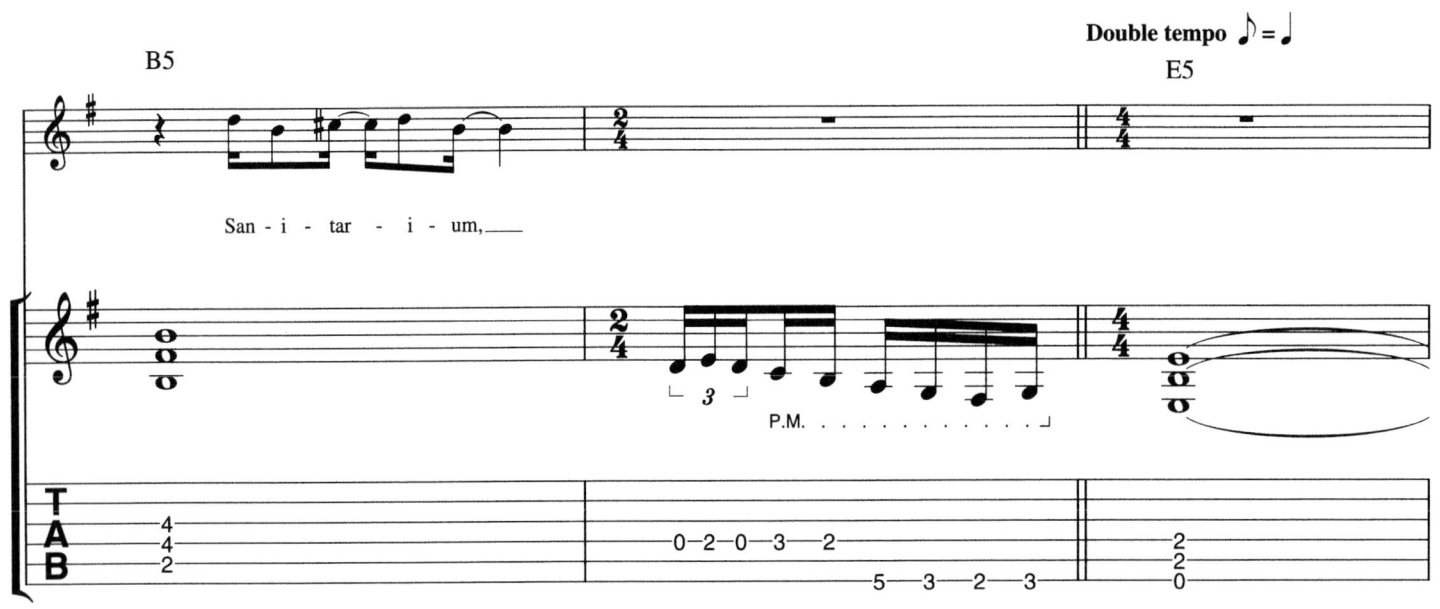

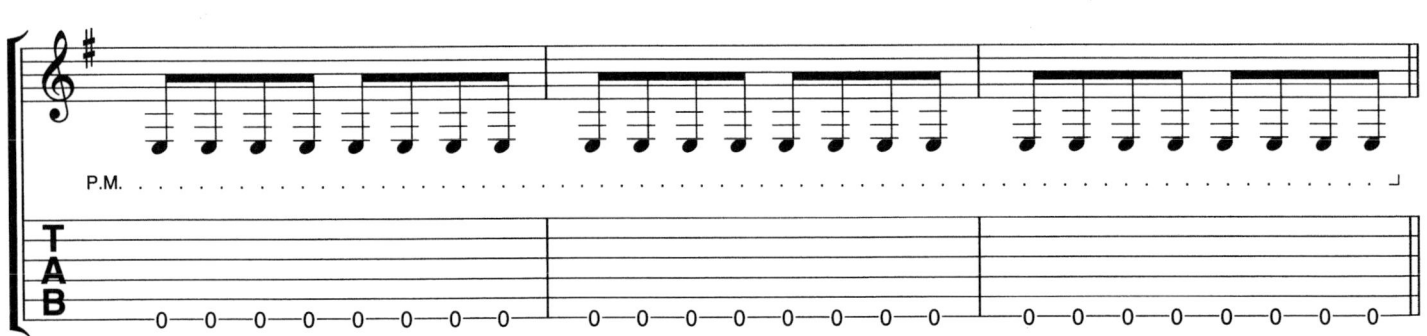

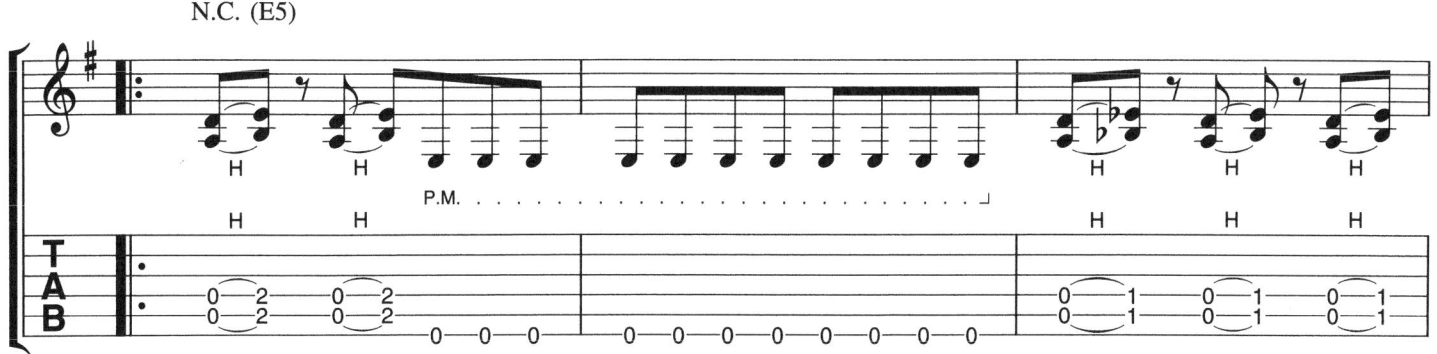
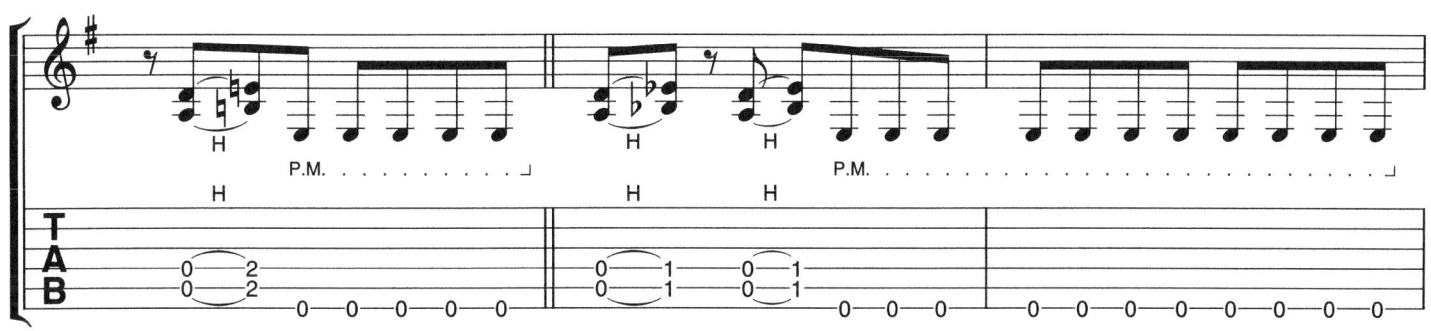
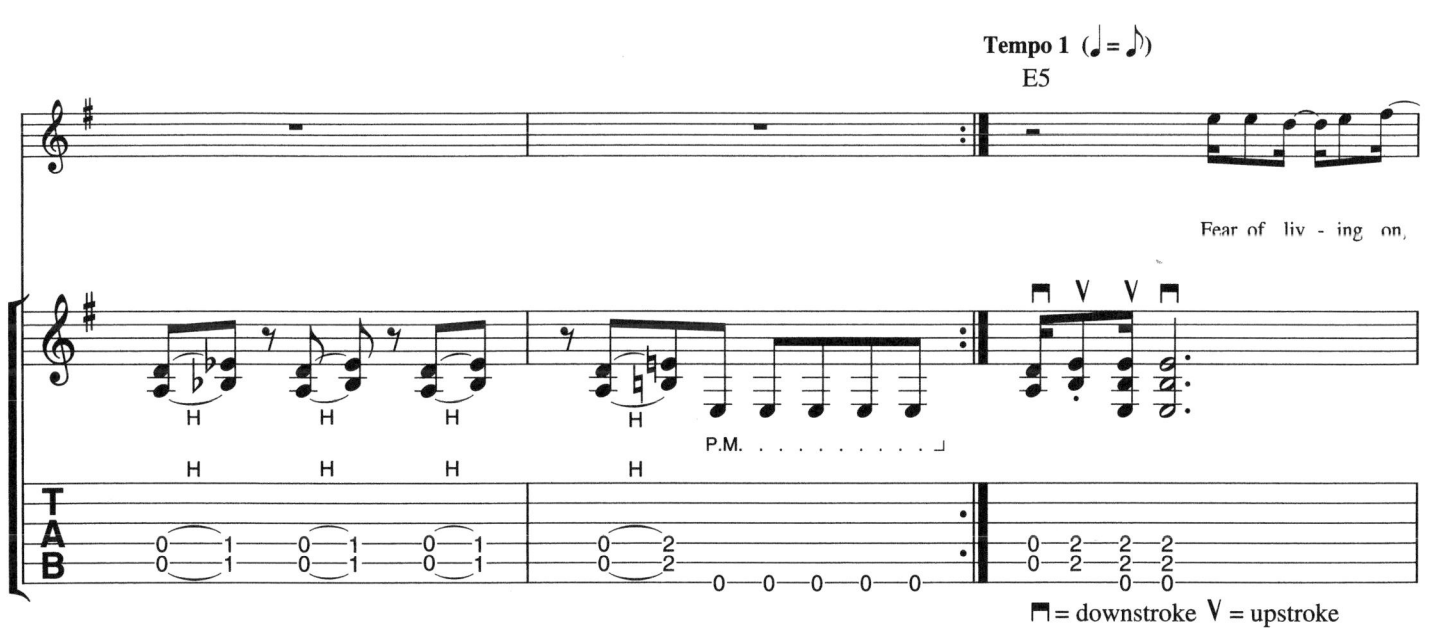

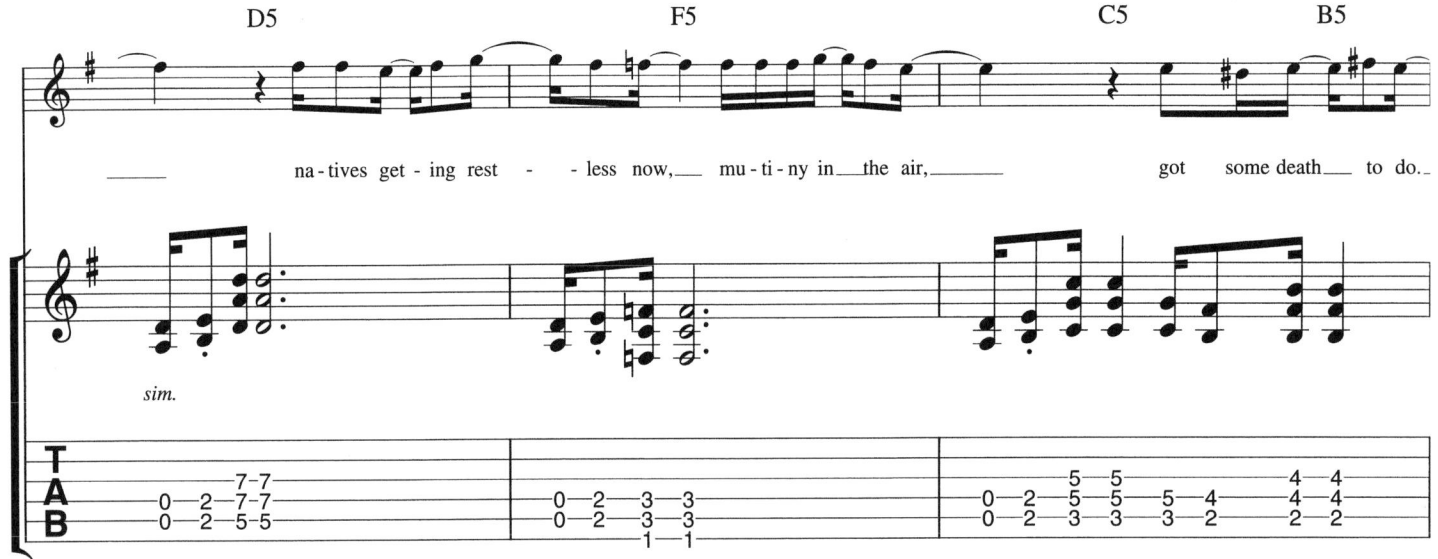
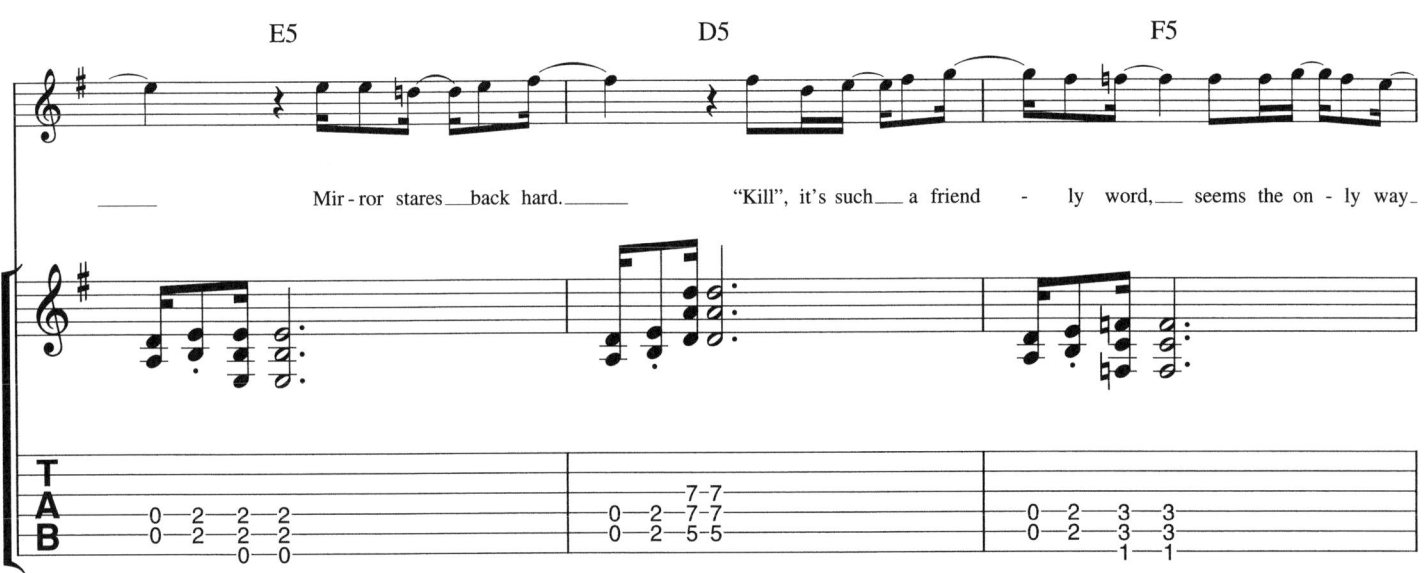
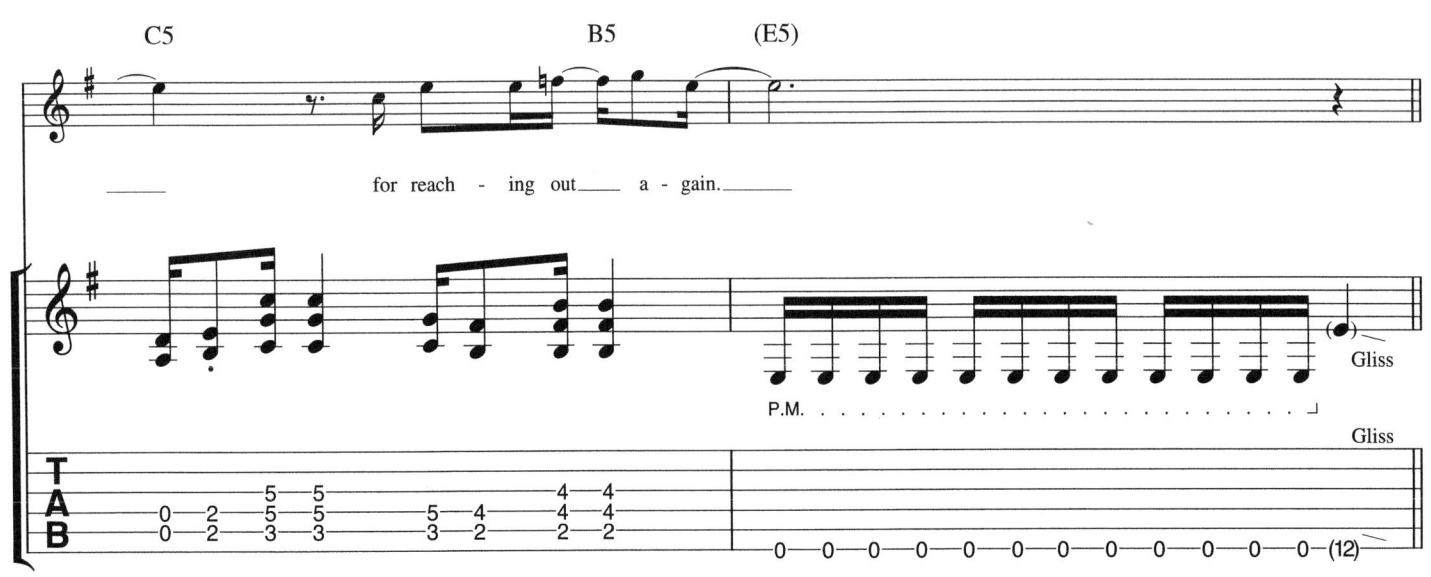

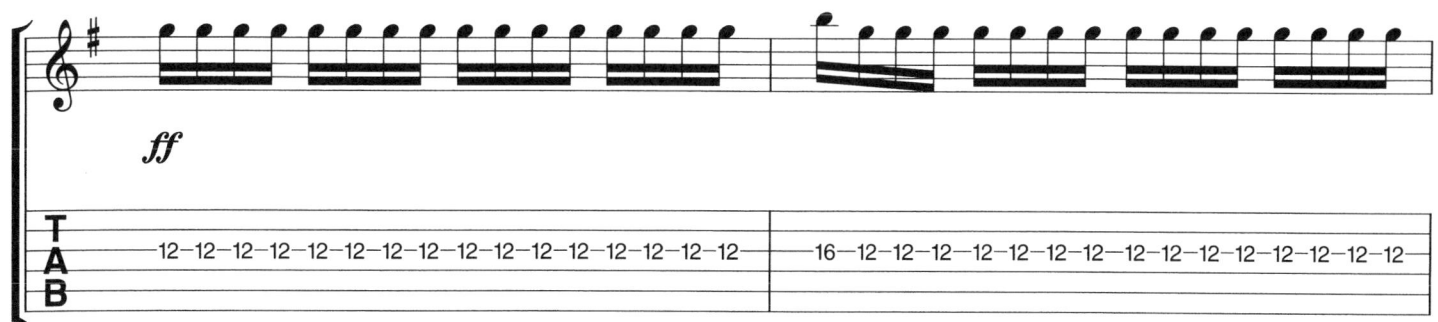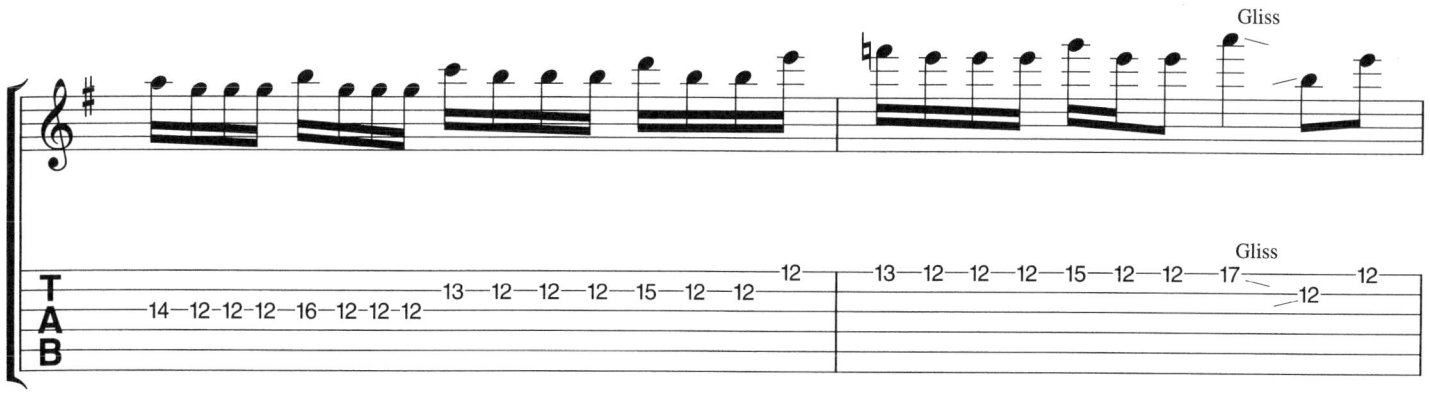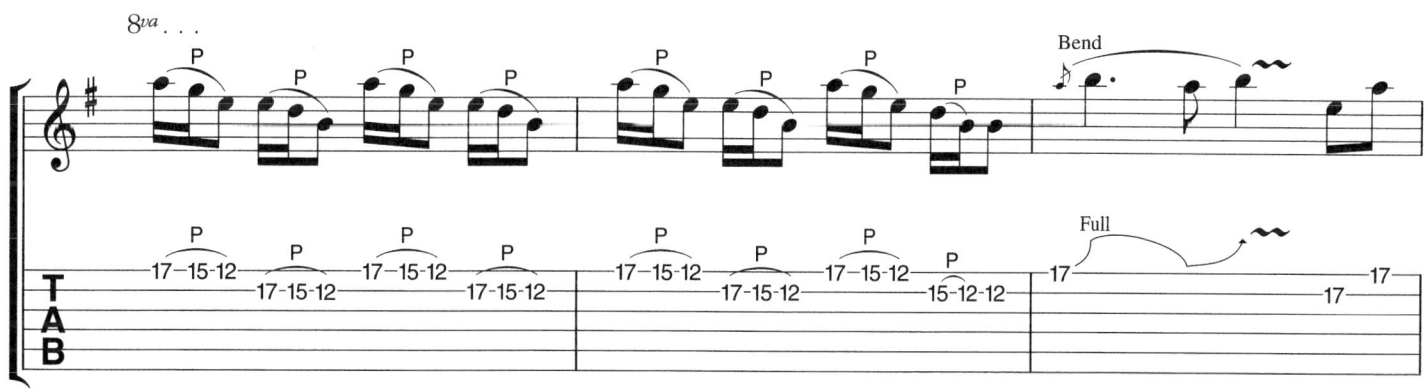

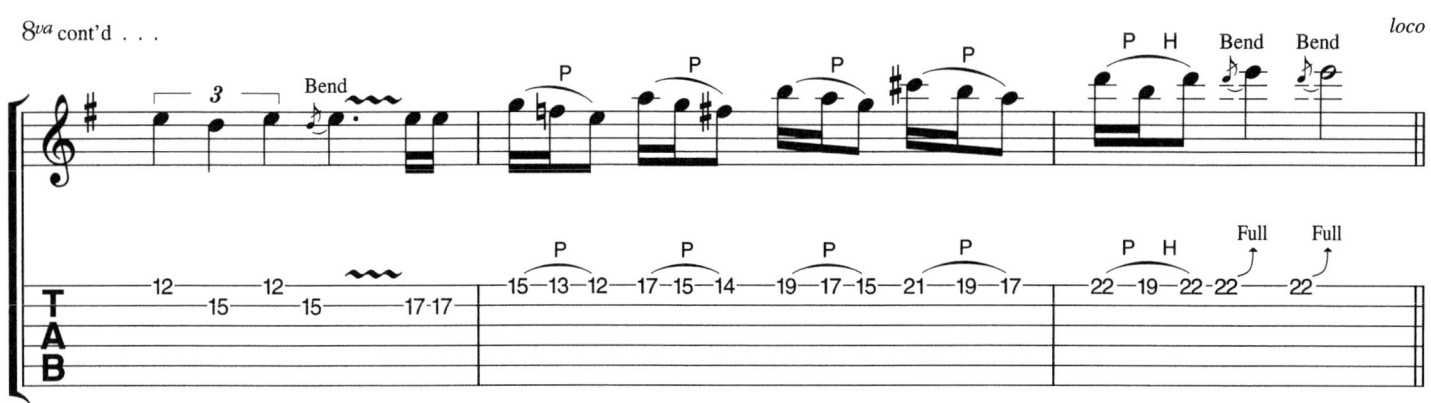

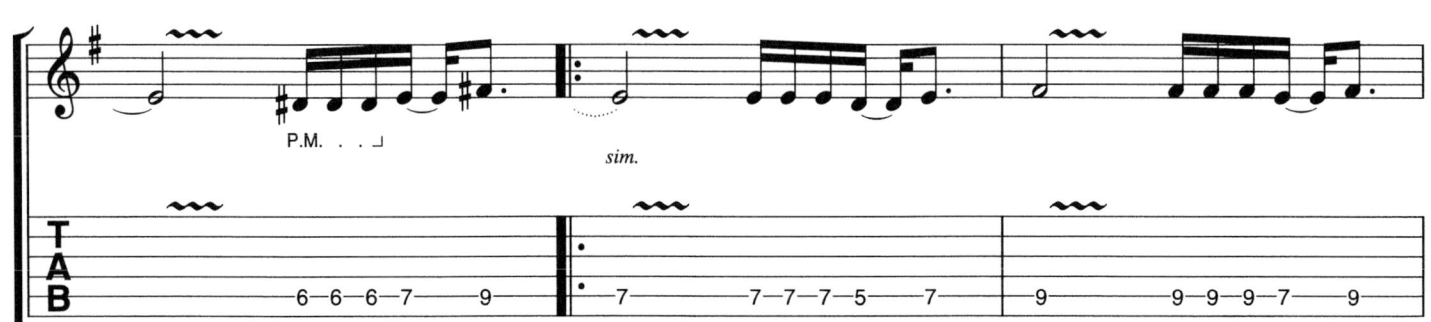

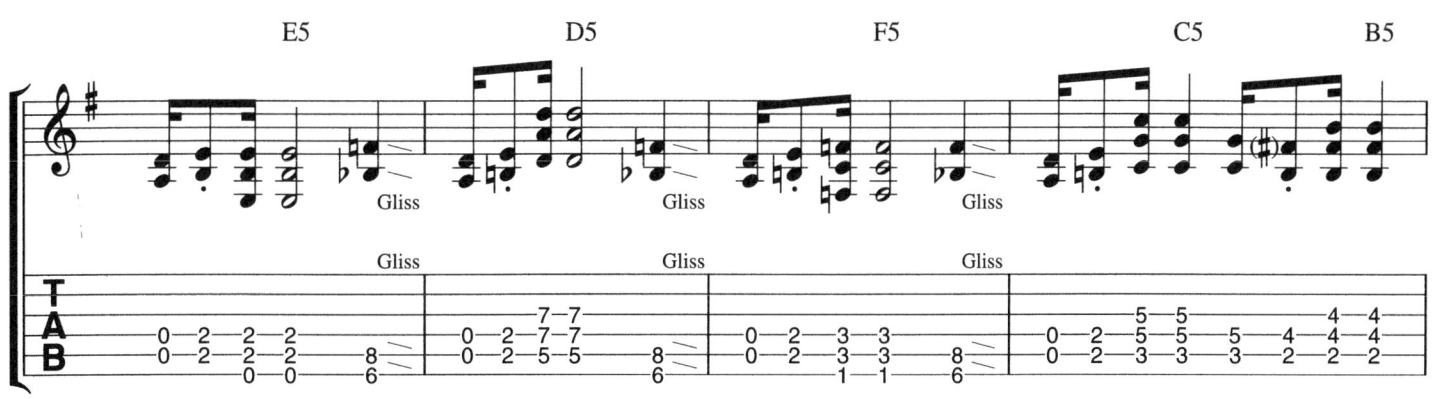
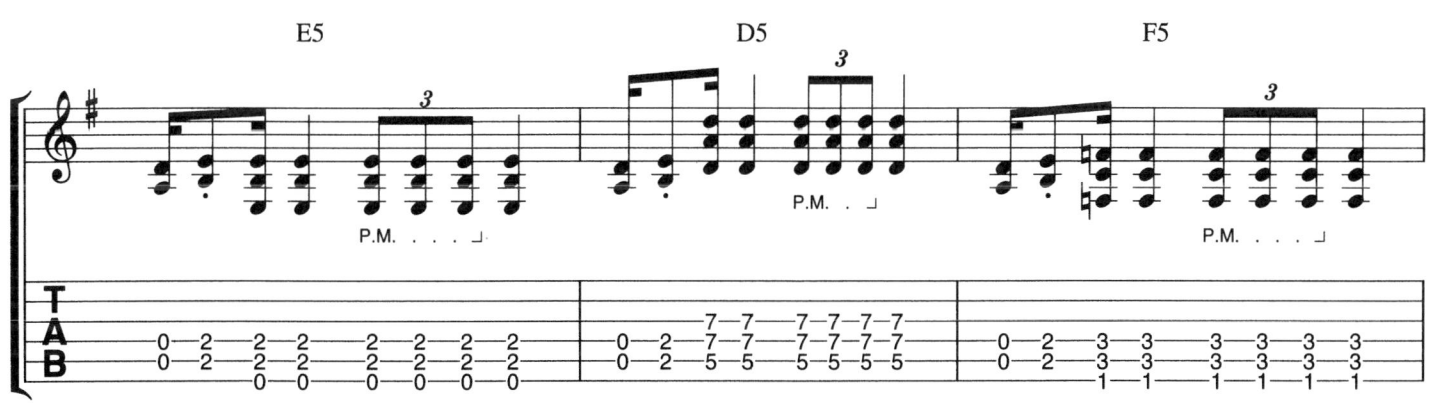
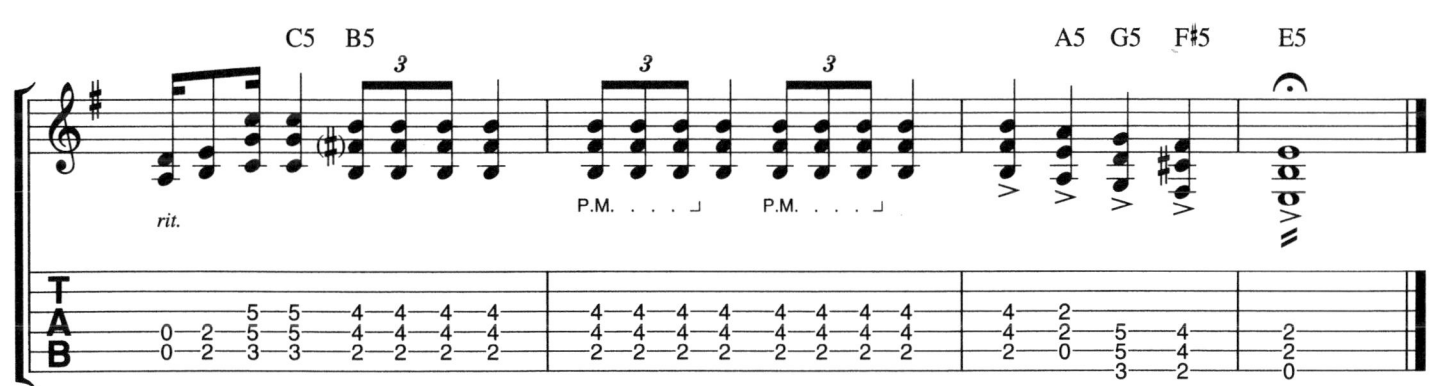

the unforgiven

Words & Music by James Hetfield, Lars Ulrich & Kirk Hammett

© Copyright 1991 Creeping Death Music, USA.
PolyGram Music Publishing Limited, 47 British Grove, London W4.
All Rights Reserved. International Copyright Secured.

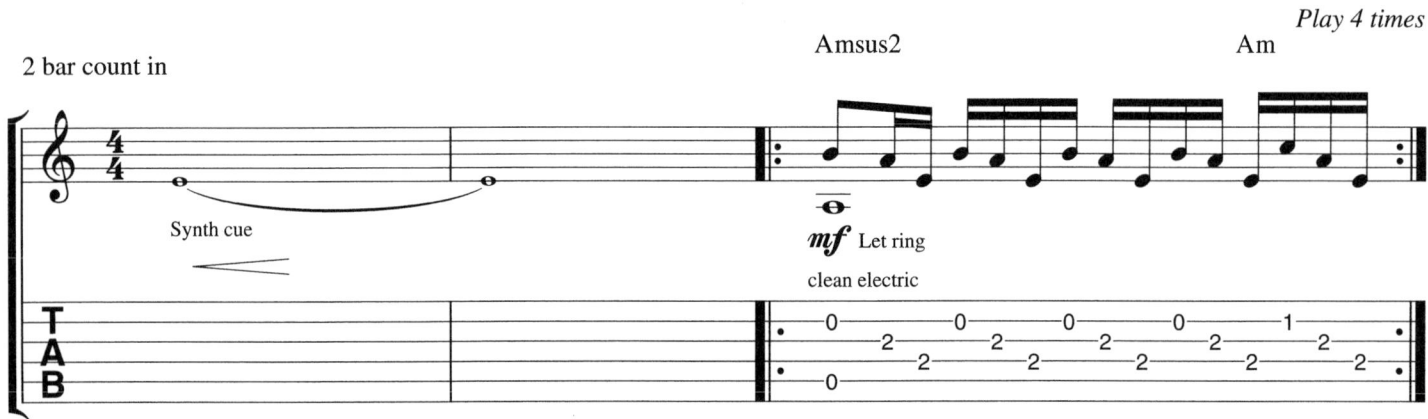

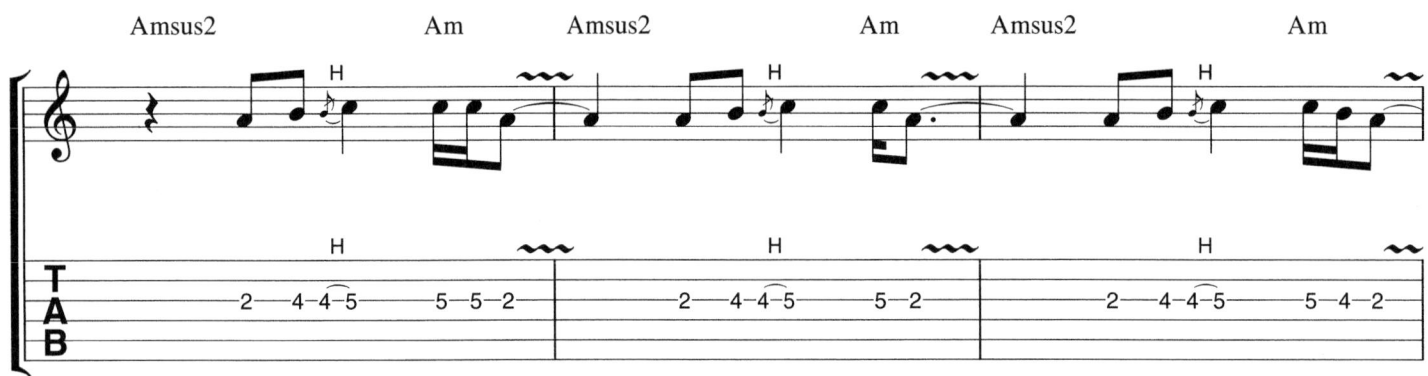

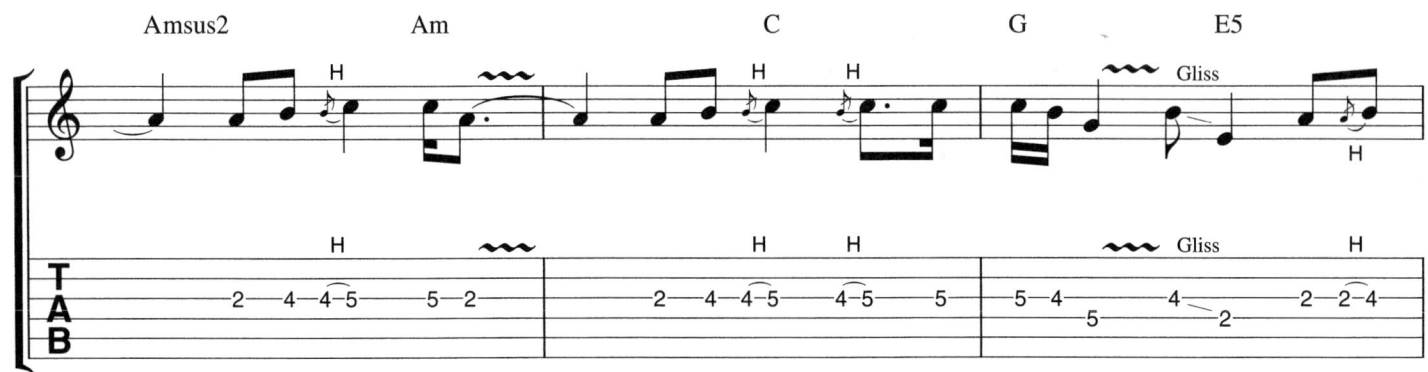

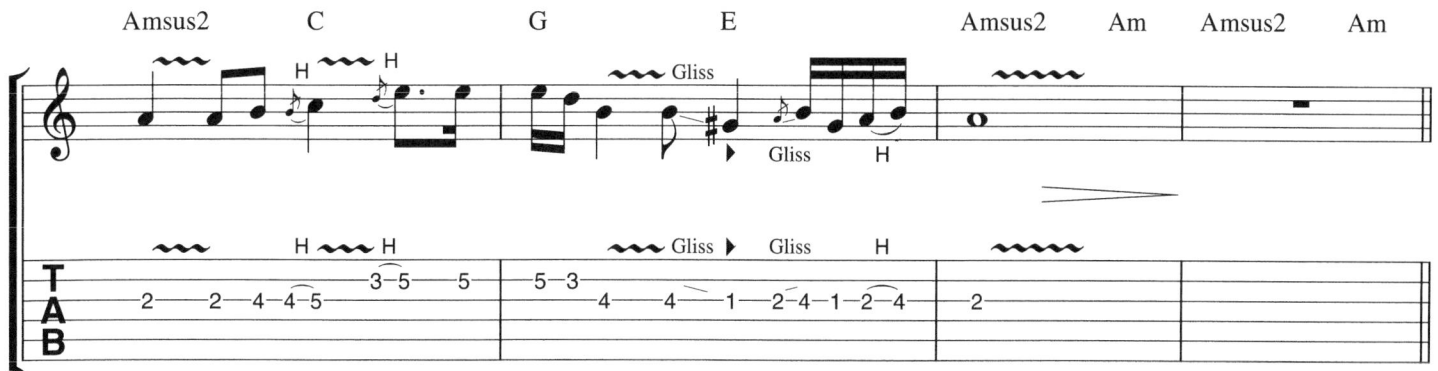
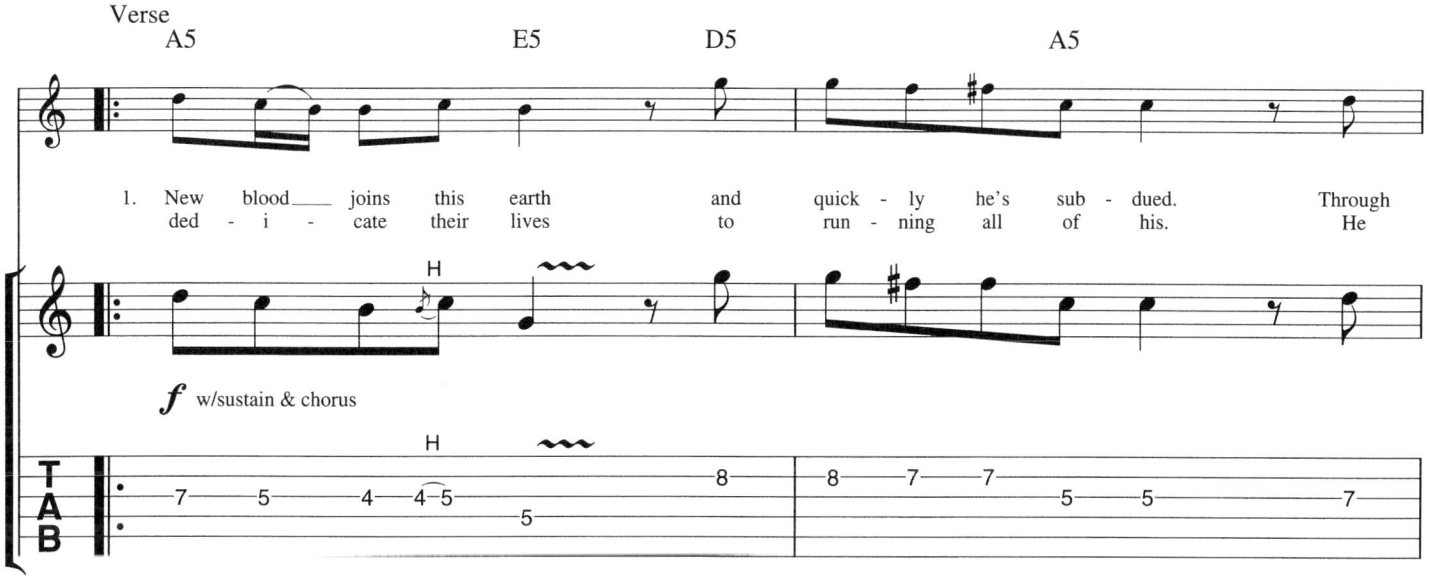
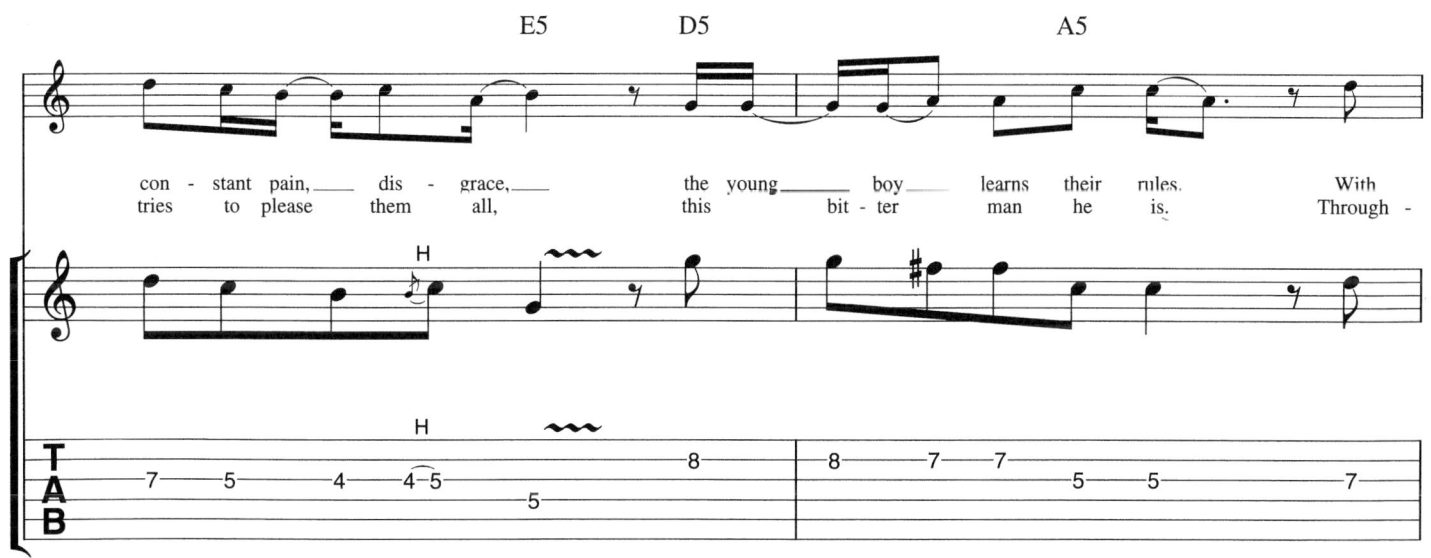

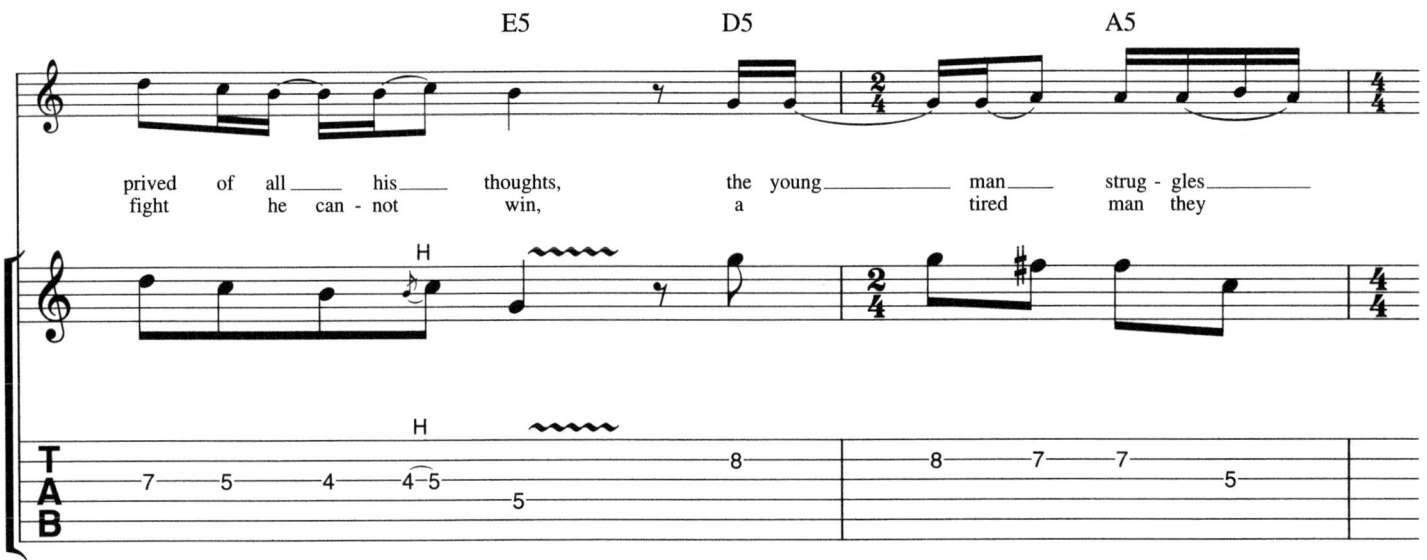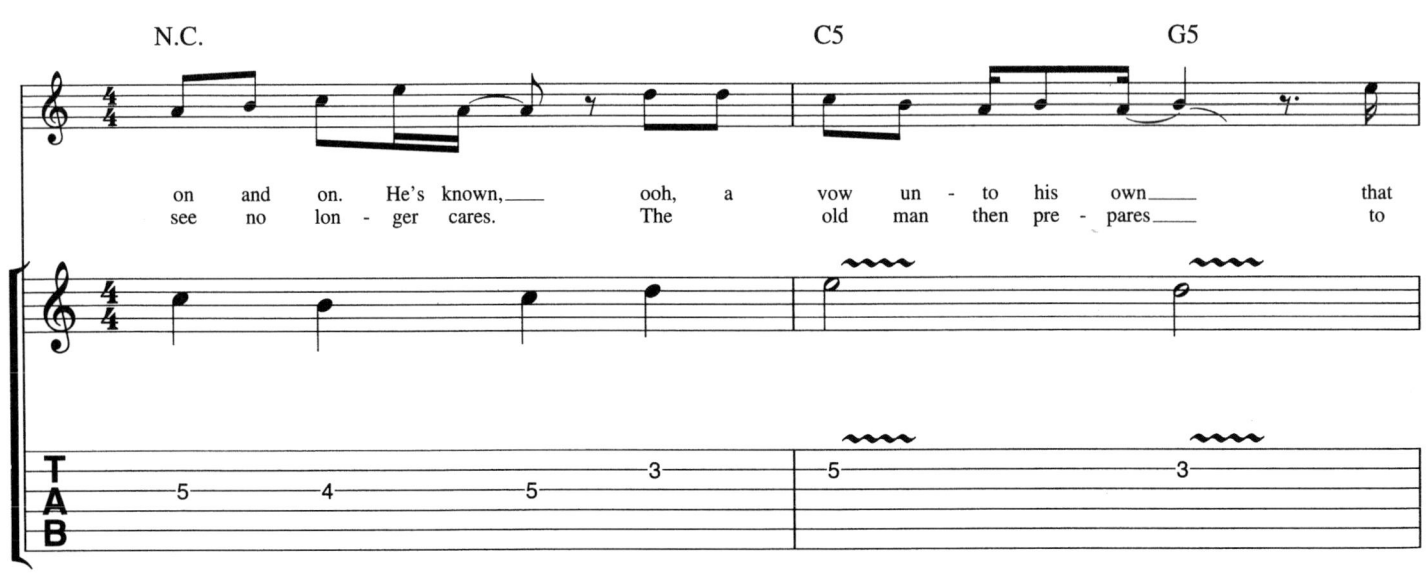

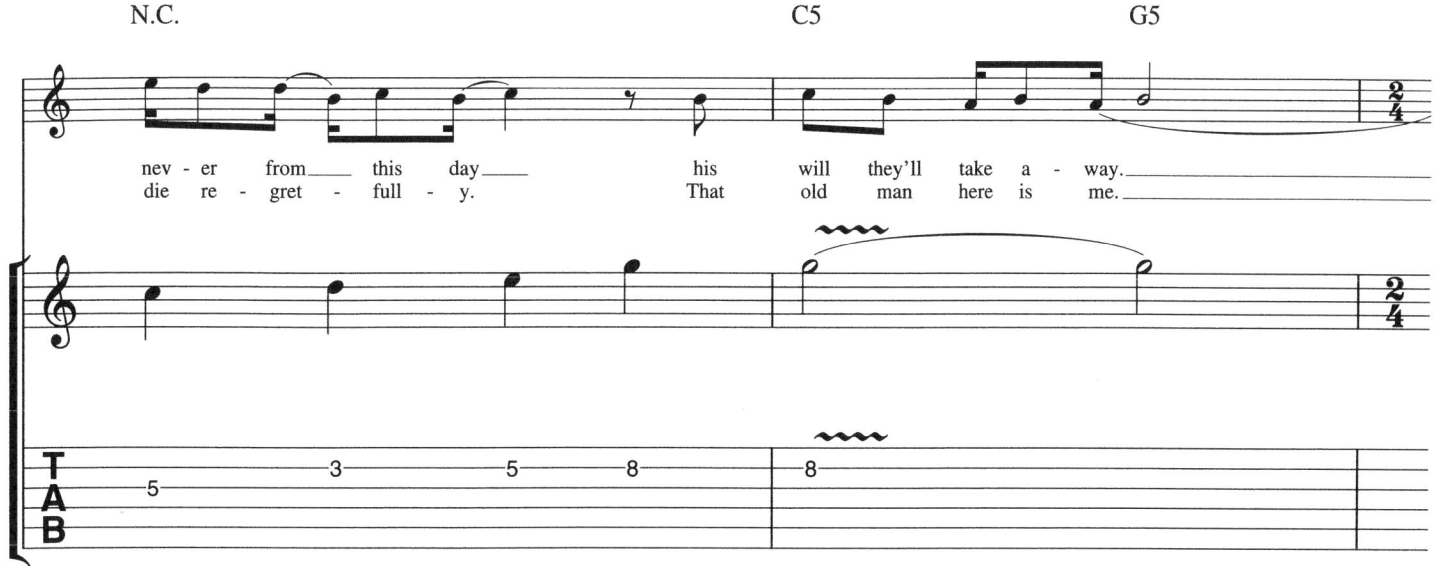

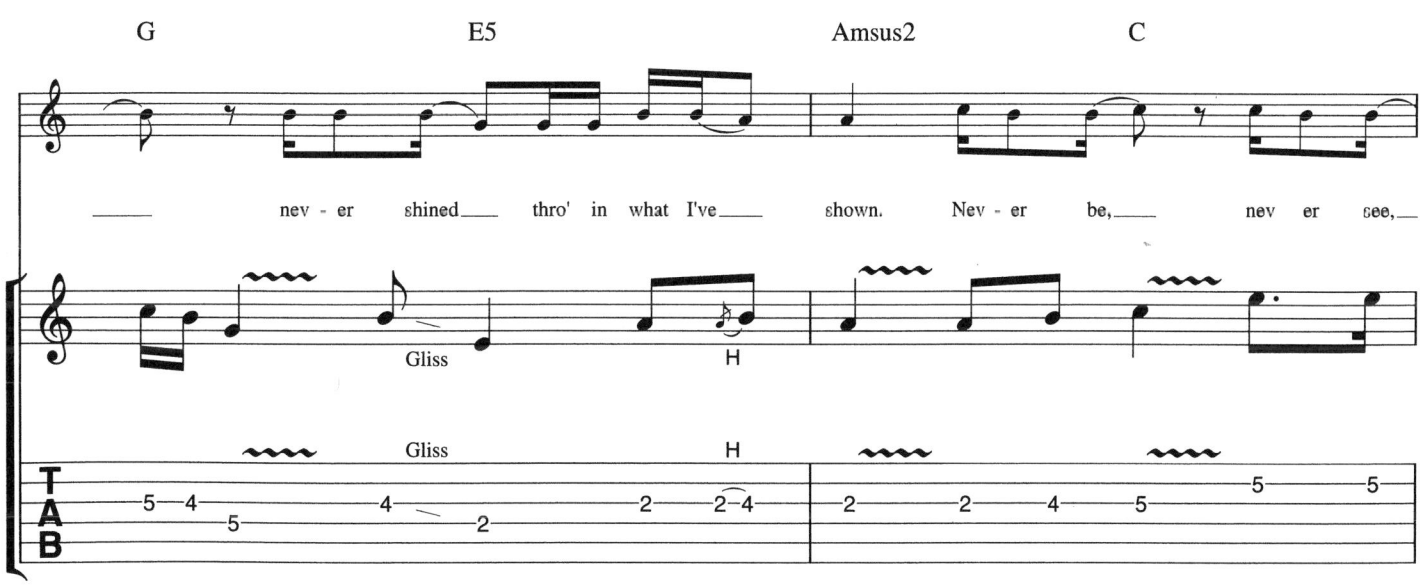

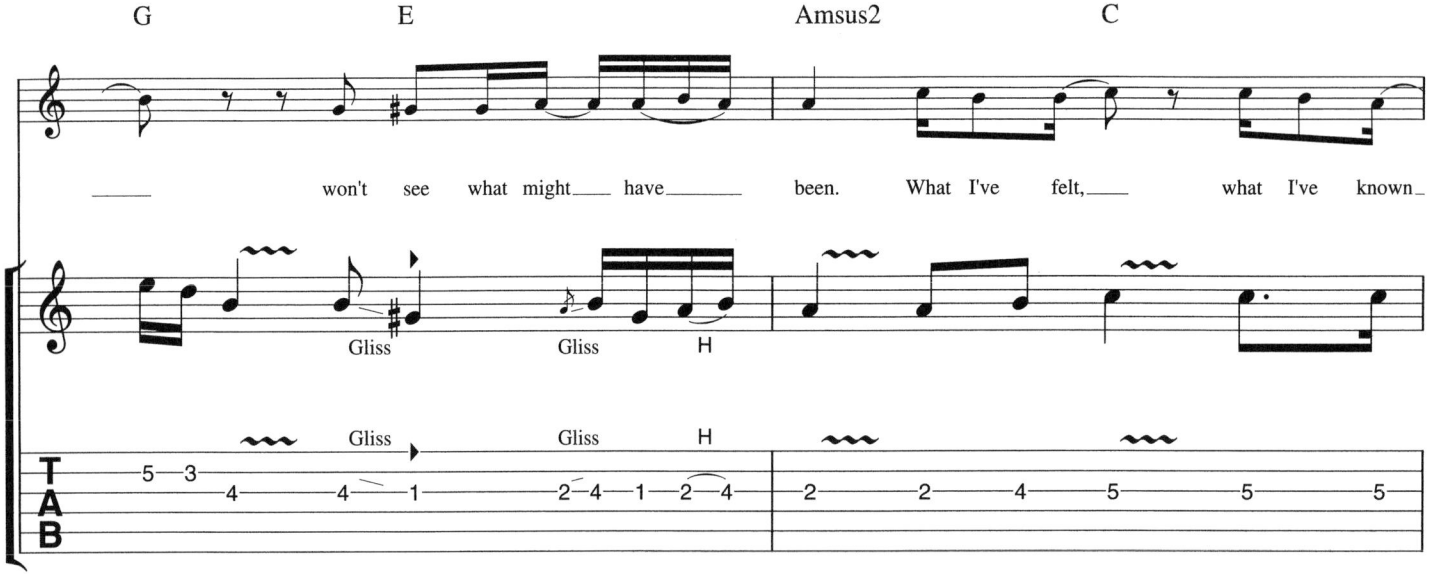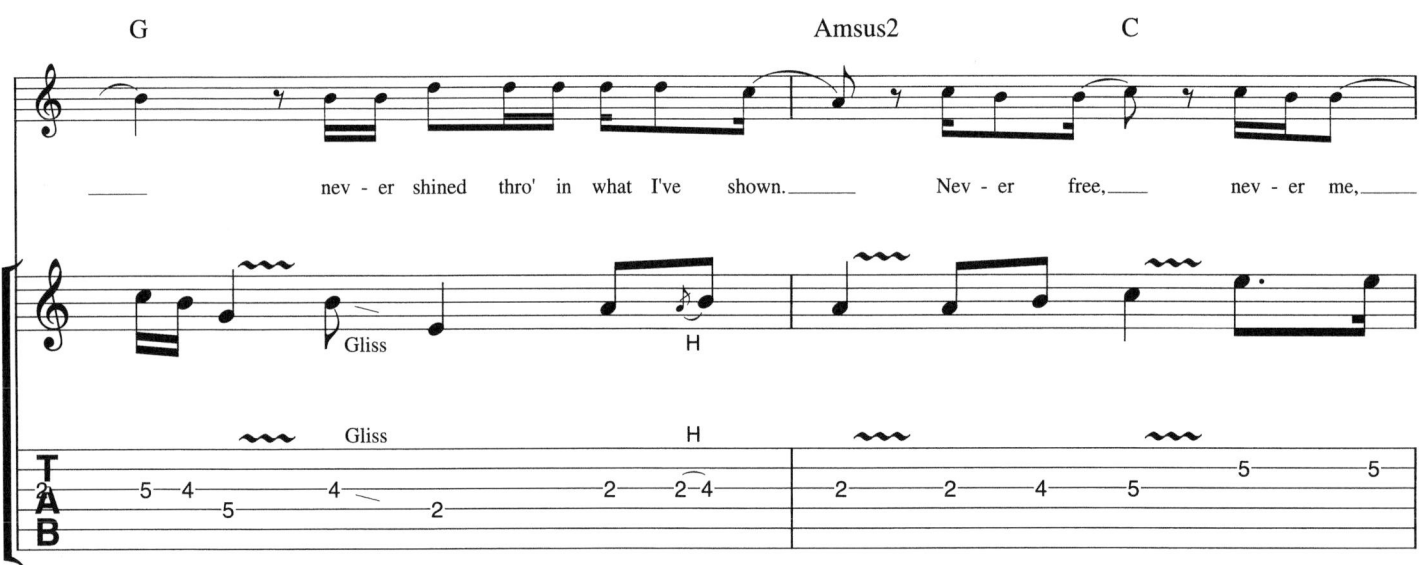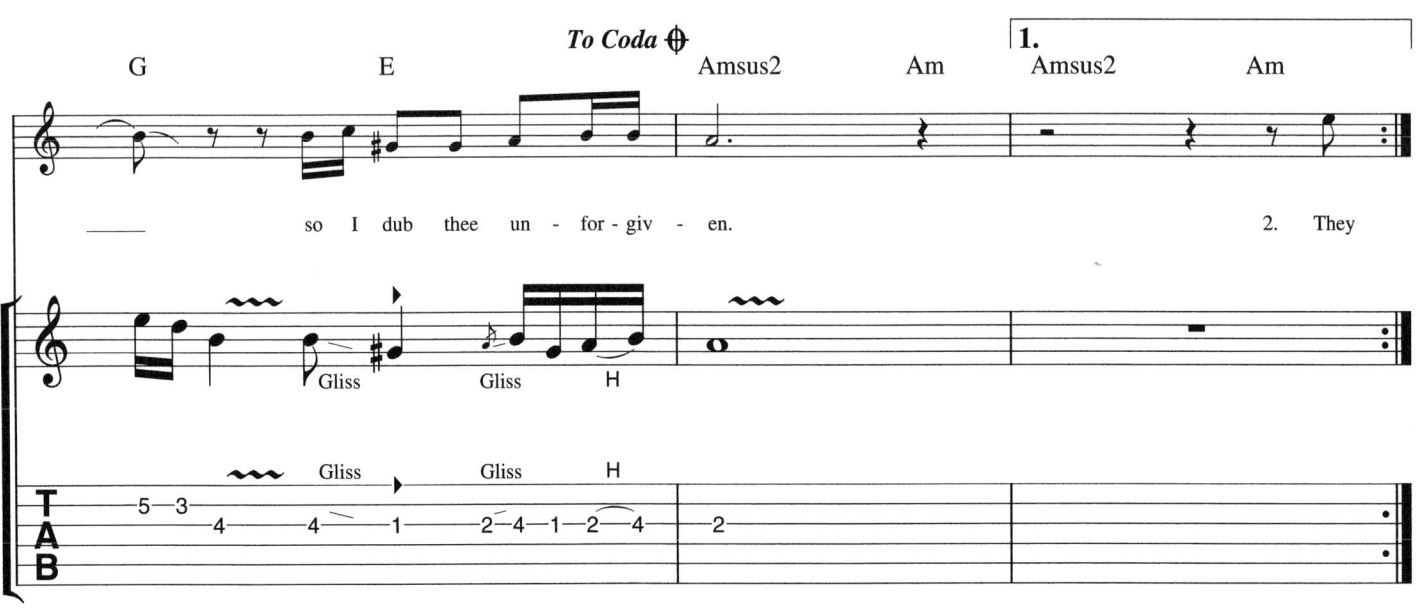

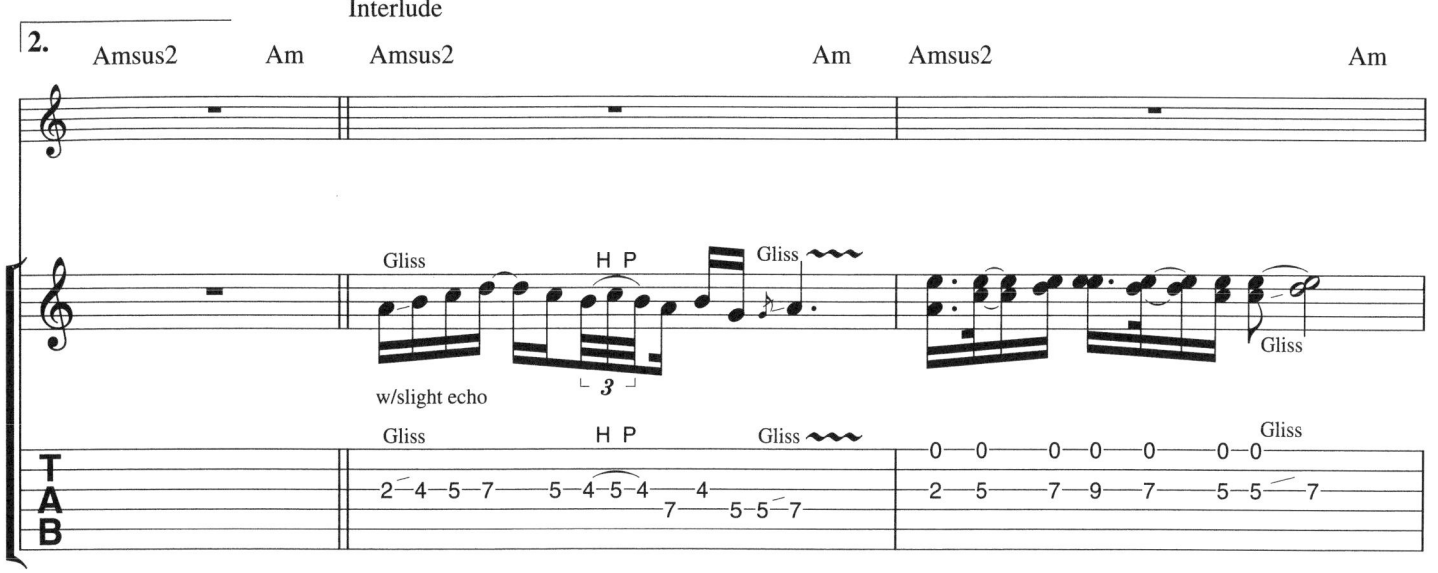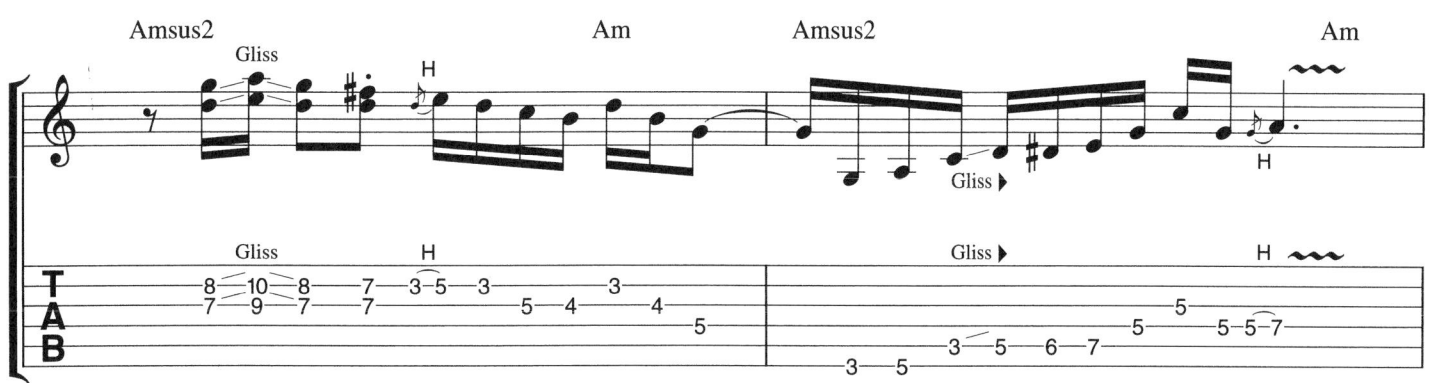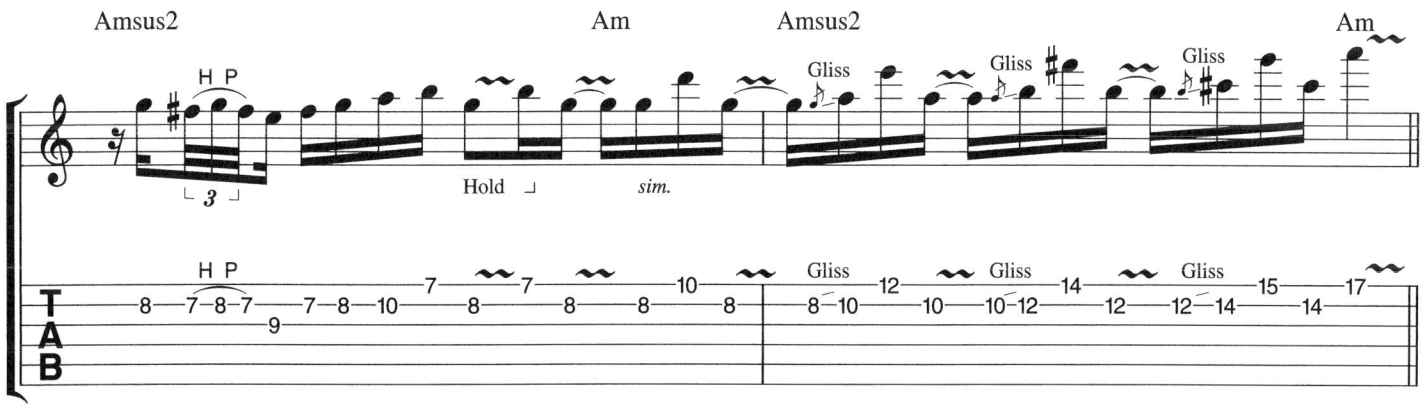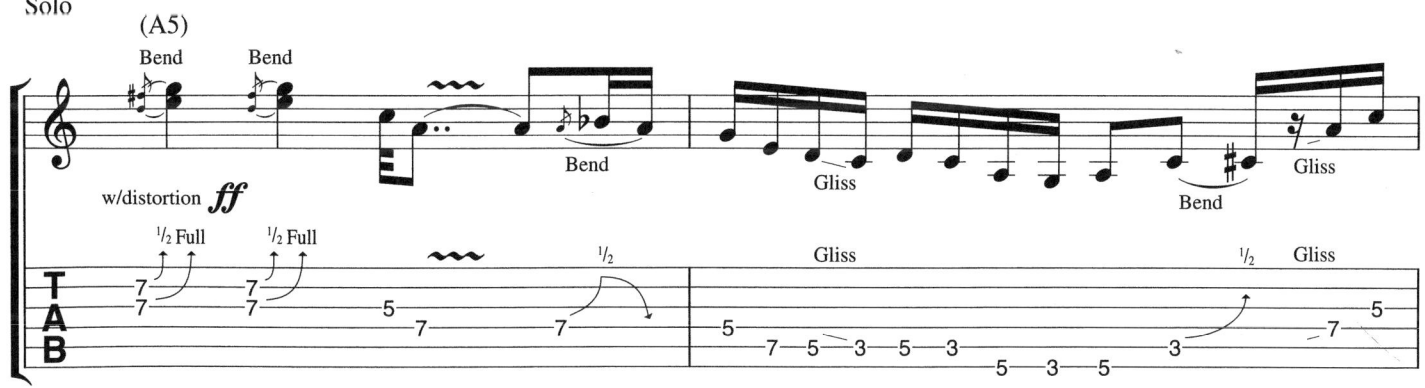

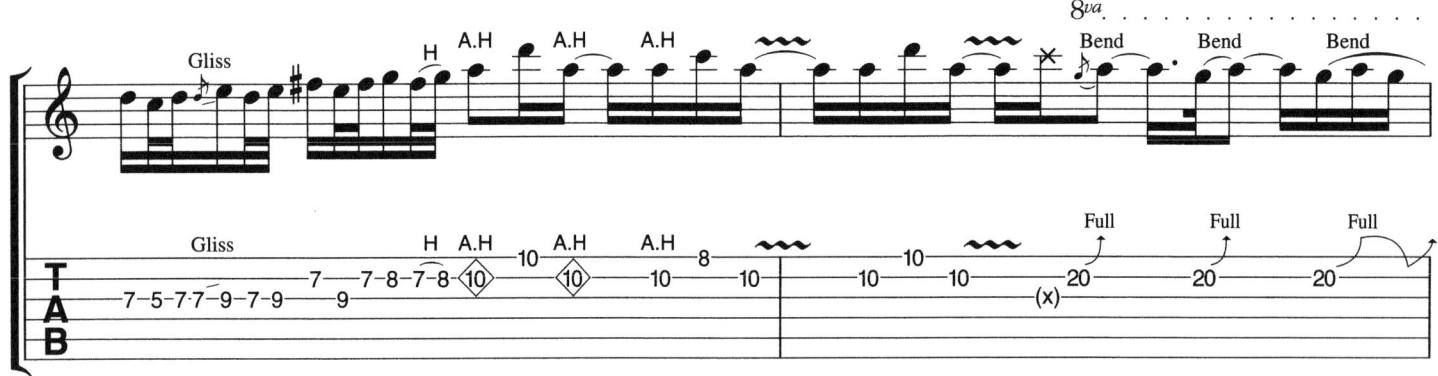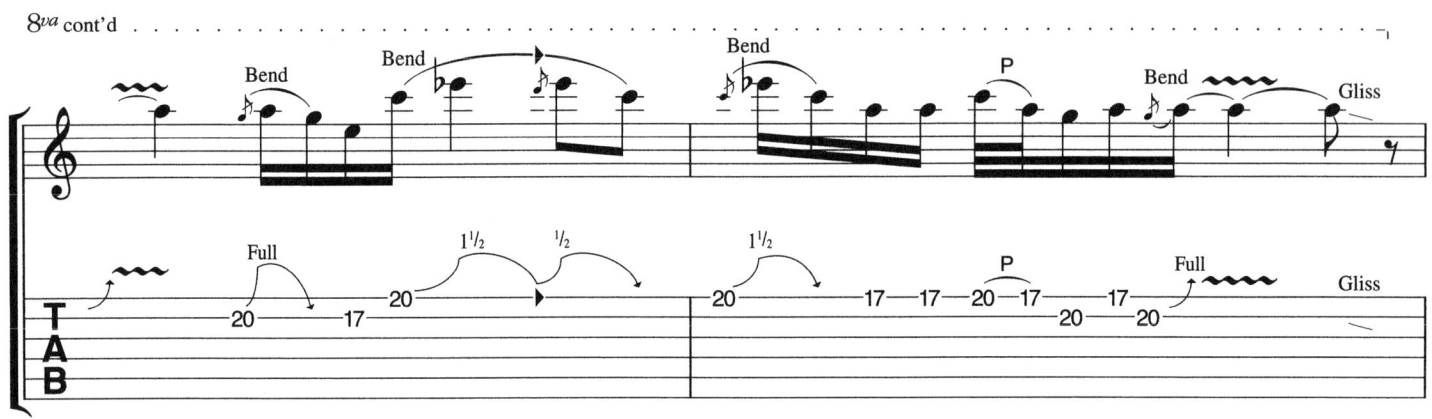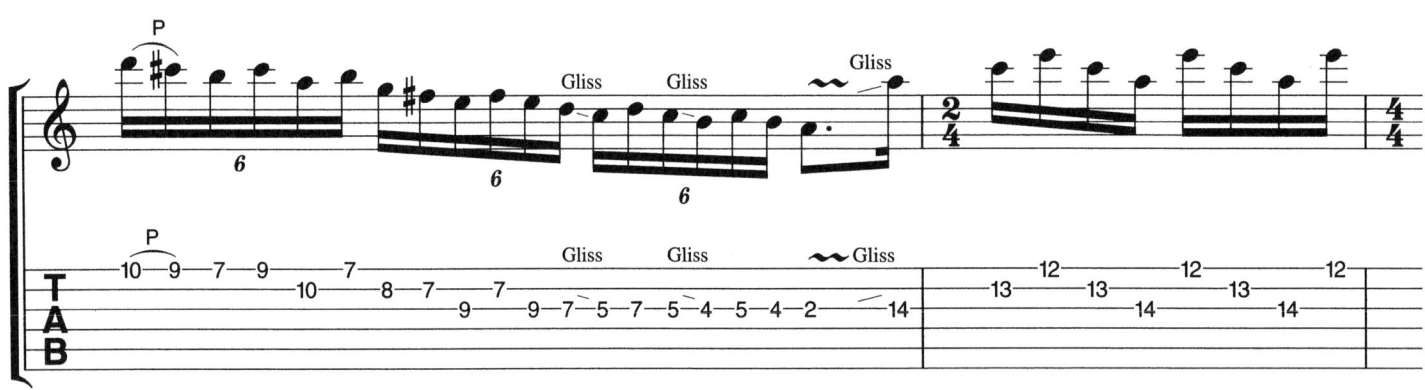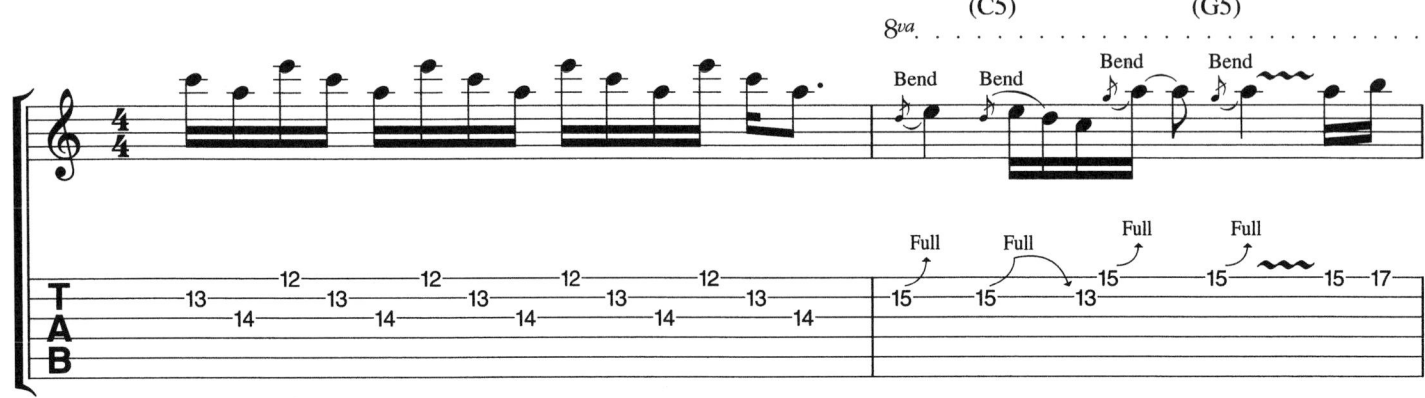

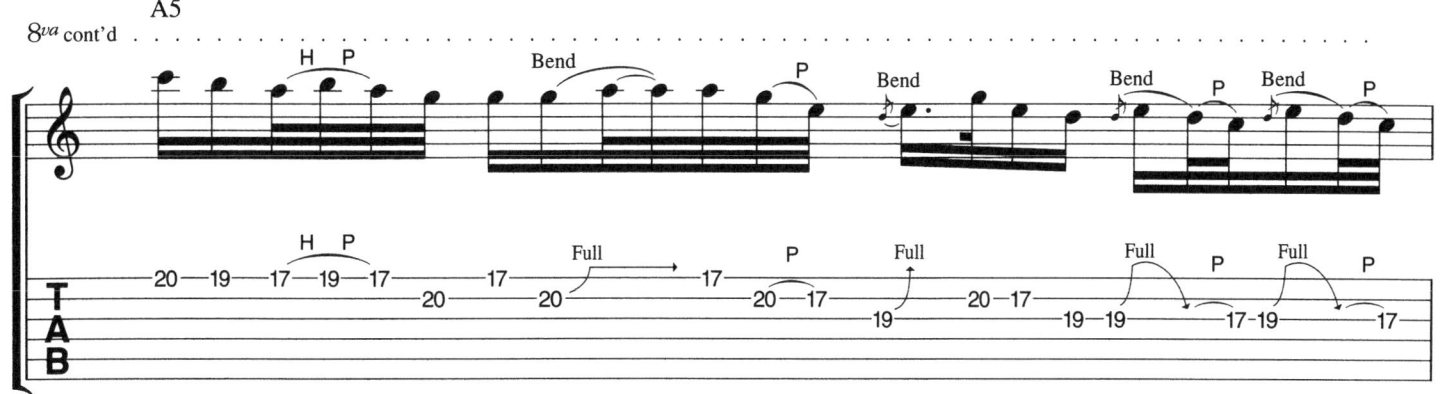
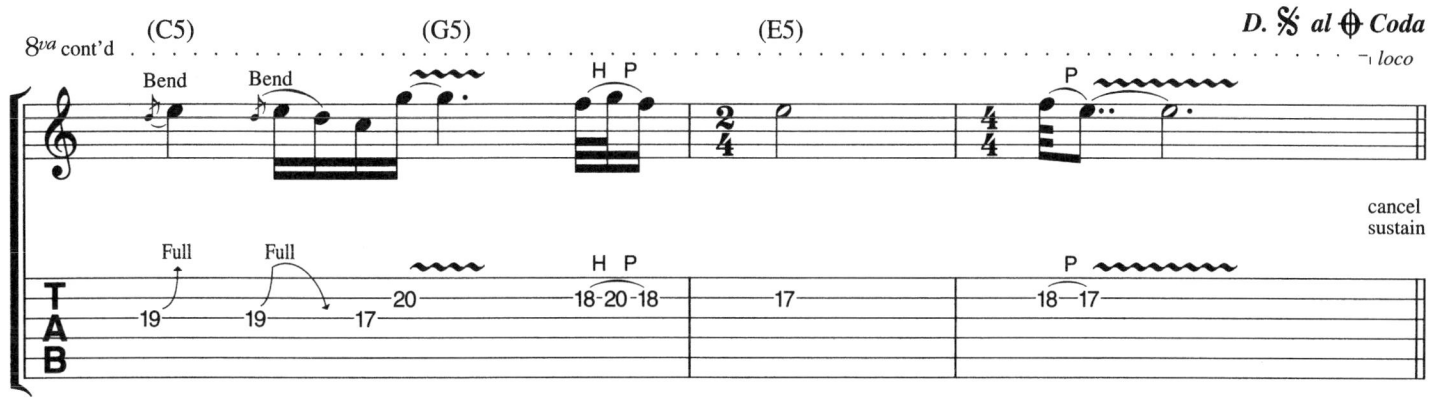
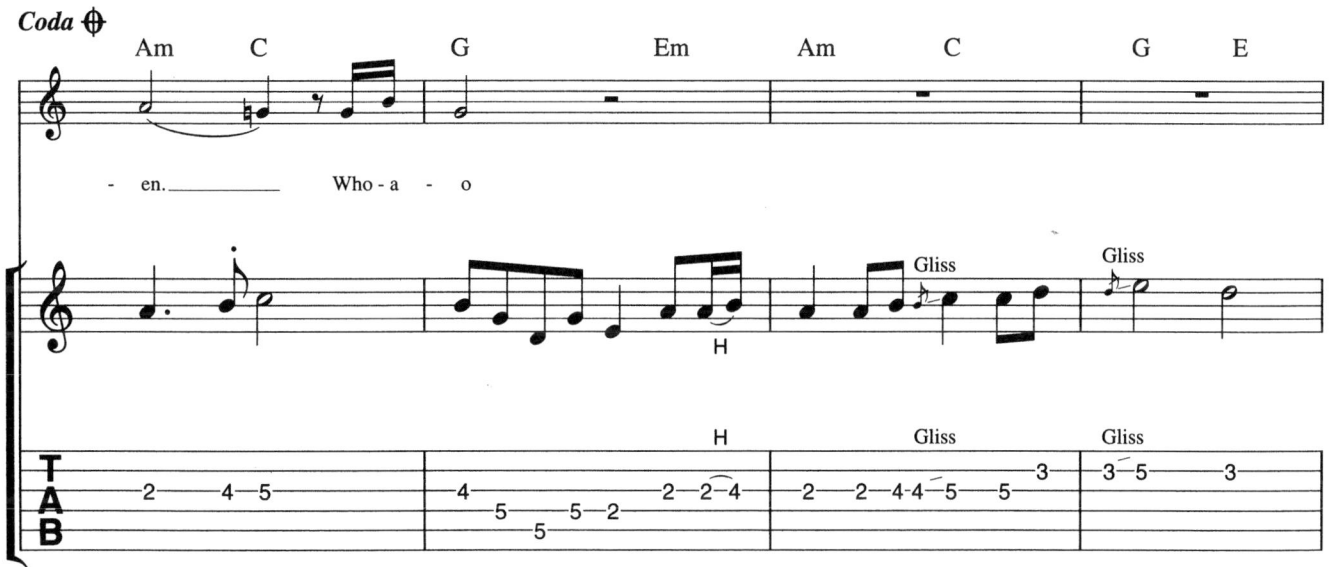

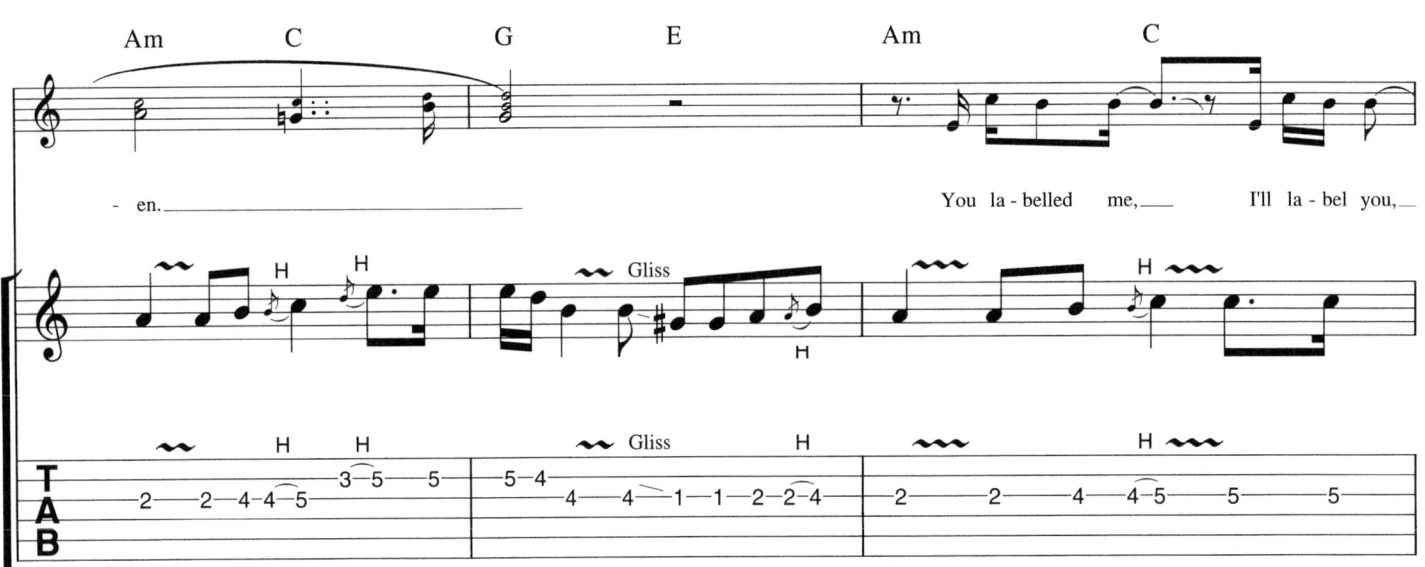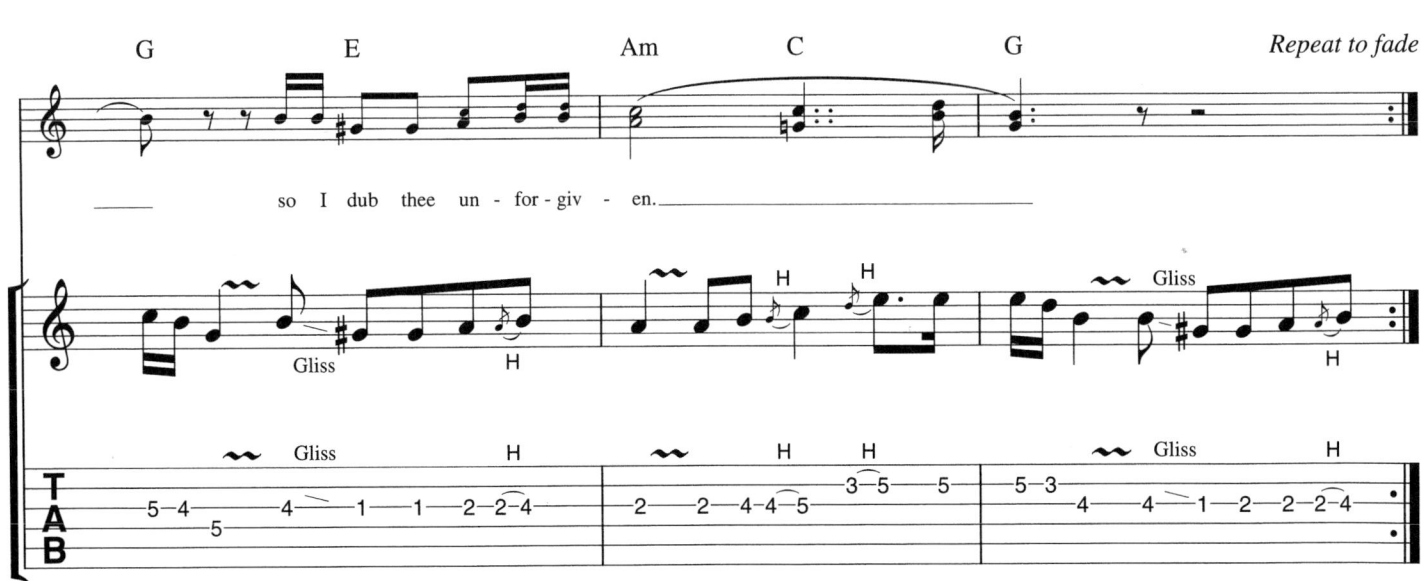

play guitar with...

the best of metallica

part 2

- 78 **carpe diem baby**
- **creeping death** 66
- 87 **leper messiah**
- **the memory remains** 106
- 98 **seek and destroy**
- **whiskey in the jar** 114

- 124 **guitar tablature explained**
- **translations** 126 & 127

creeping death

Words & Music by James Hetfield, Lars Ulrich, Cliff Burton & Kirk Hammett

© Copyright 1984 Creeping Death Music, USA.
PolyGram Music Publishing Limited, 47 British Grove, London W4.
All Rights Reserved. International Copyright Secured.

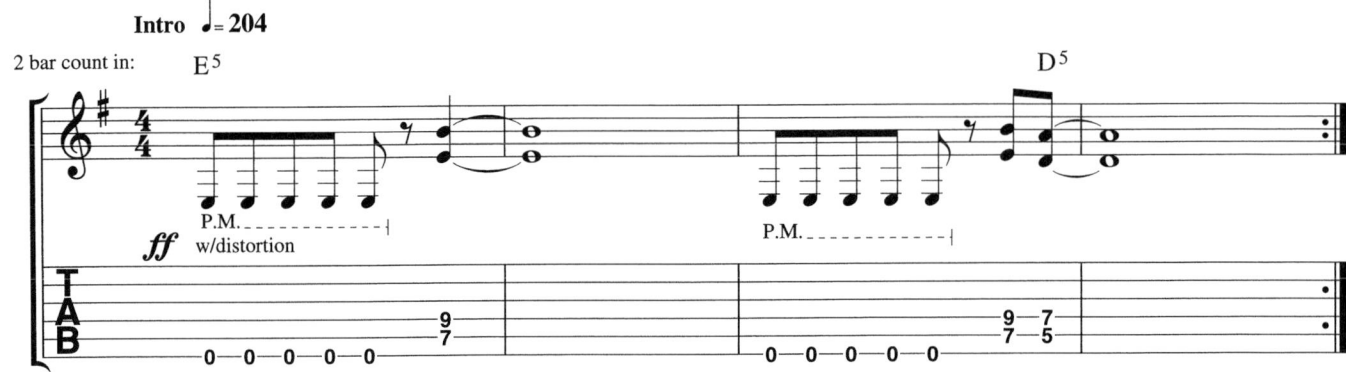

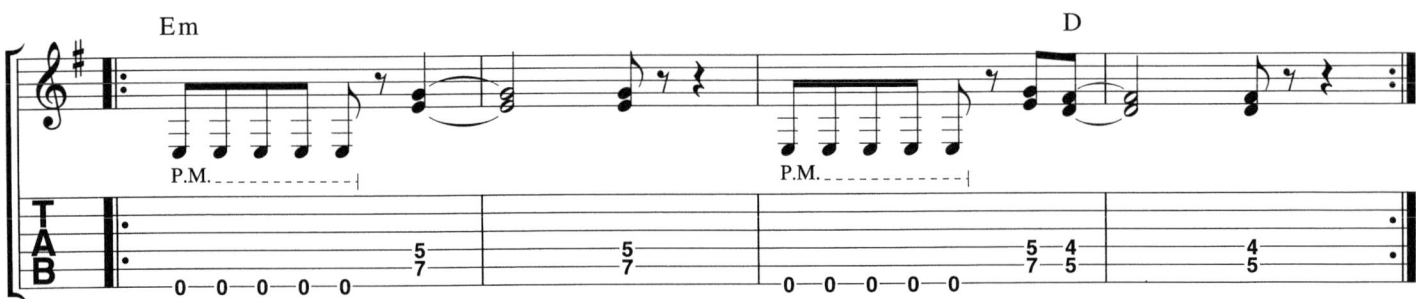

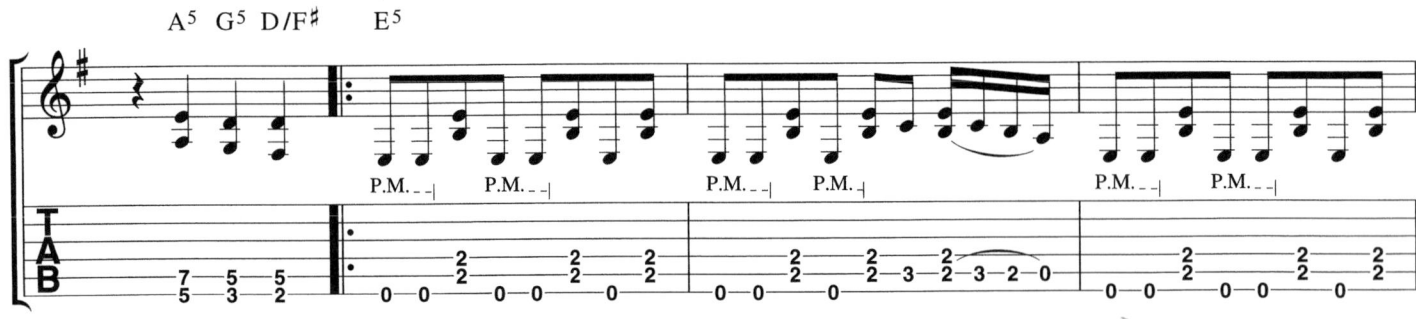

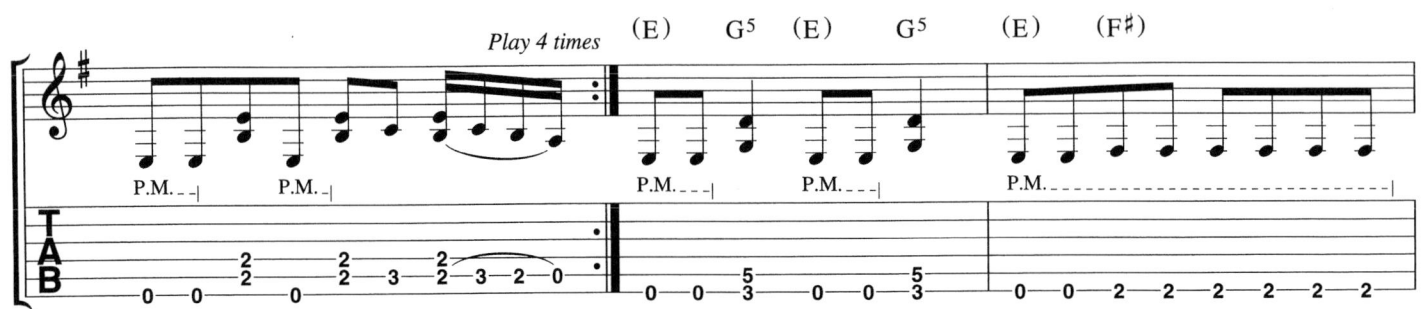

66

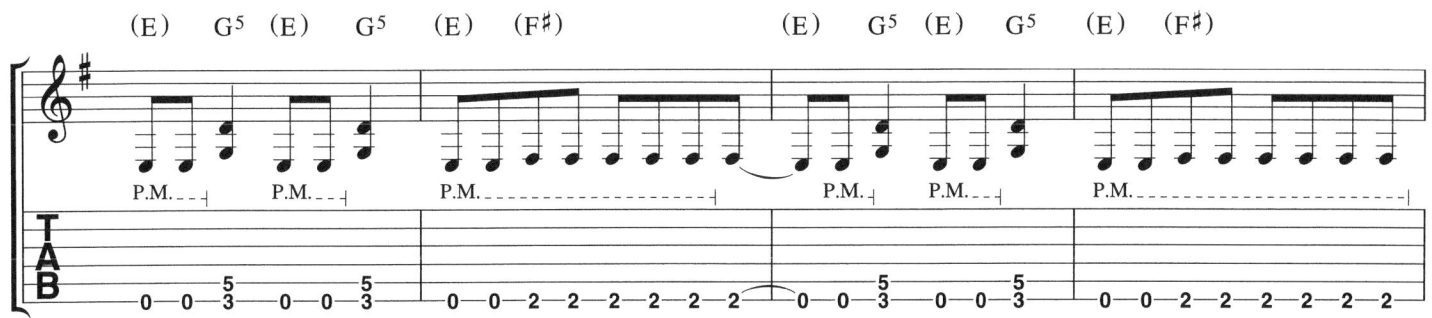
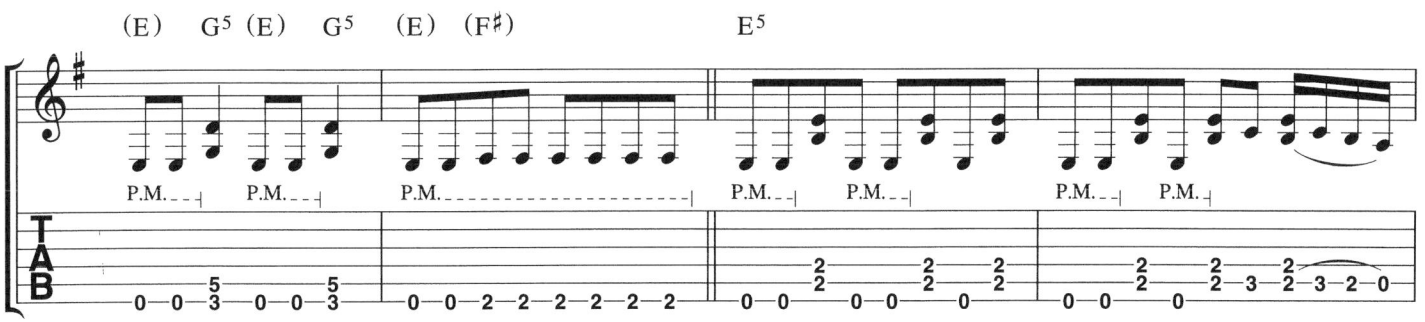
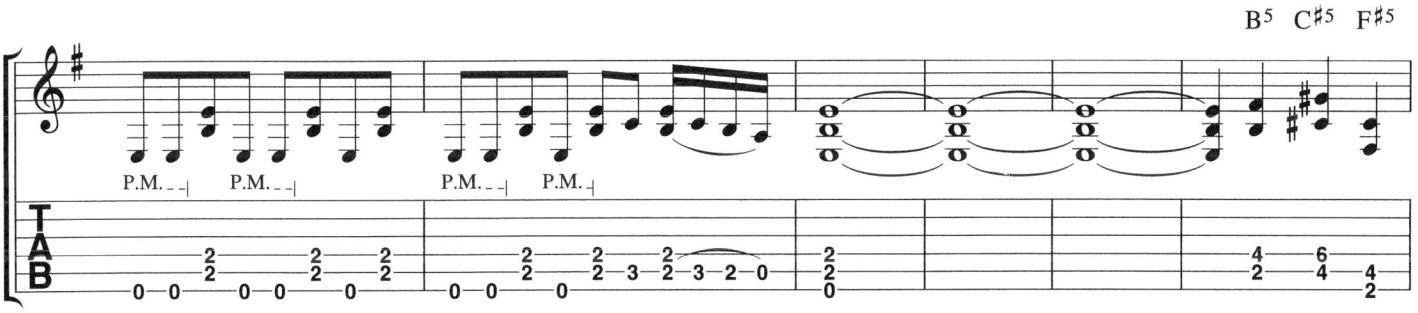

Verse

1. Slaves, Hebrews born to serve, to the Pha-
2. Now, let my people go, land of Gosh-
3. I rule the midnight air, the destroy-

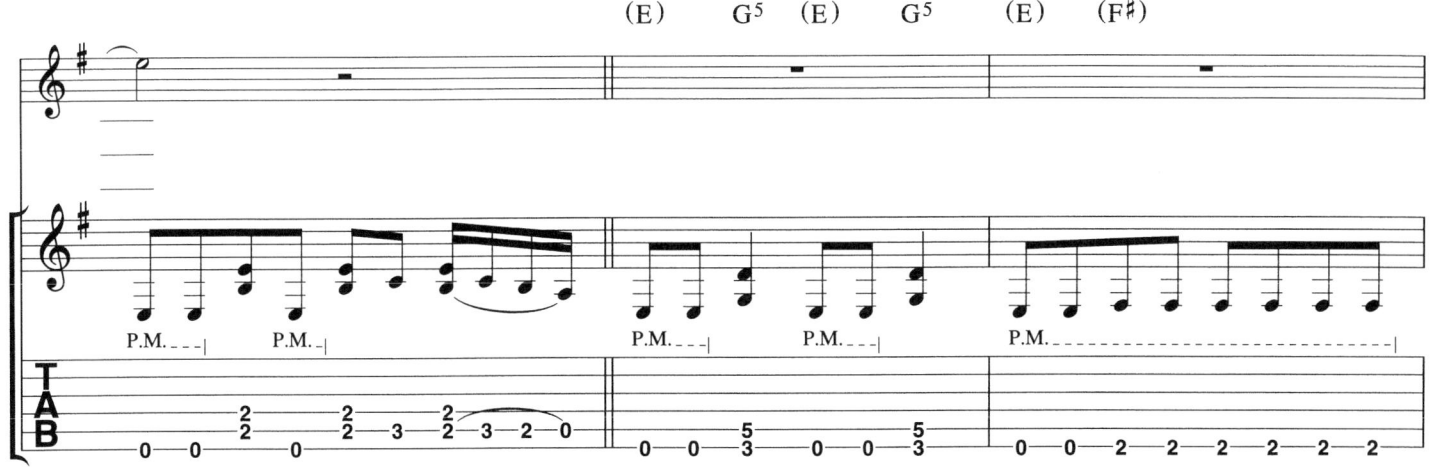
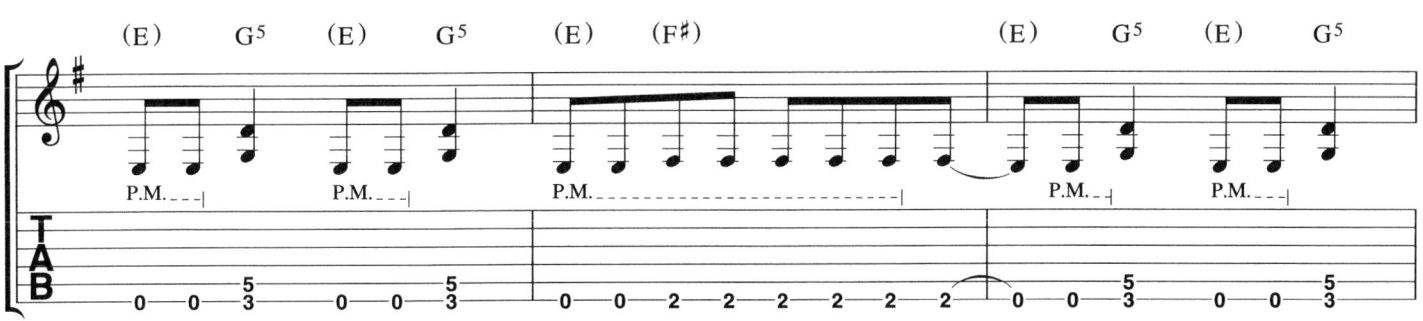
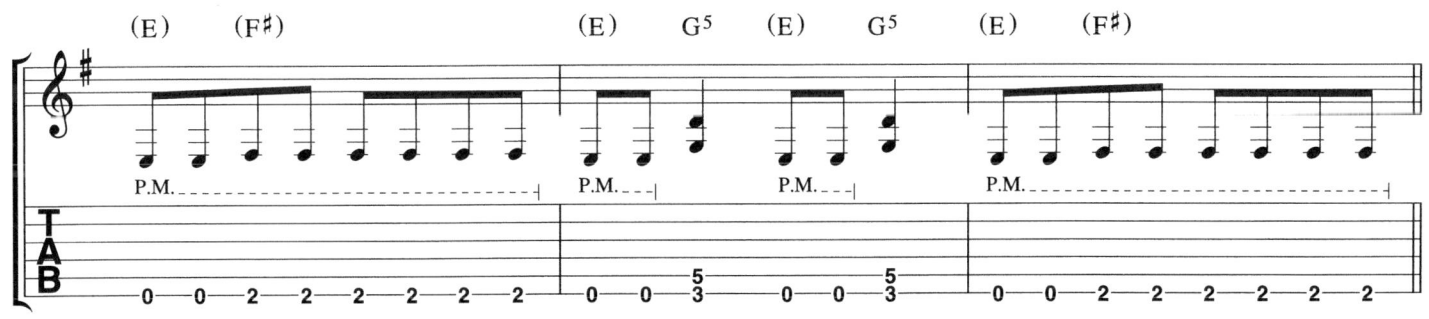

Chorus

So let it be writ-ten, so let it be done___

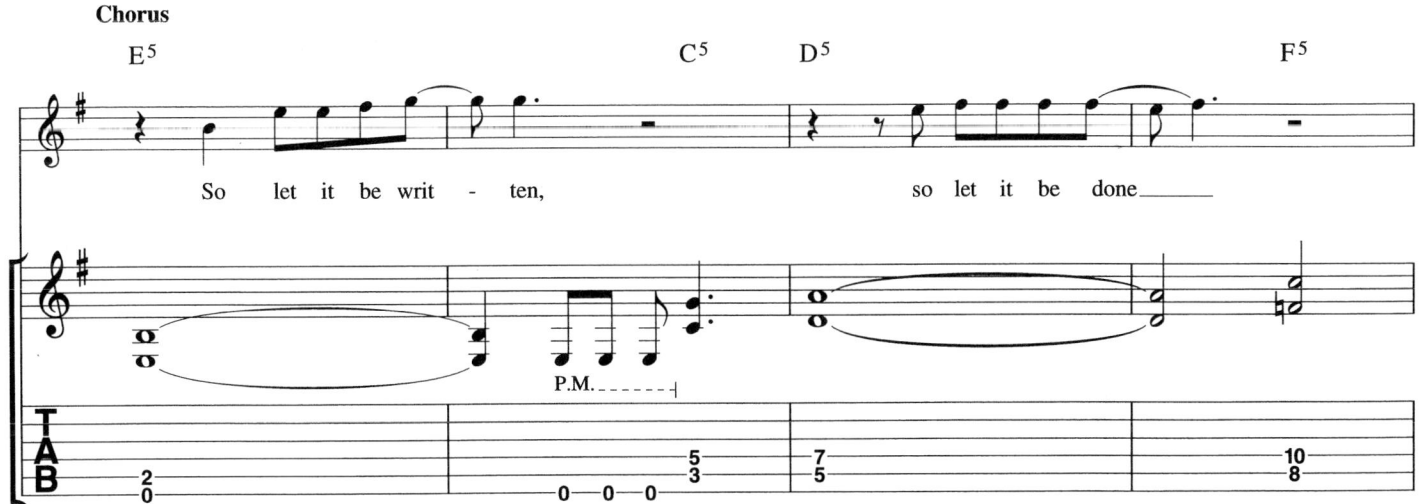

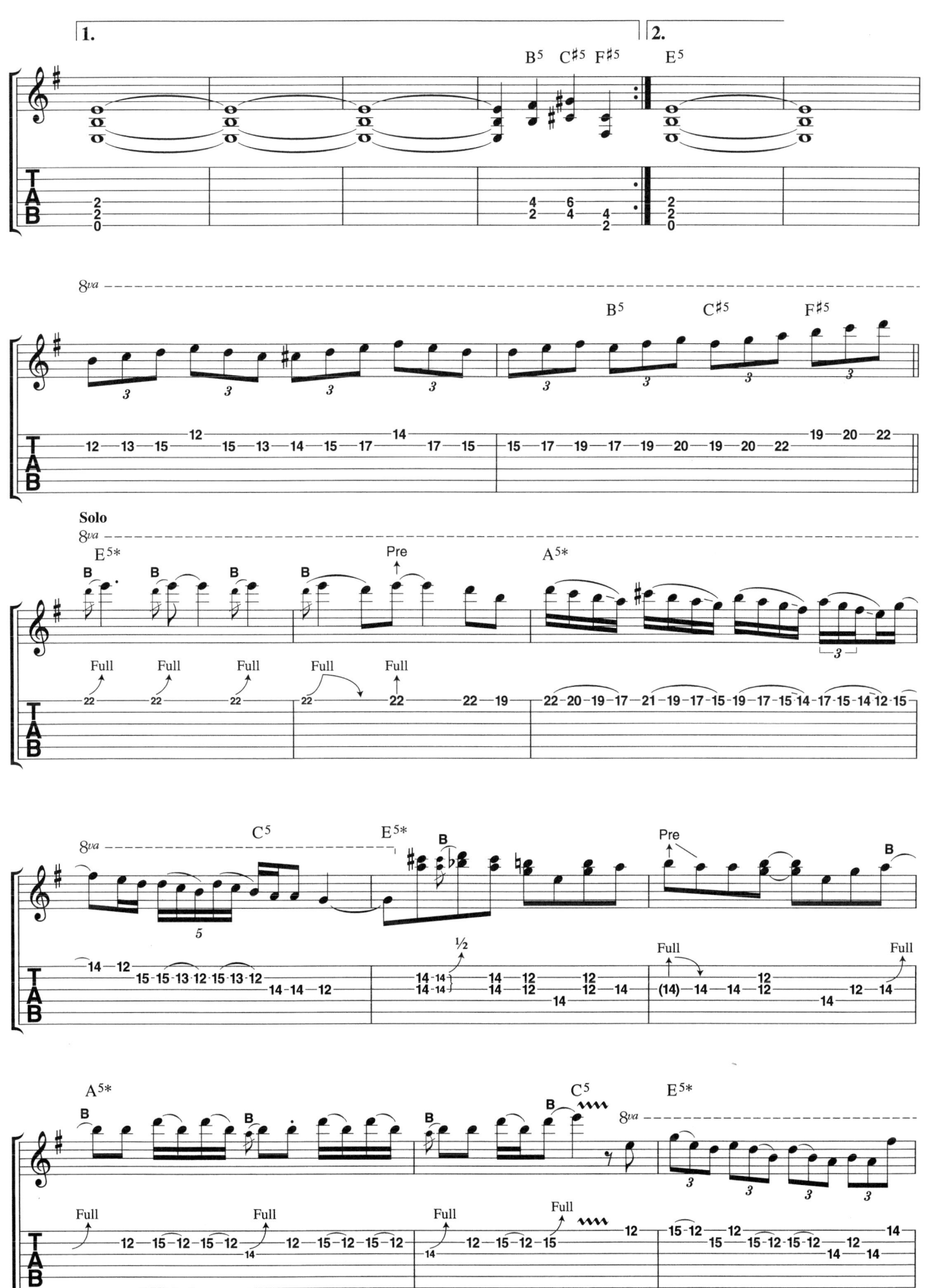

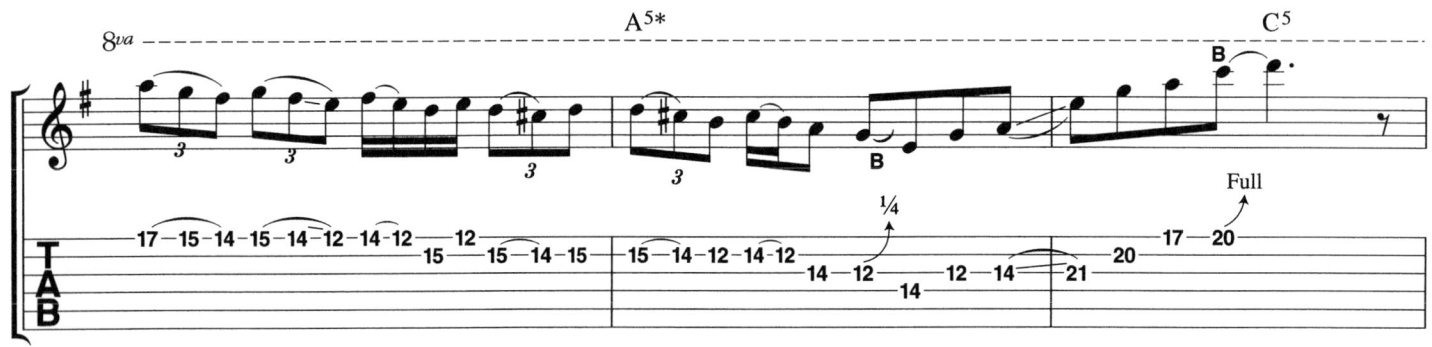

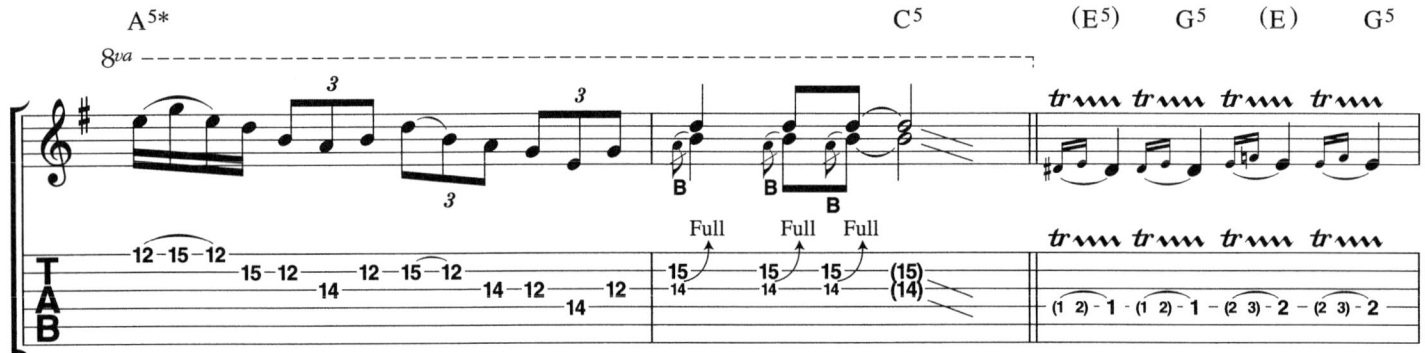
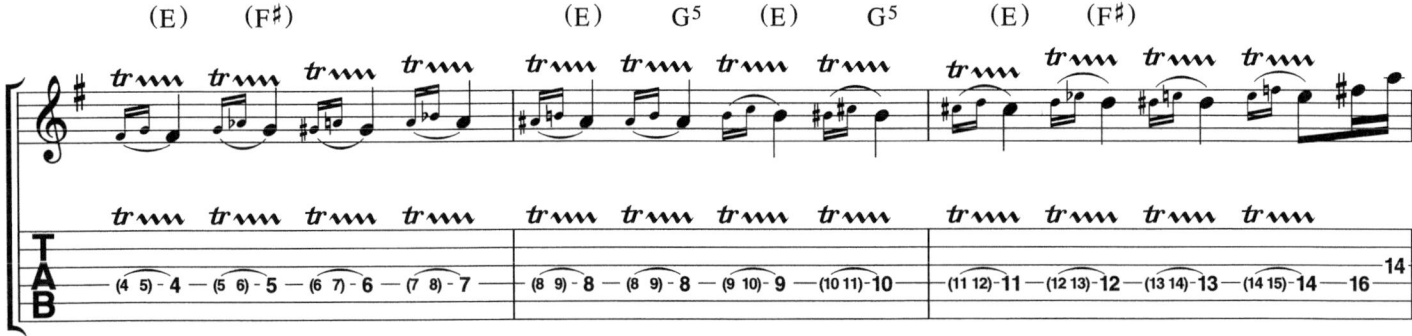
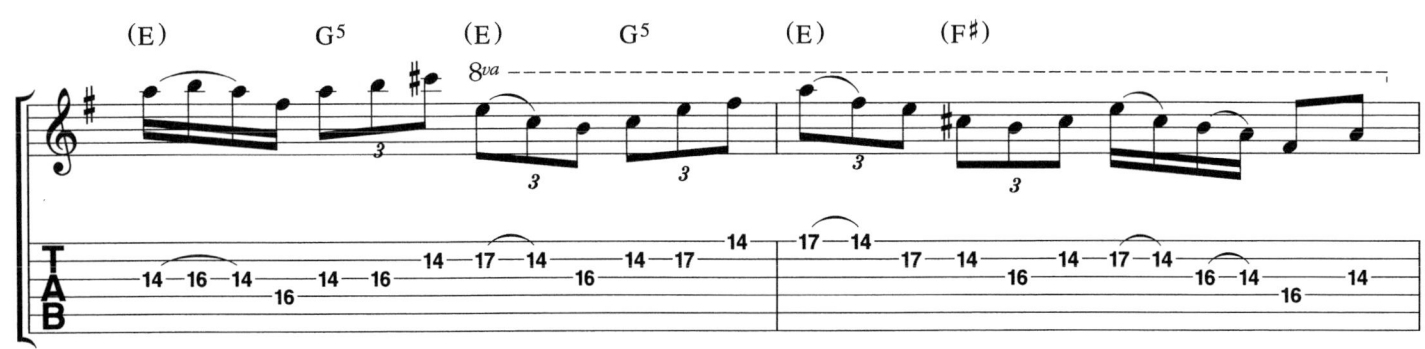

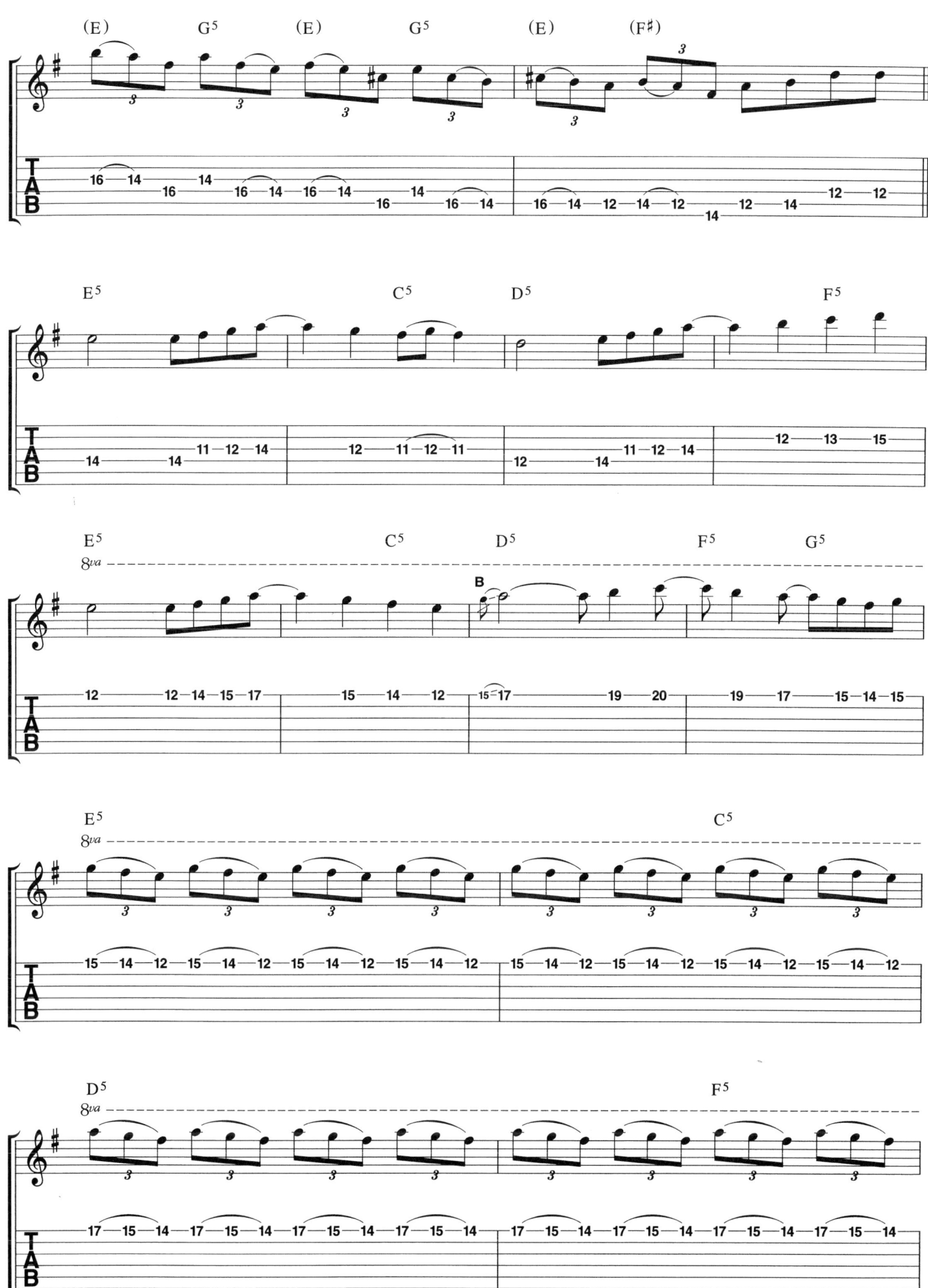

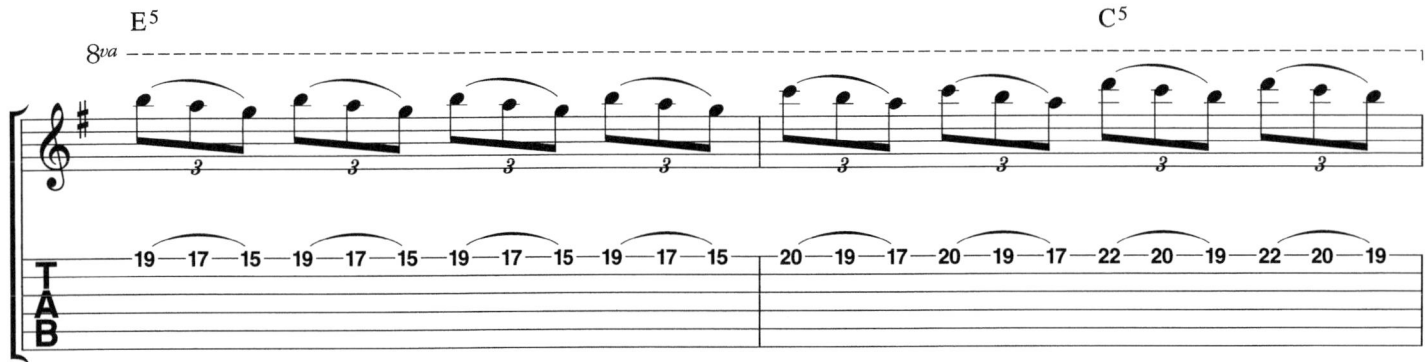
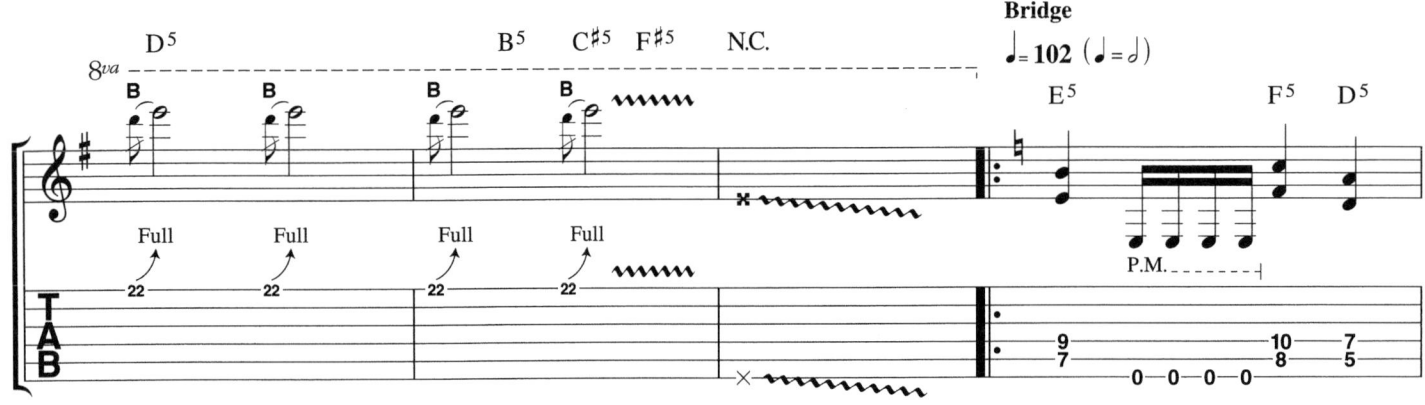
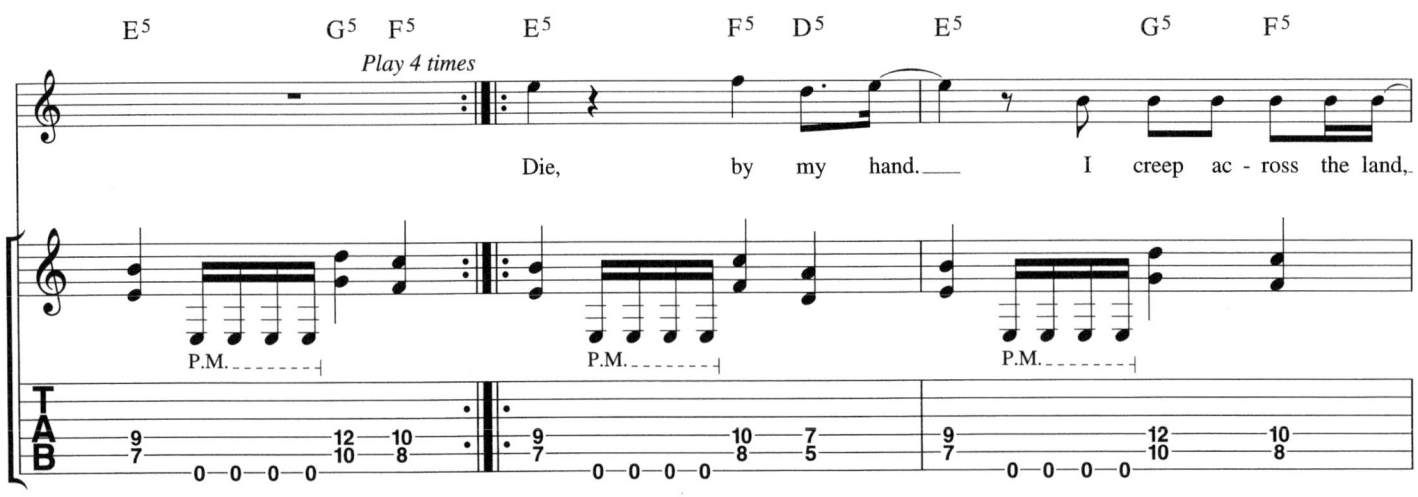

Die, by my hand. I creep across the land,

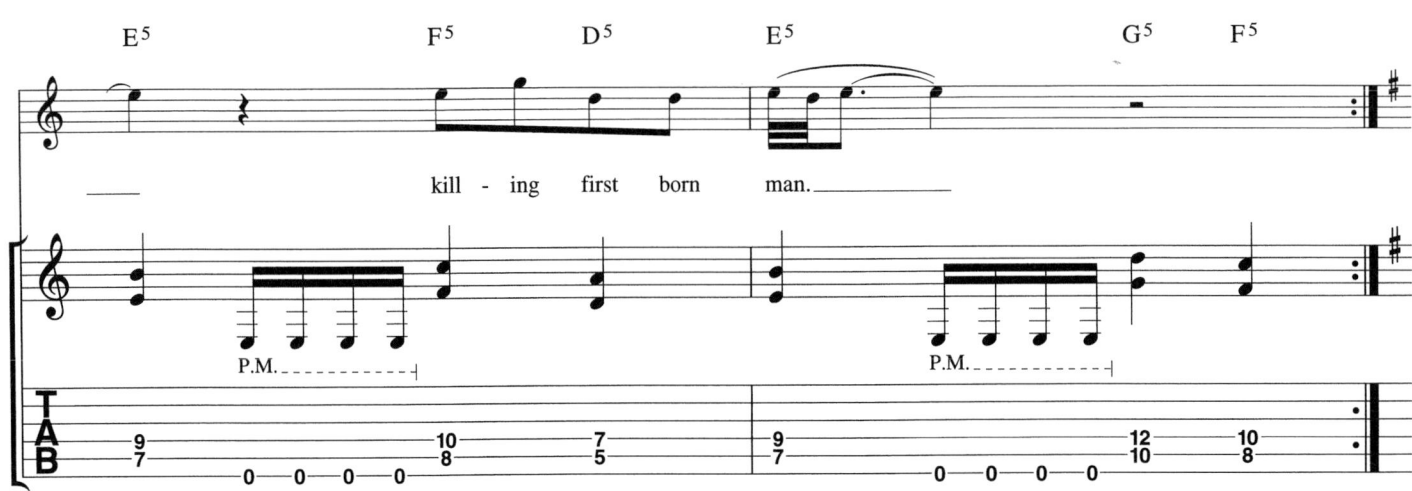

killing first born man.

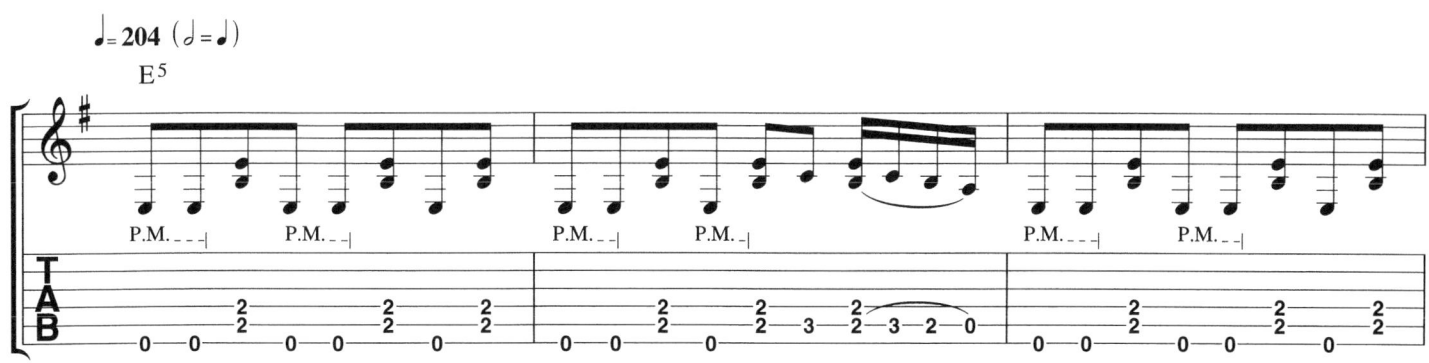
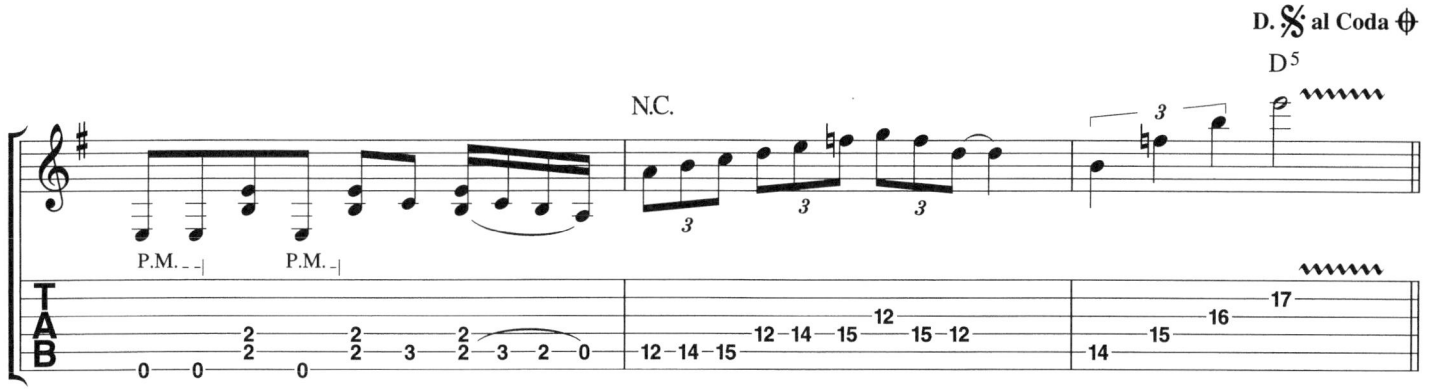

⊕ Coda

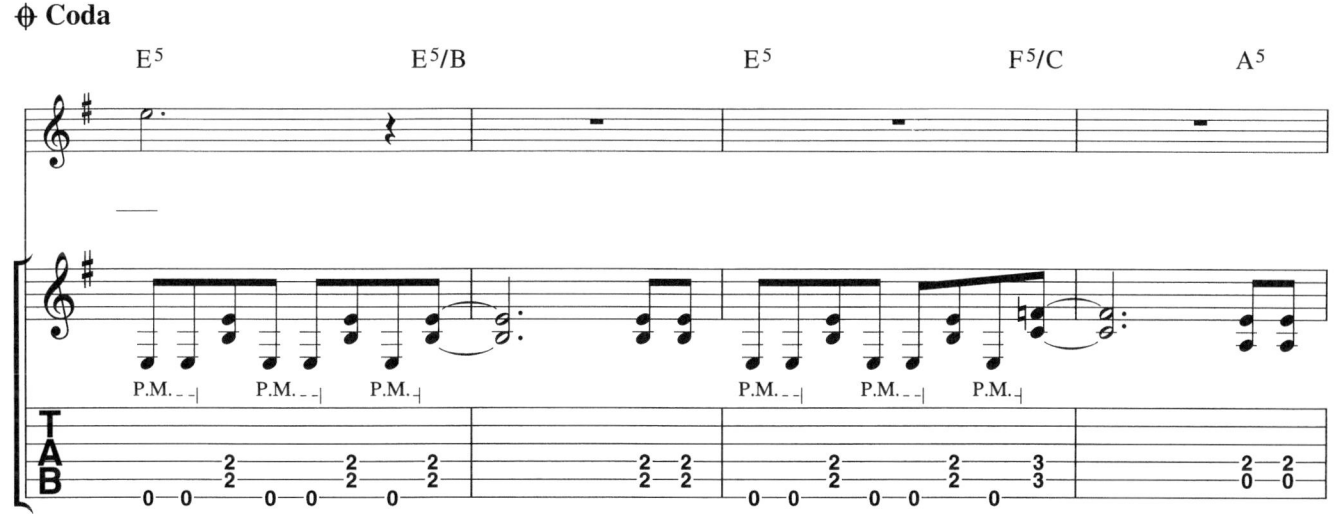
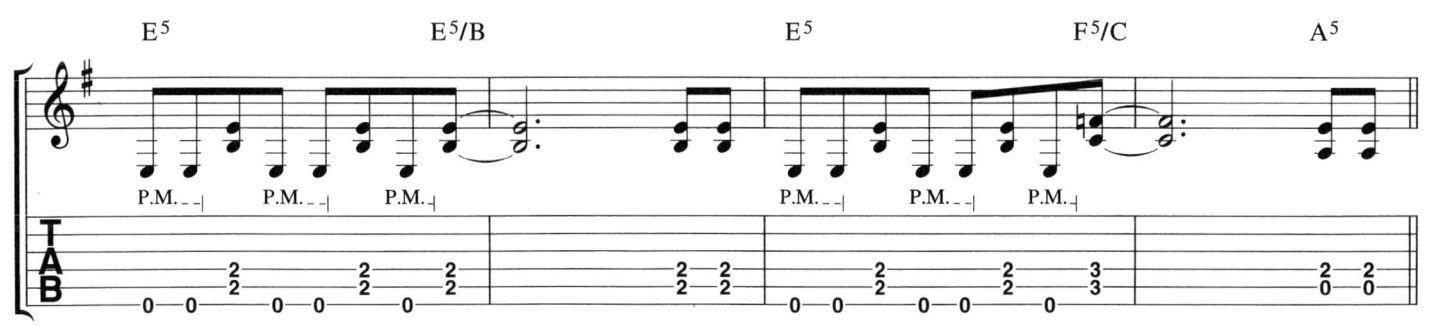

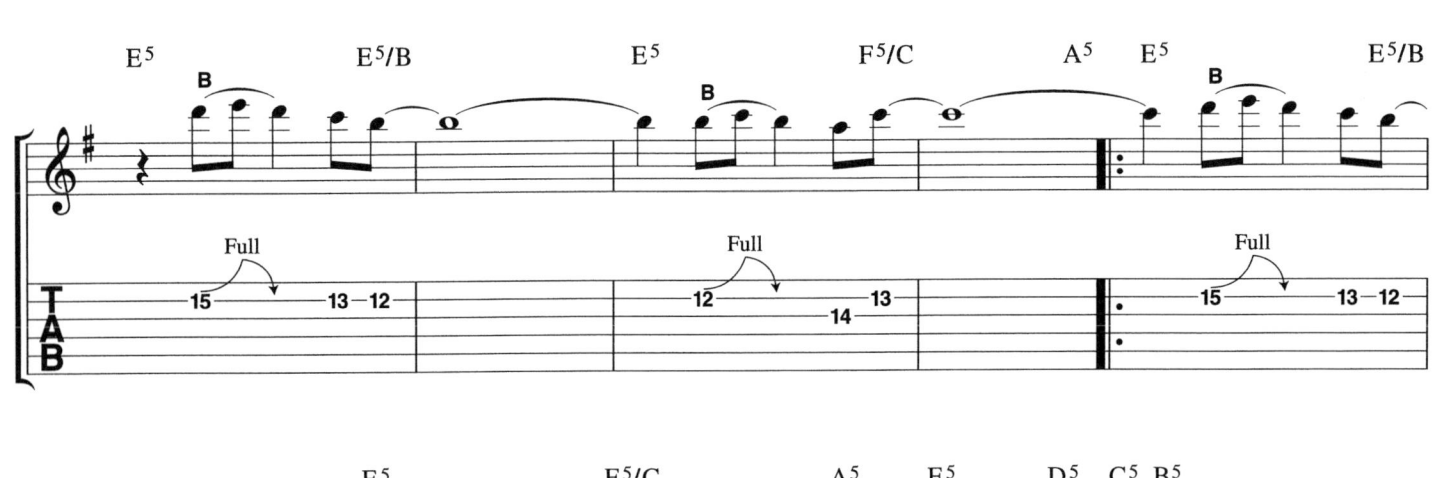
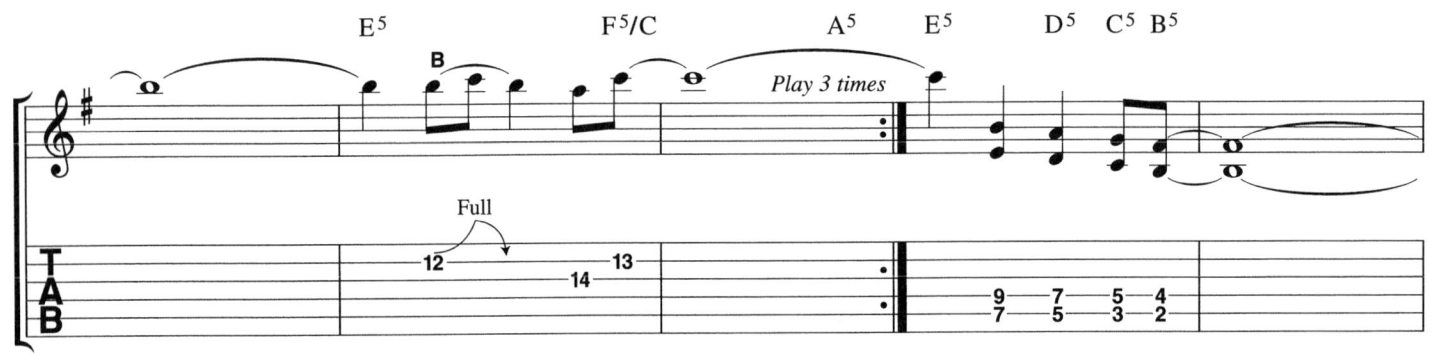
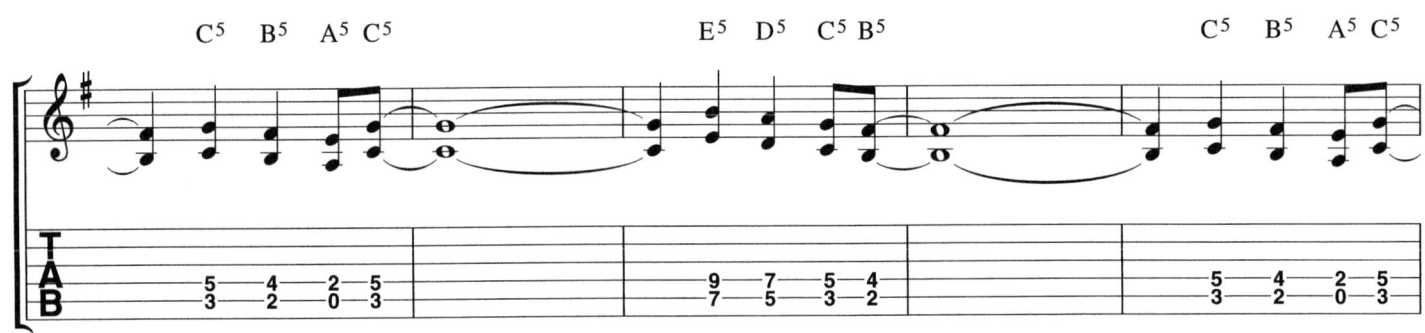
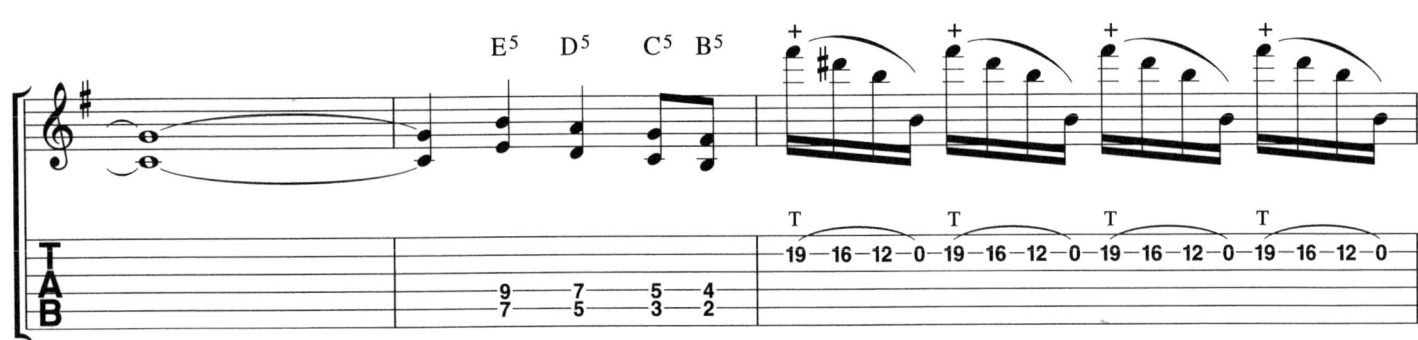
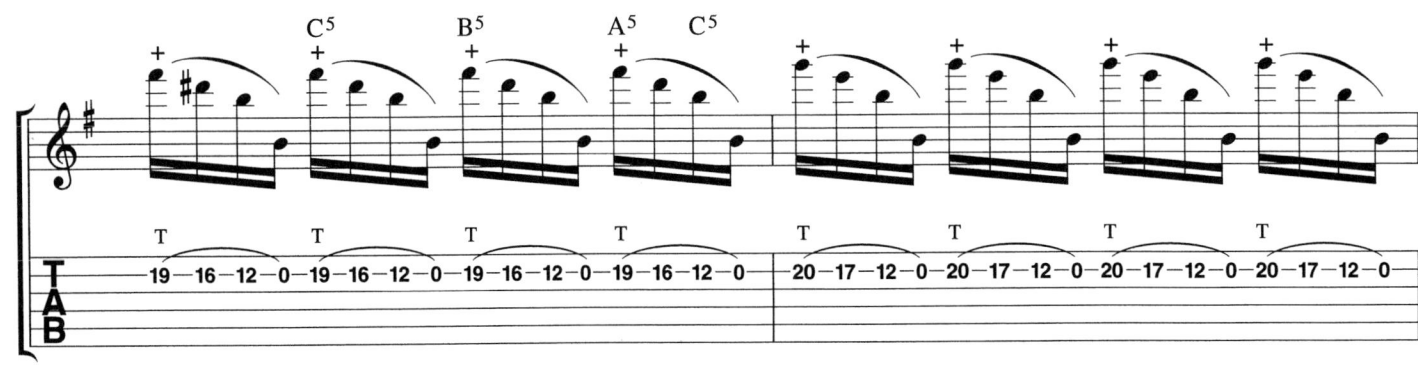

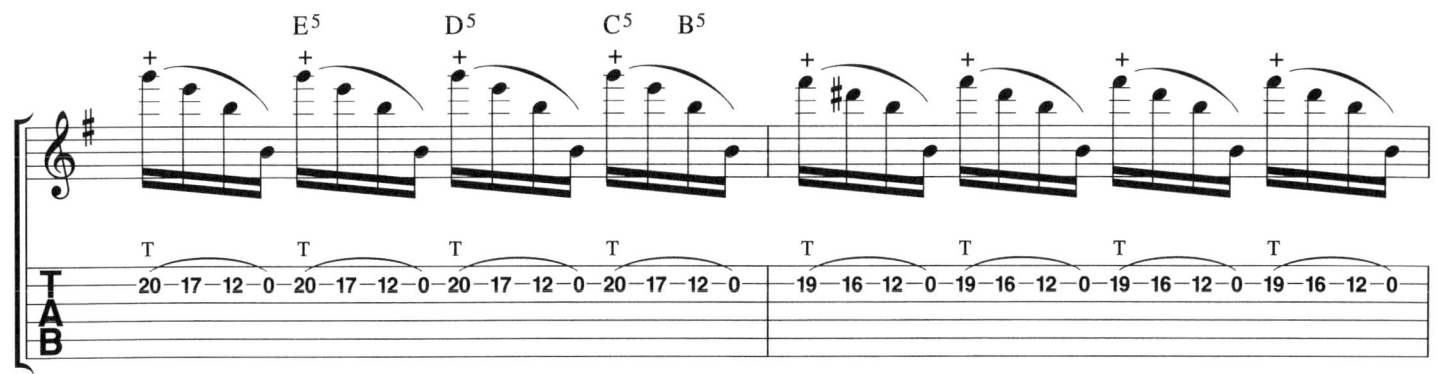
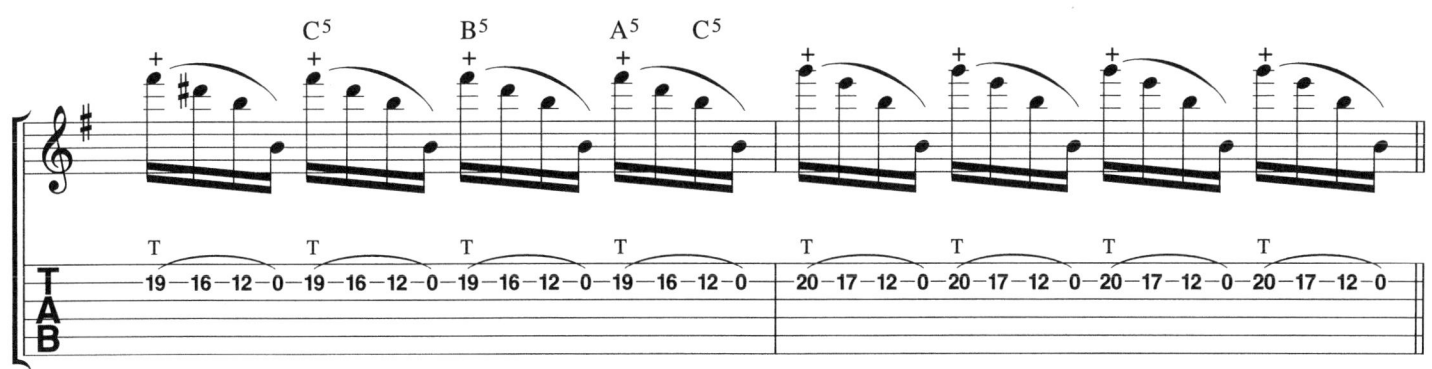

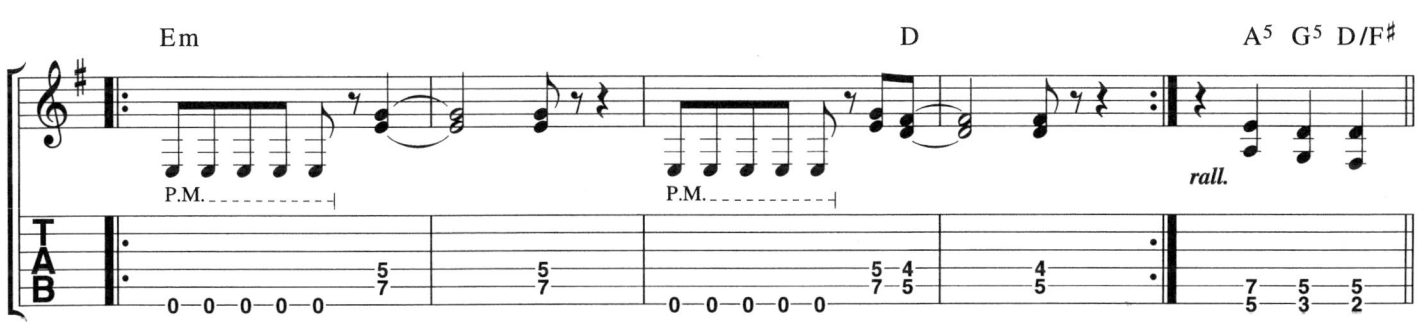
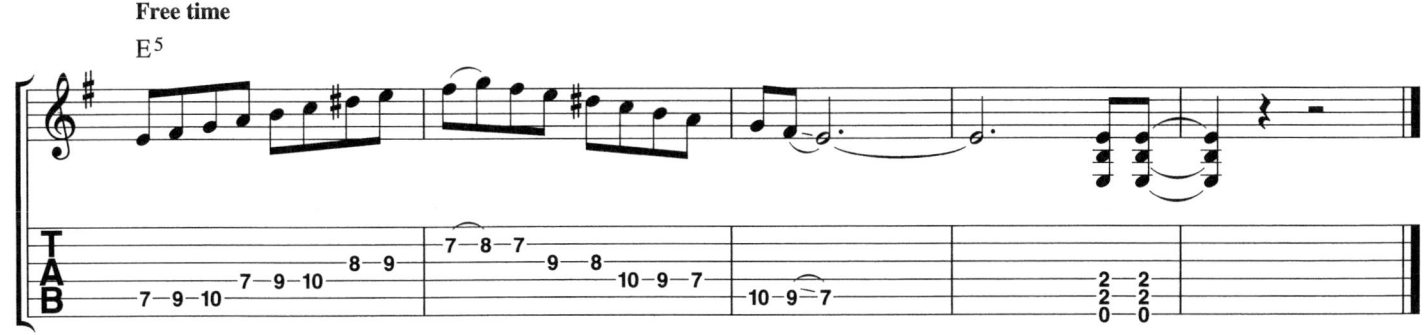

carpe diem baby

Words & Music by James Hetfield, Lars Ulrich & Kirk Hammett

© Copyright 1997 Creeping Death Music, USA.
PolyGram Music Publishing Limited, 47 British Grove, London W4.
All Rights Reserved. International Copyright Secured.

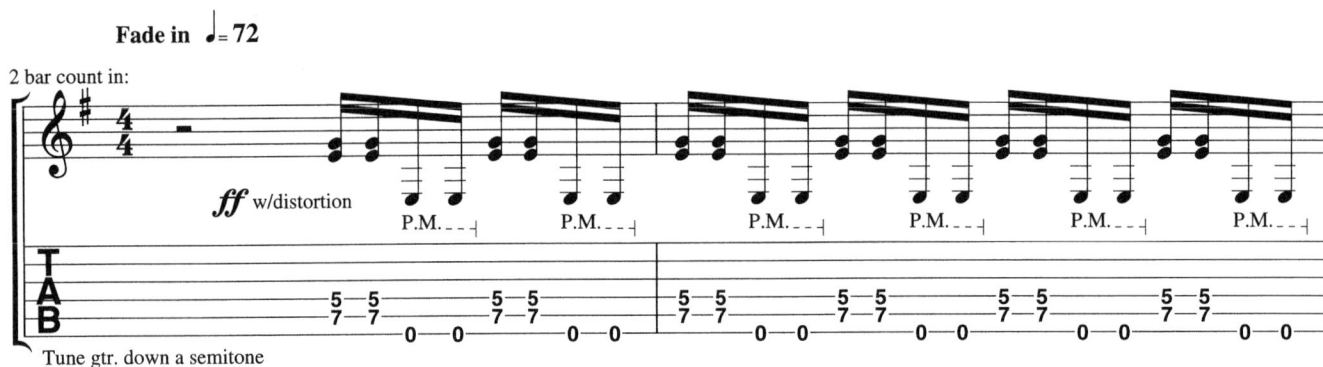

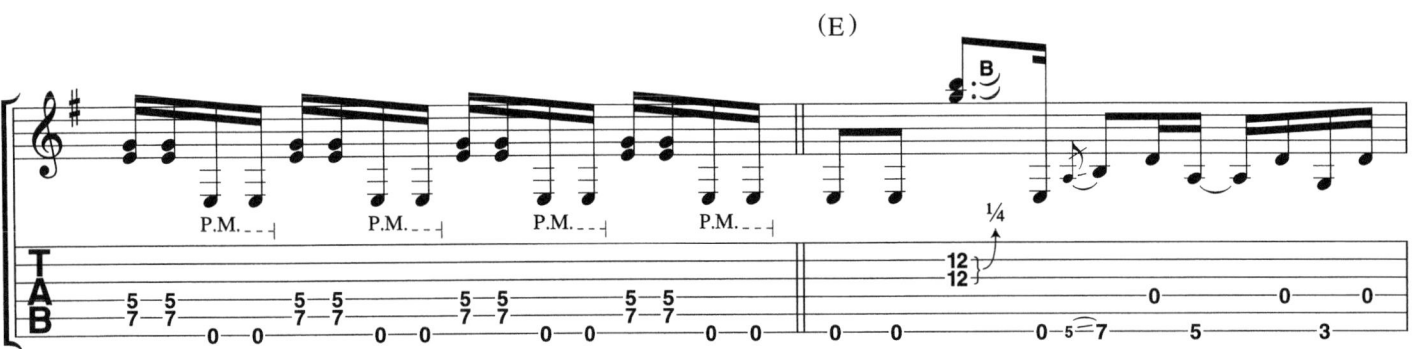

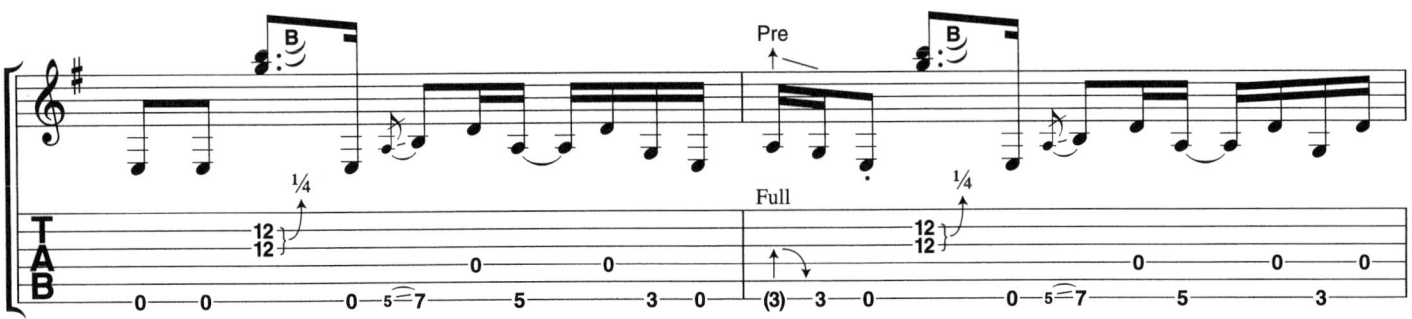

78

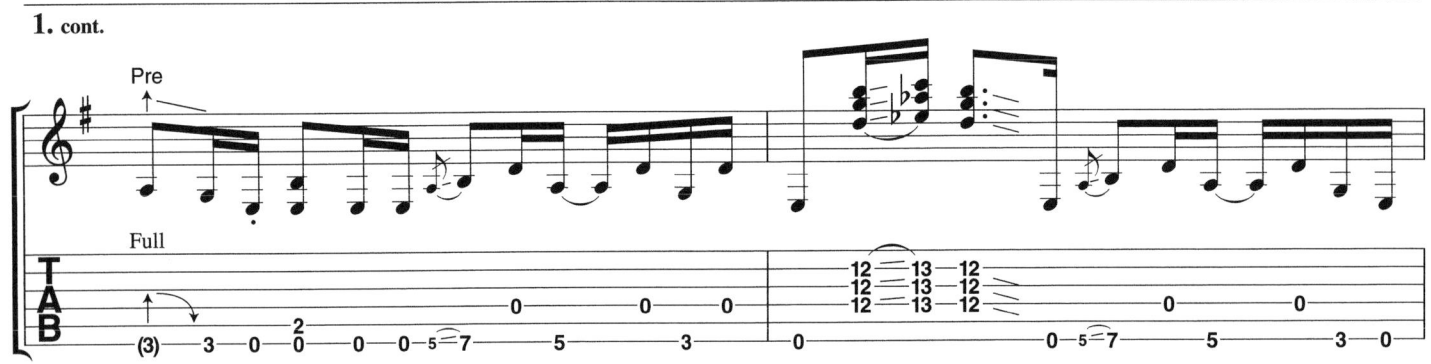
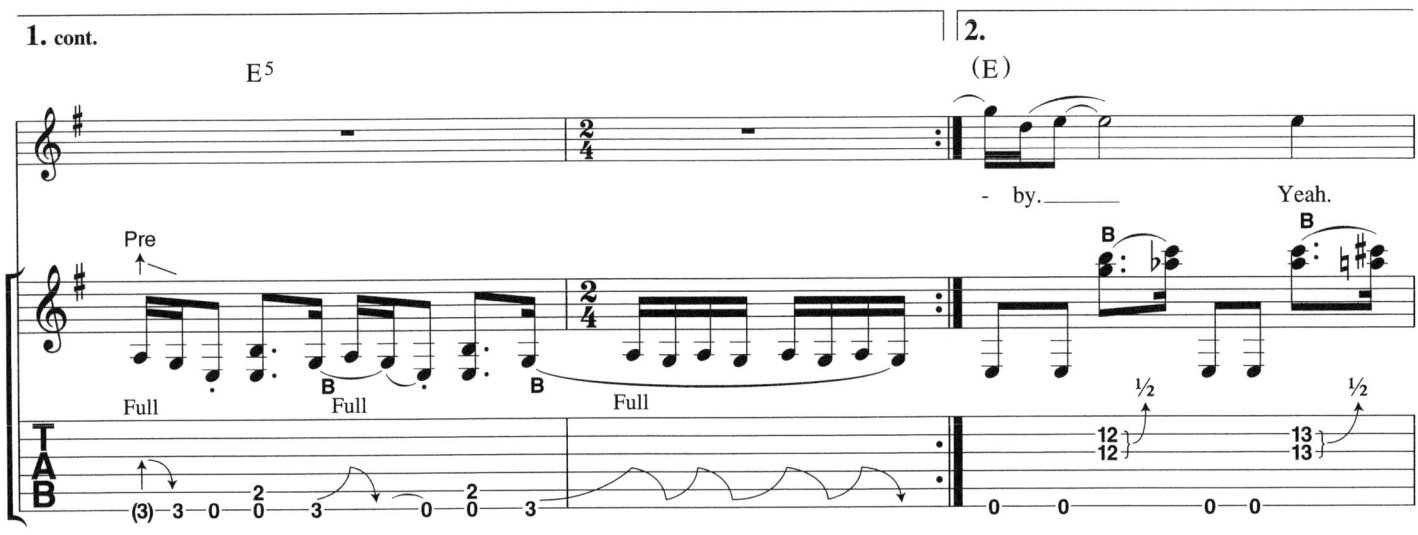
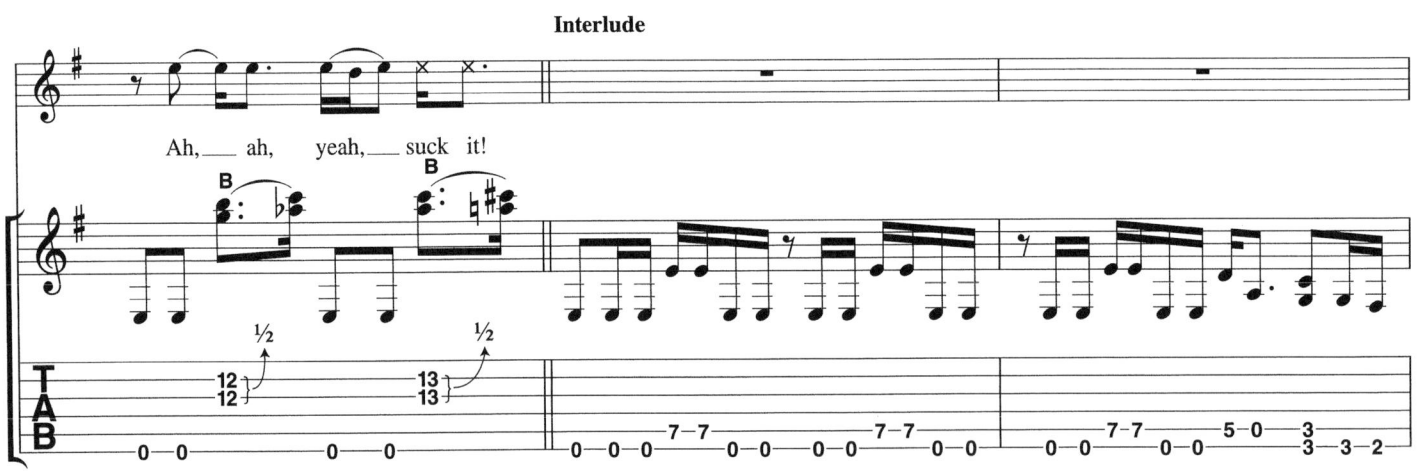

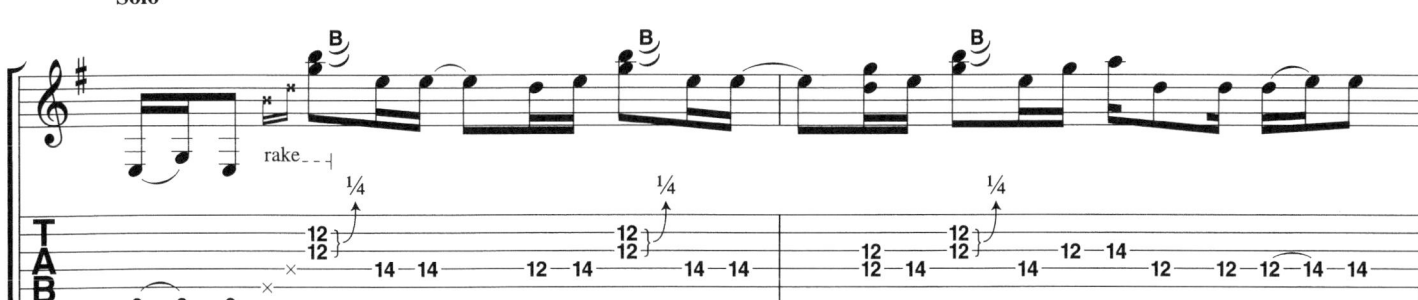
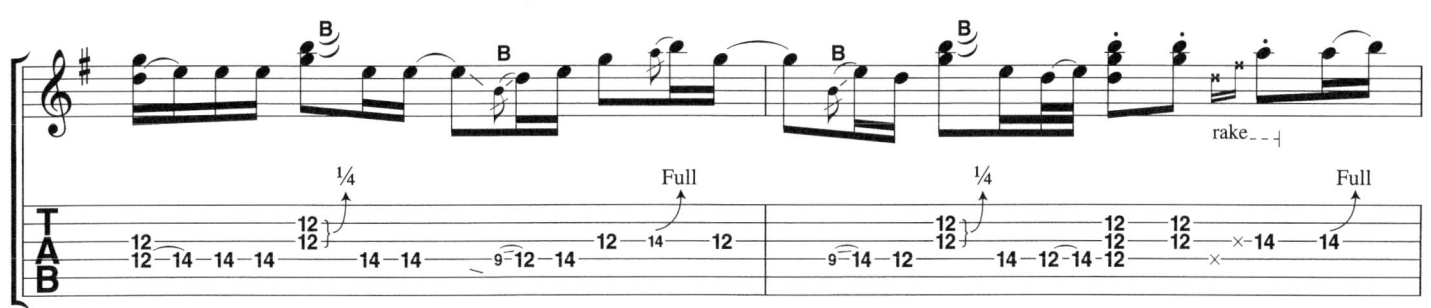
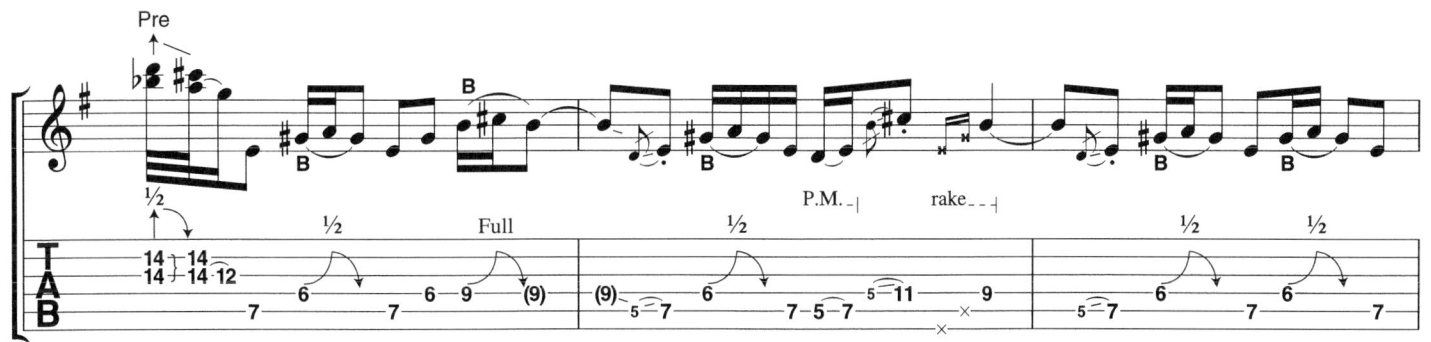
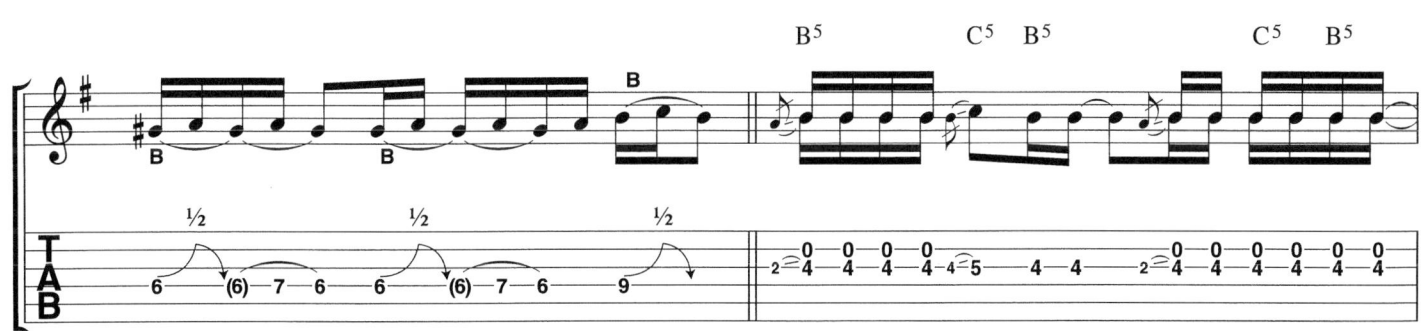
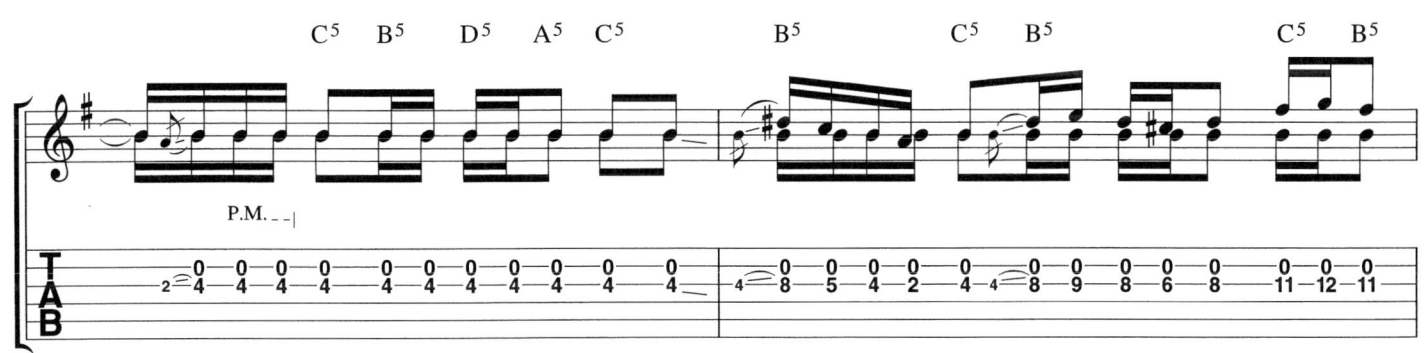

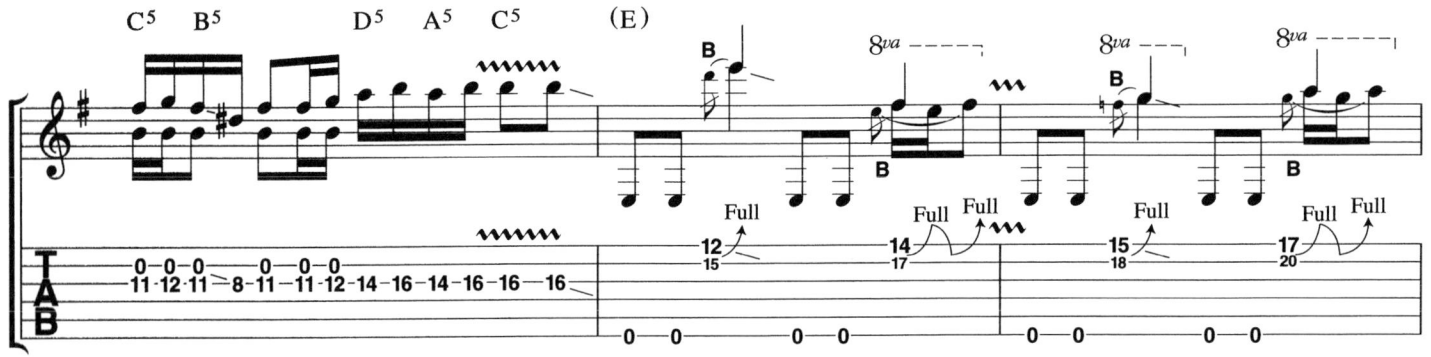
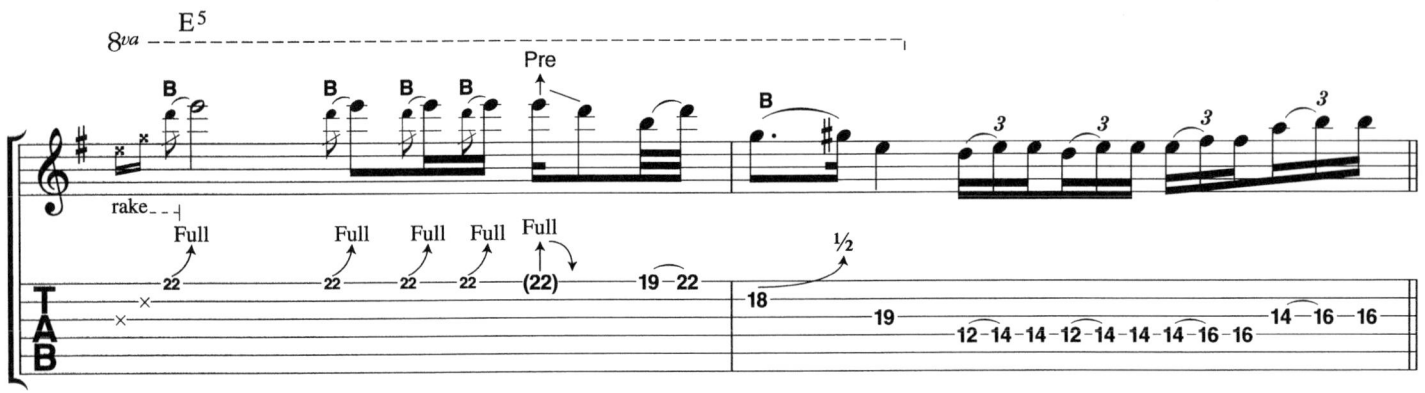
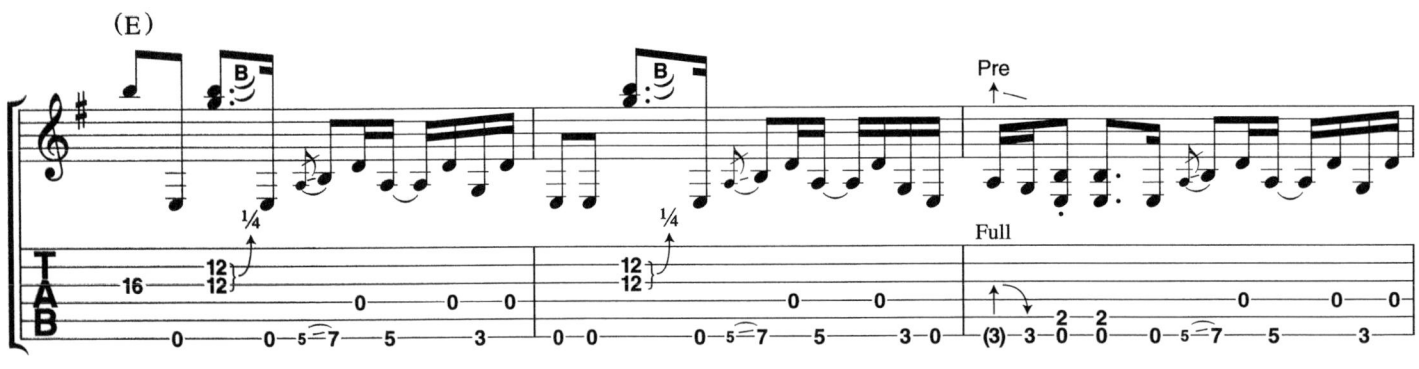
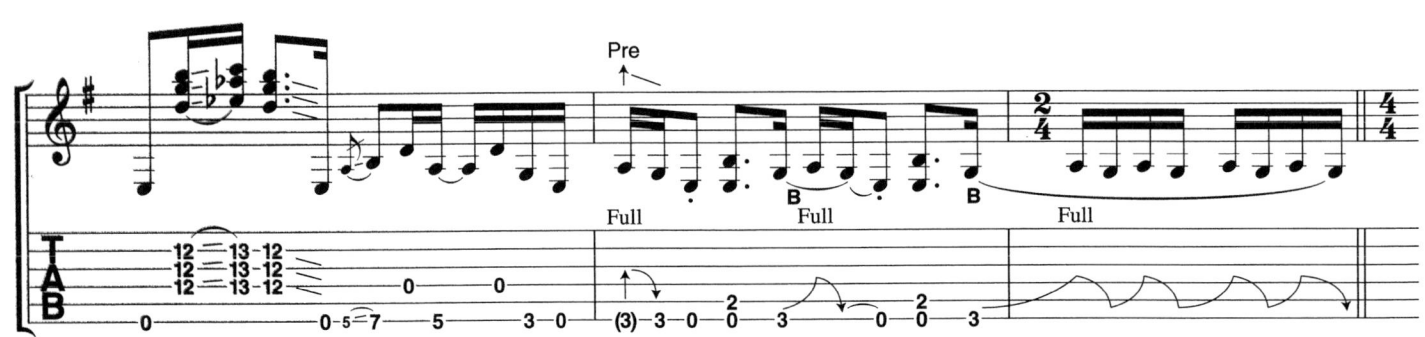

leper messiah

Words & Music by James Hetfield & Lars Ulrich

© Copyright 1986 Creeping Death Music, USA.
PolyGram Music Publishing Limited, 47 British Grove, London W4.
All Rights Reserved. International Copyright Secured.

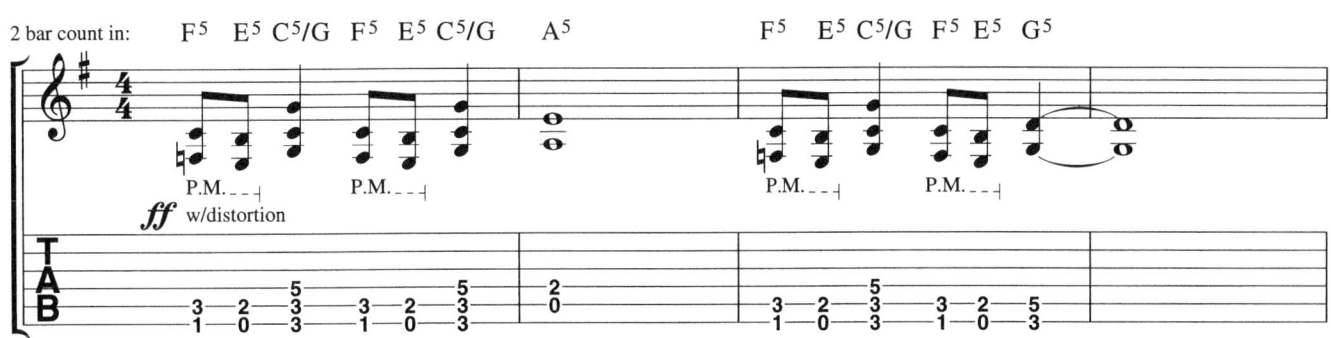

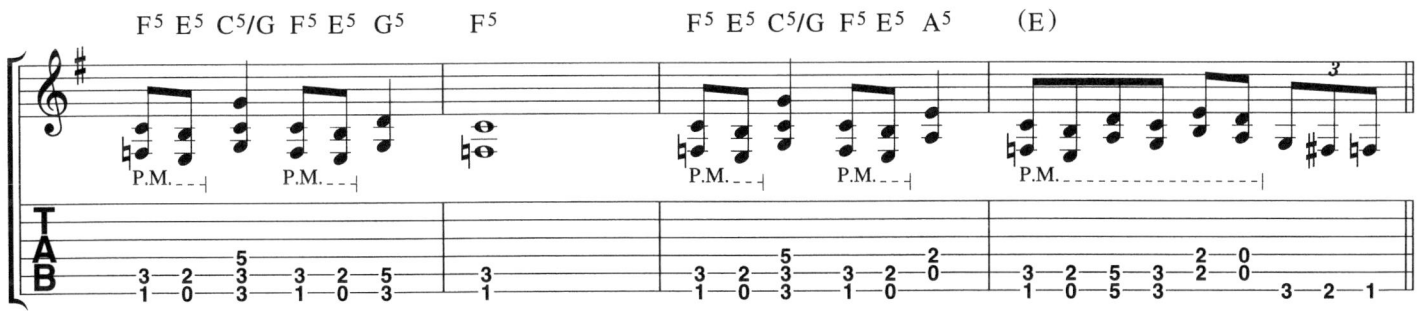

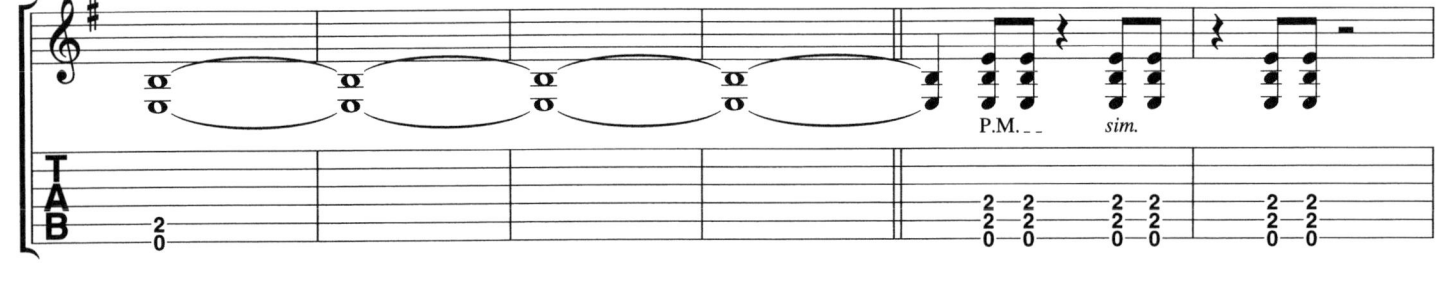

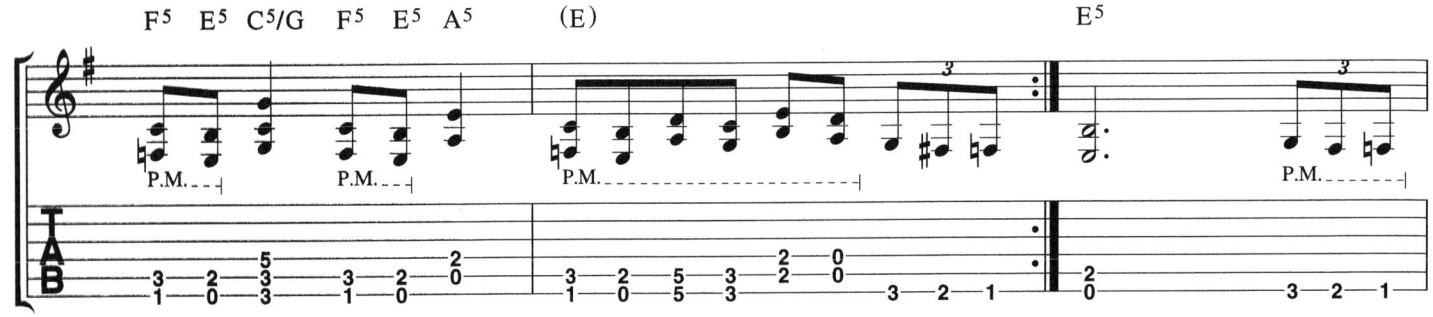

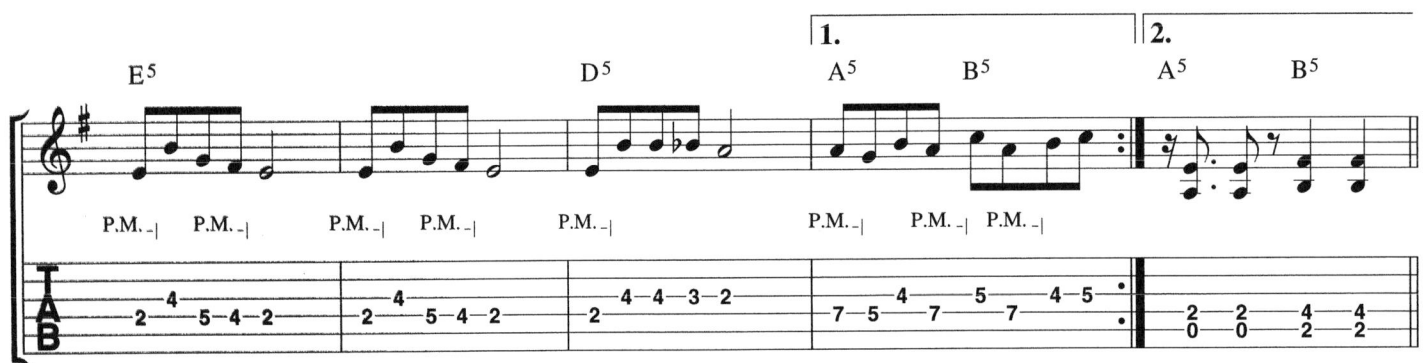

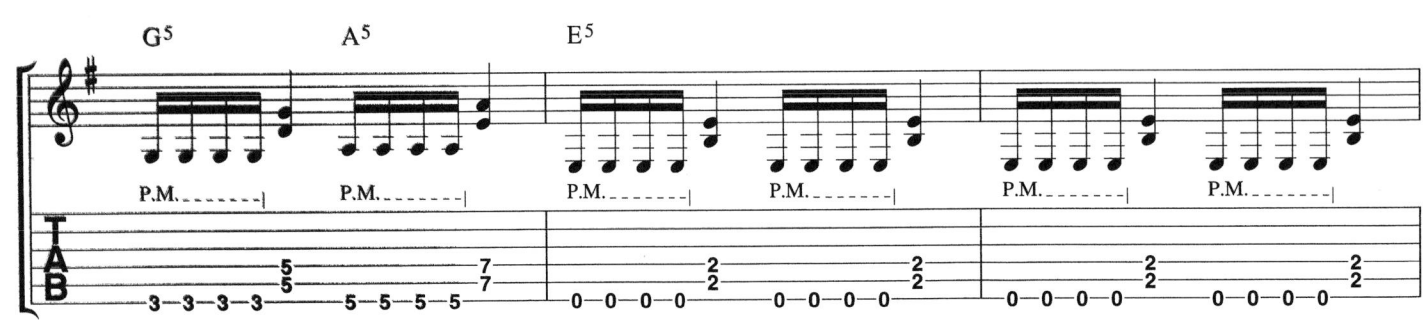

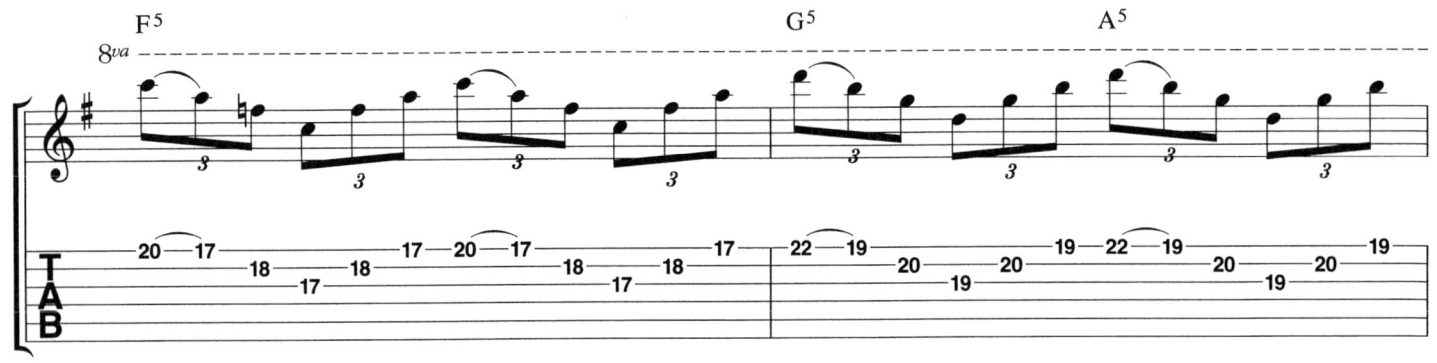
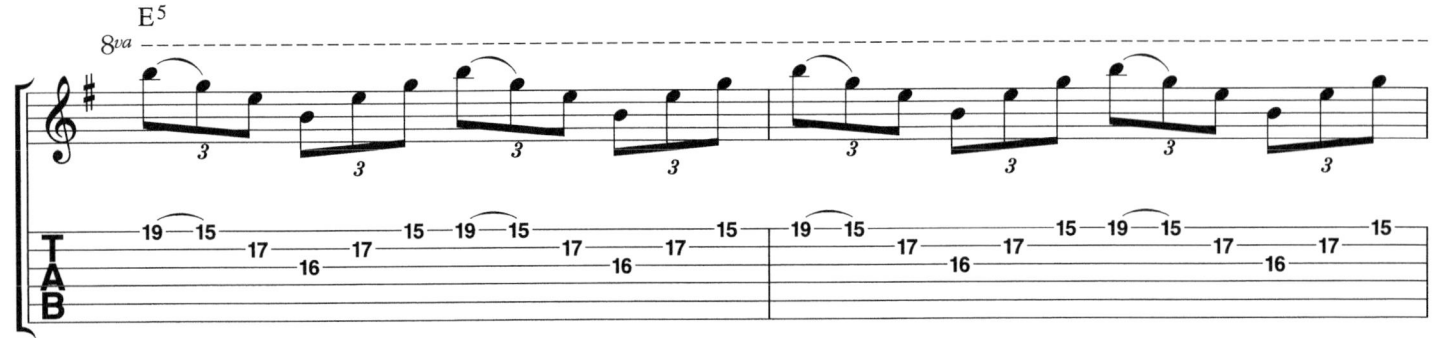
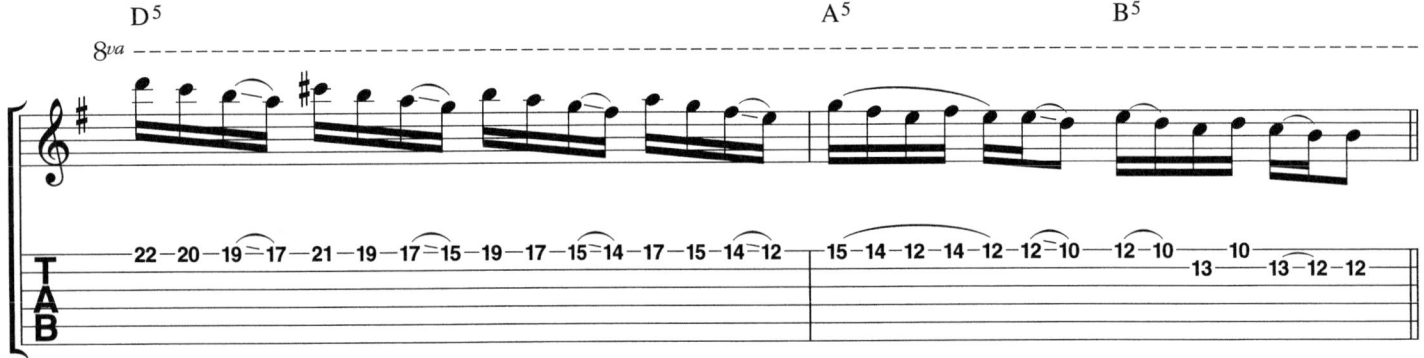
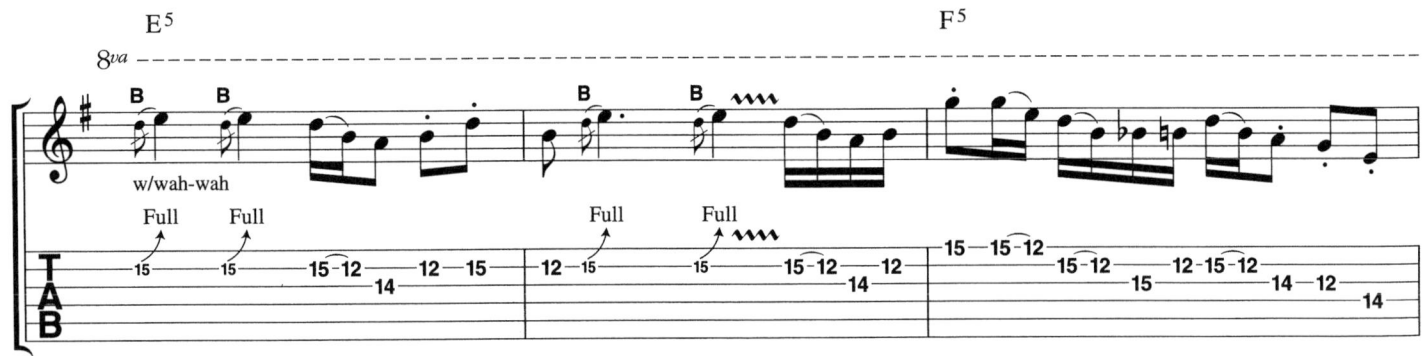
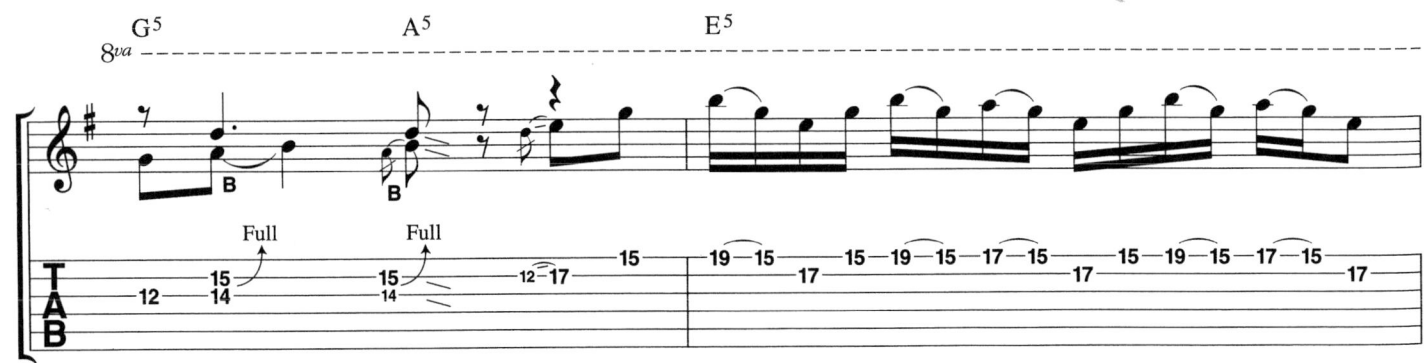

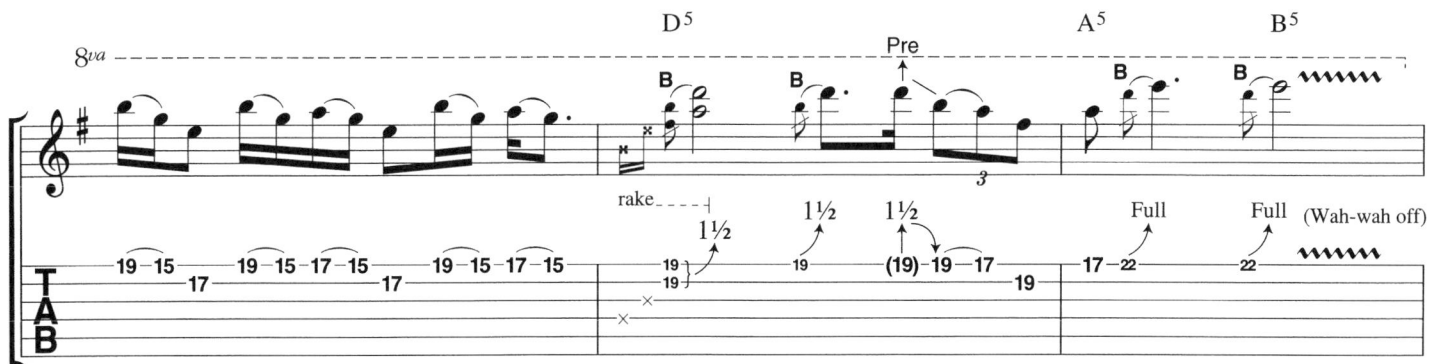

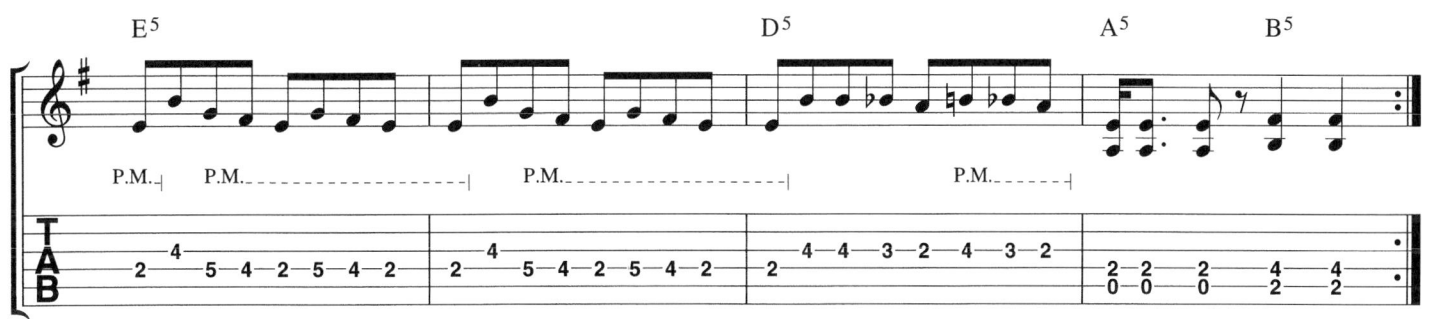
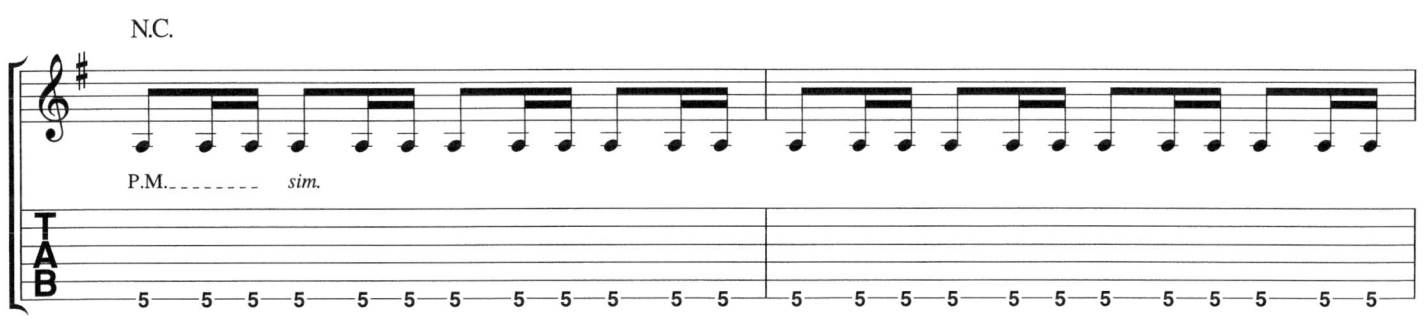
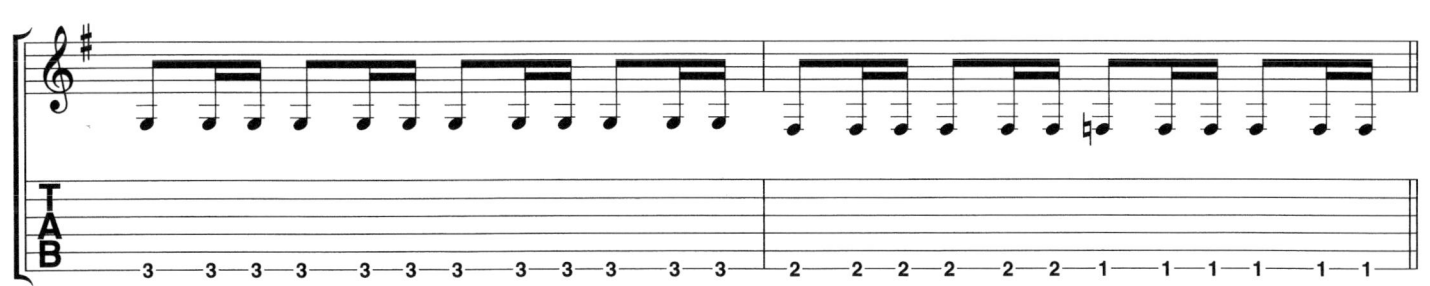

seek and destroy

Words & Music by James Hetfield & Lars Ulrich

© Copyright 1983 Creeping Death Music, USA.
PolyGram Music Publishing Limited, 47 British Grove, London W4.
All Rights Reserved. International Copyright Secured.

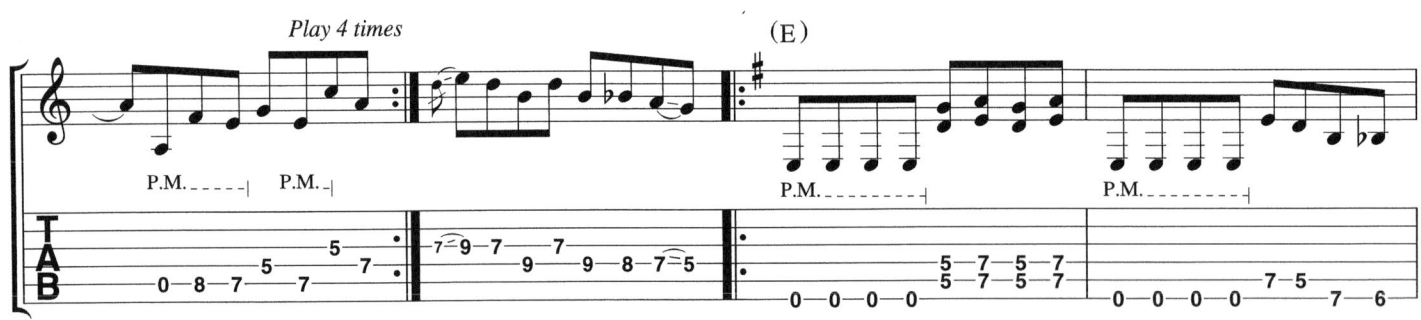

G5 F♯5 F5 E5
Search - ing seek and des - troy.
P.M.
G5 F♯5 F5 To Coda (E)
1.
Search - ing seek and des - troy.
P.M. P.M.
1. cont.
P.M. P.M. P.M. P.M.
1. cont.
2.
E5
♩= 208 (𝅗𝅥 = ♩)
E
Solo drums
2. There is - troy.
P.M. P.M.

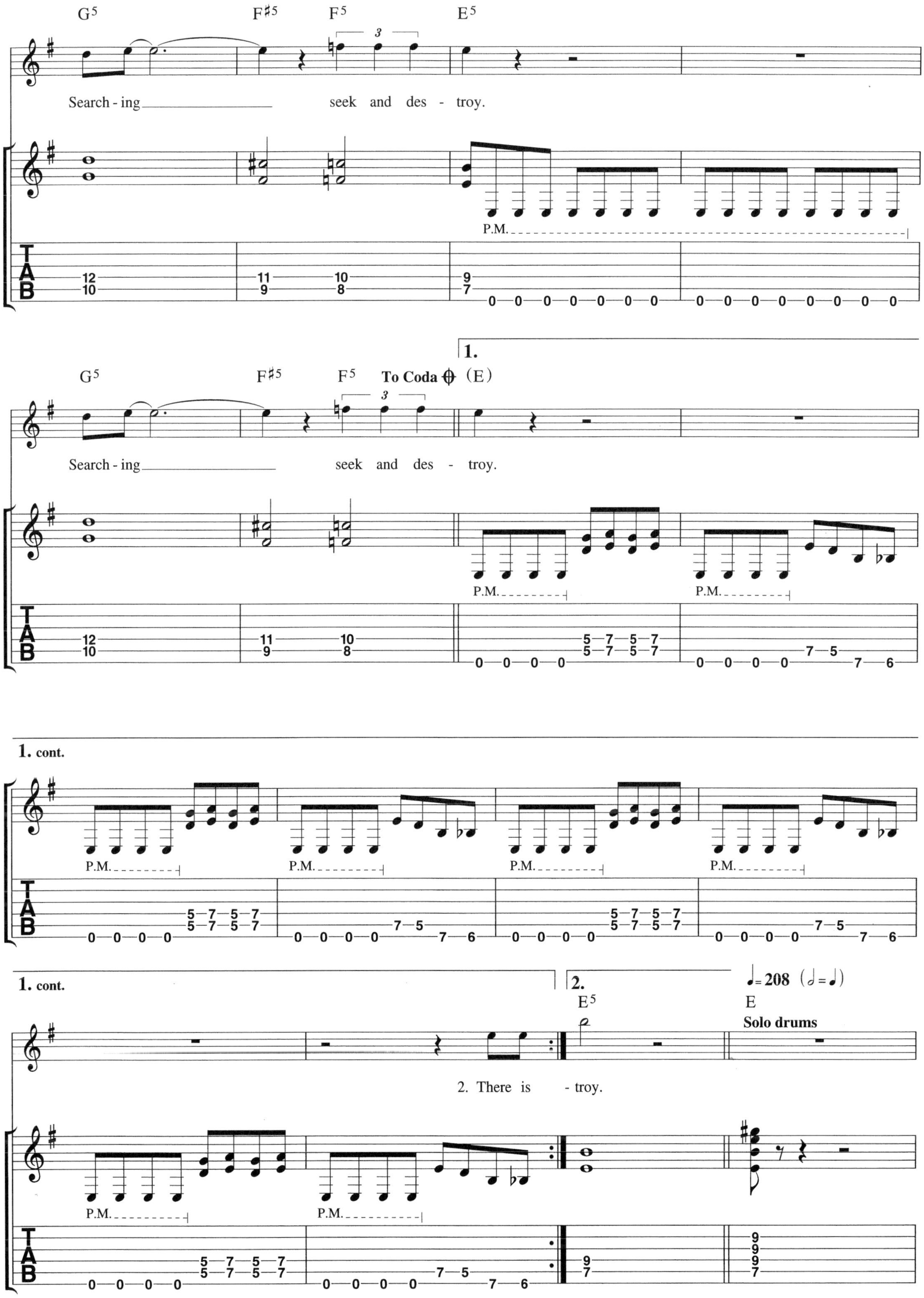

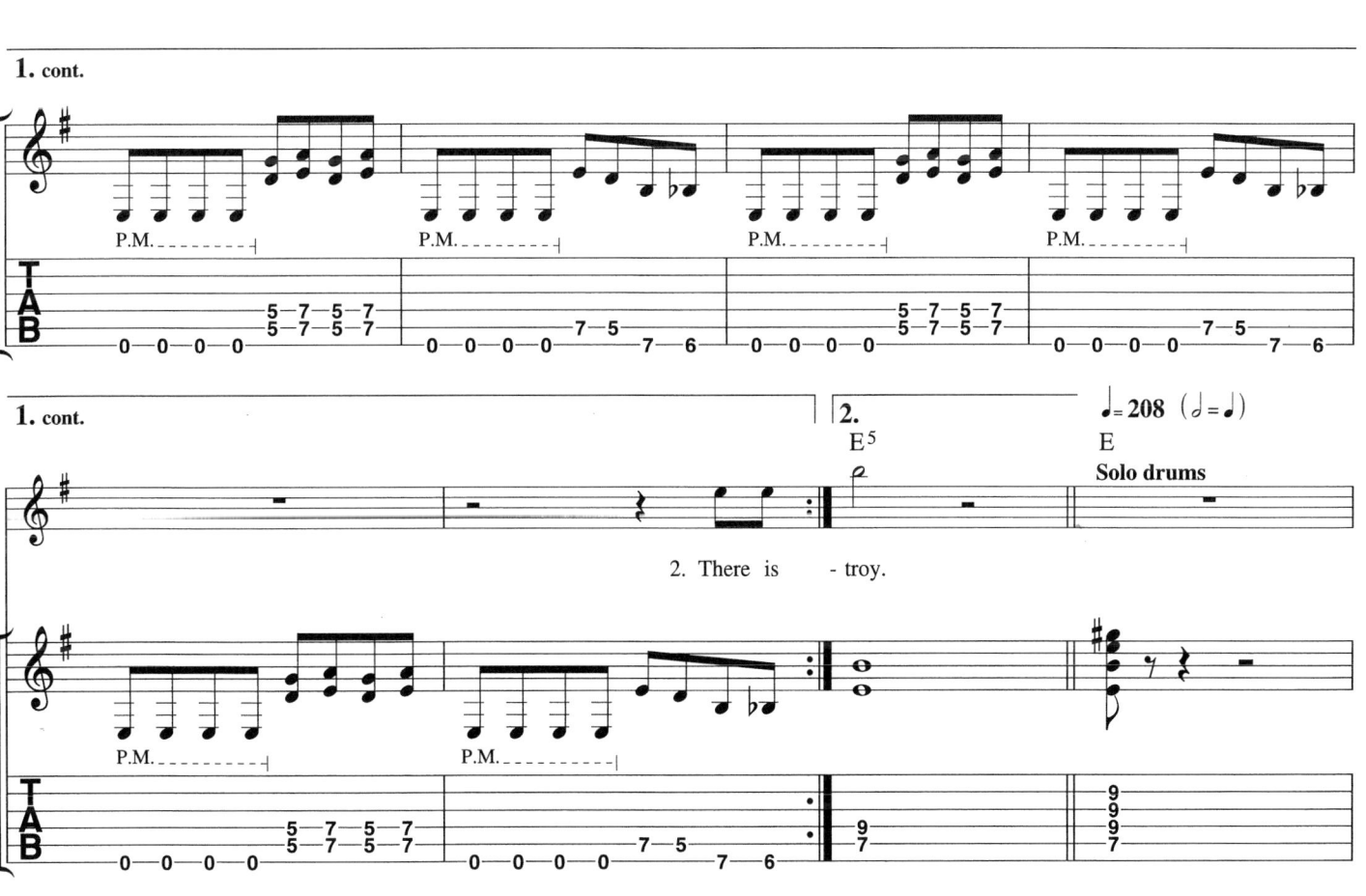

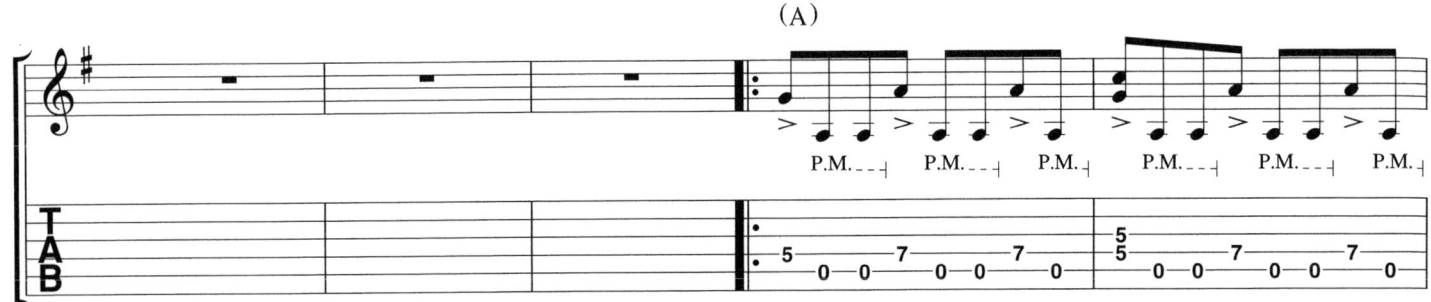

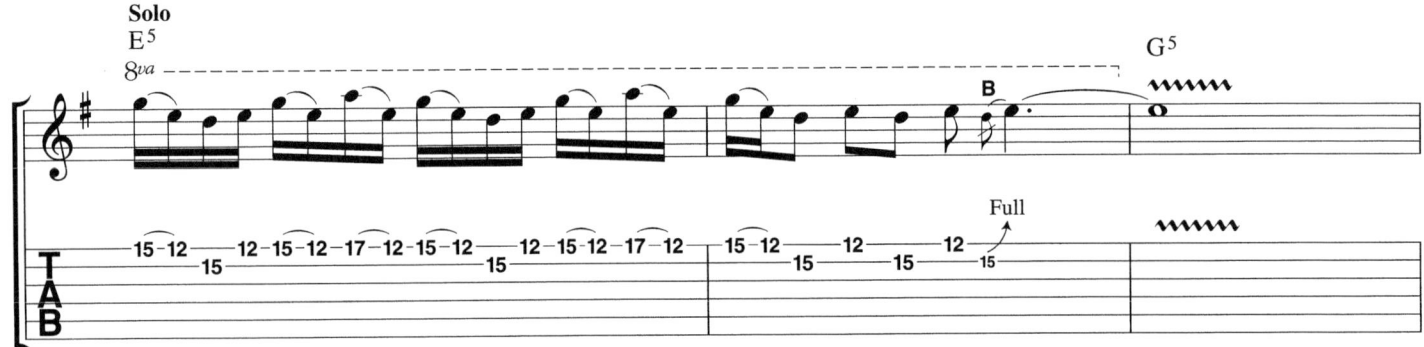
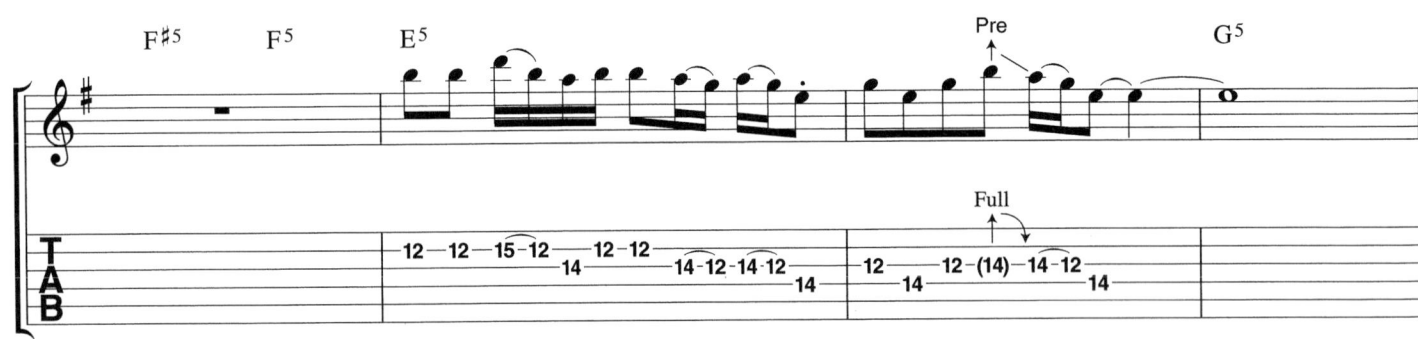
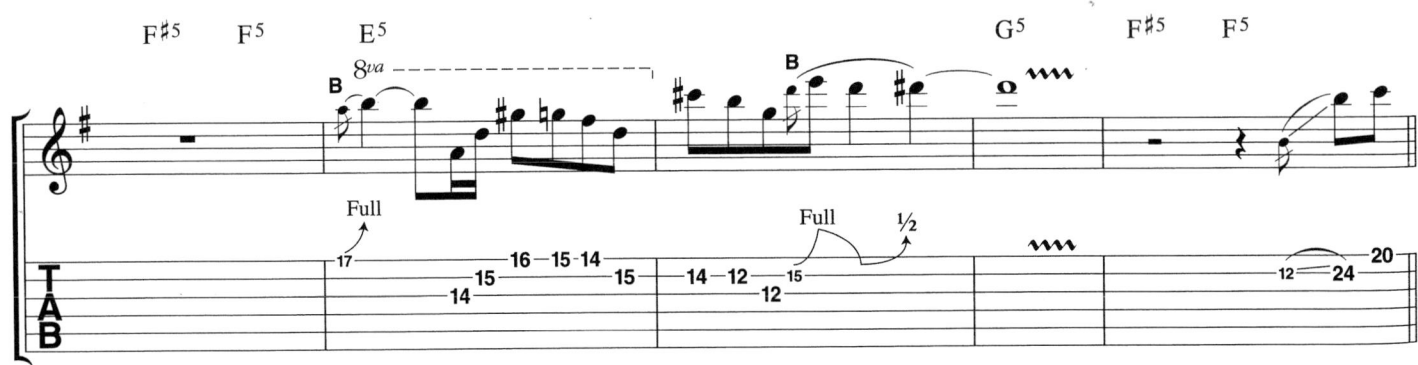

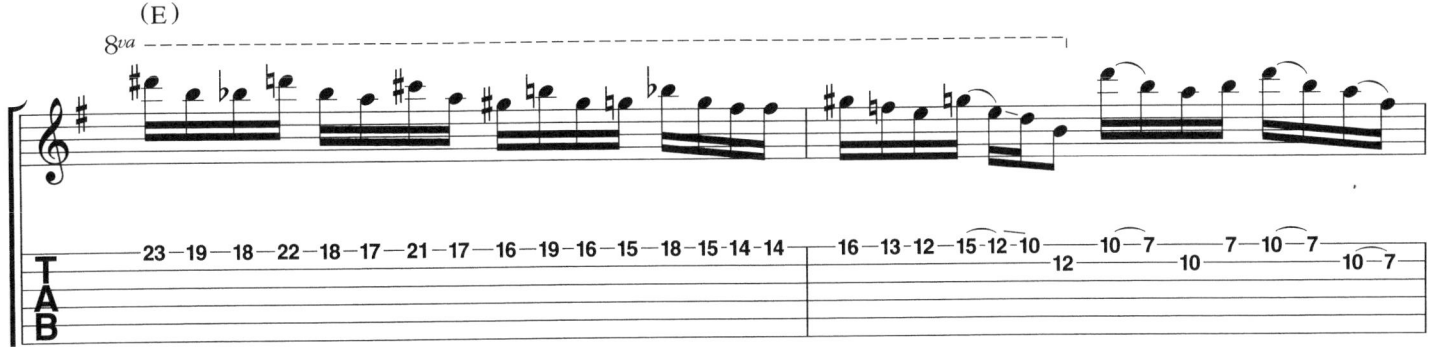

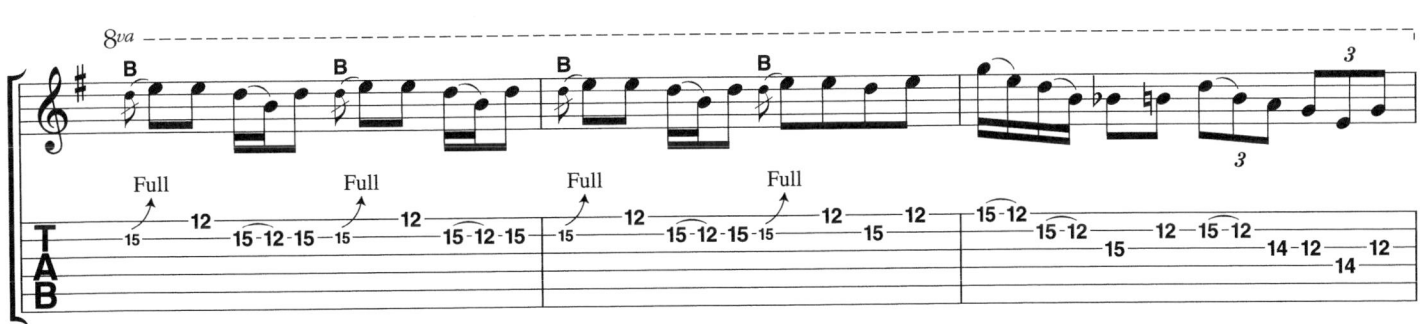

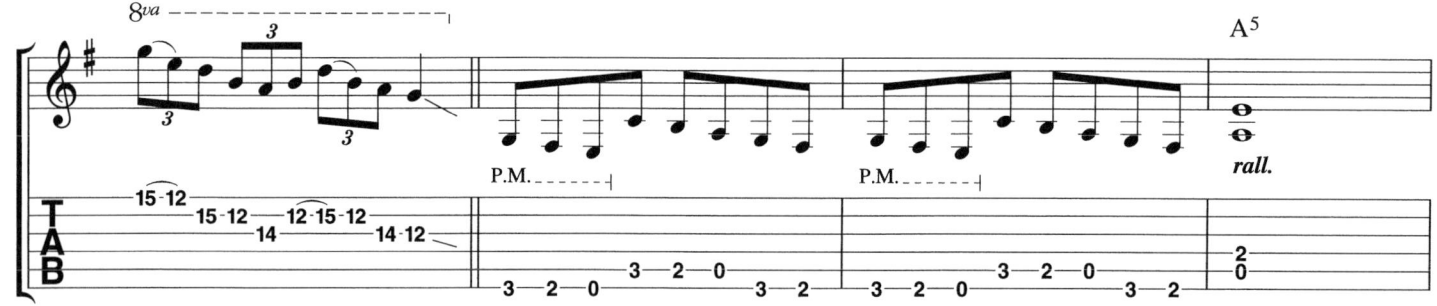

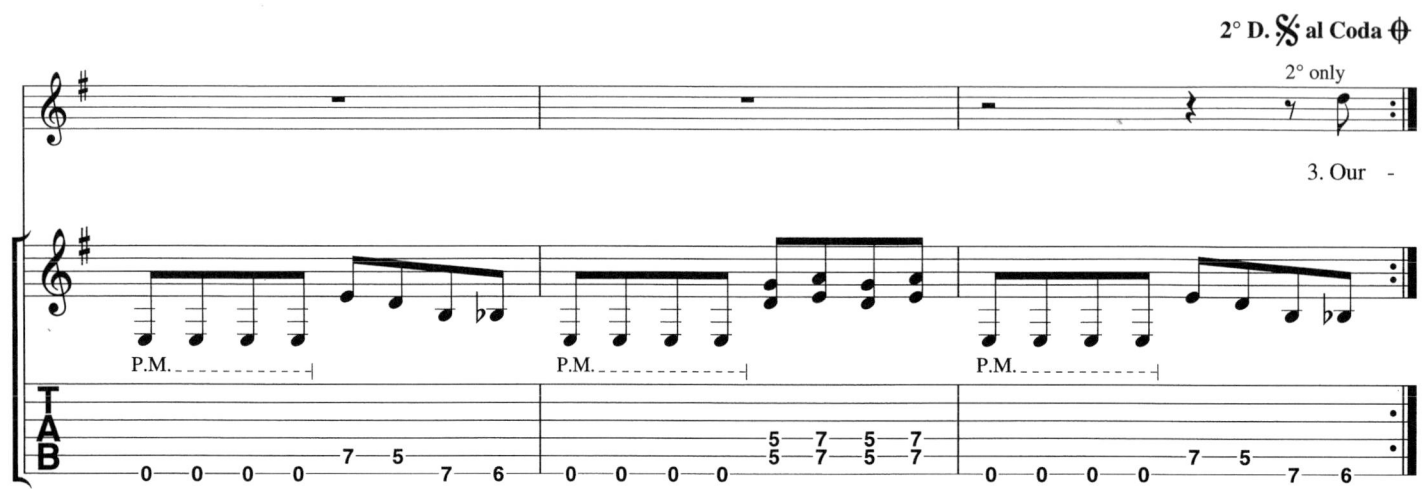

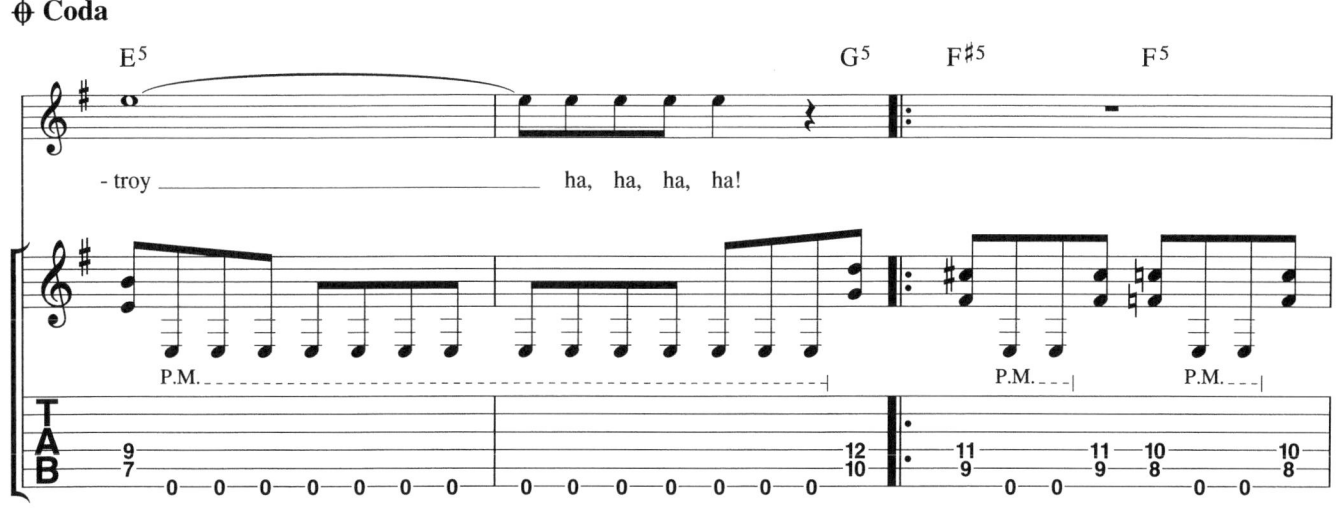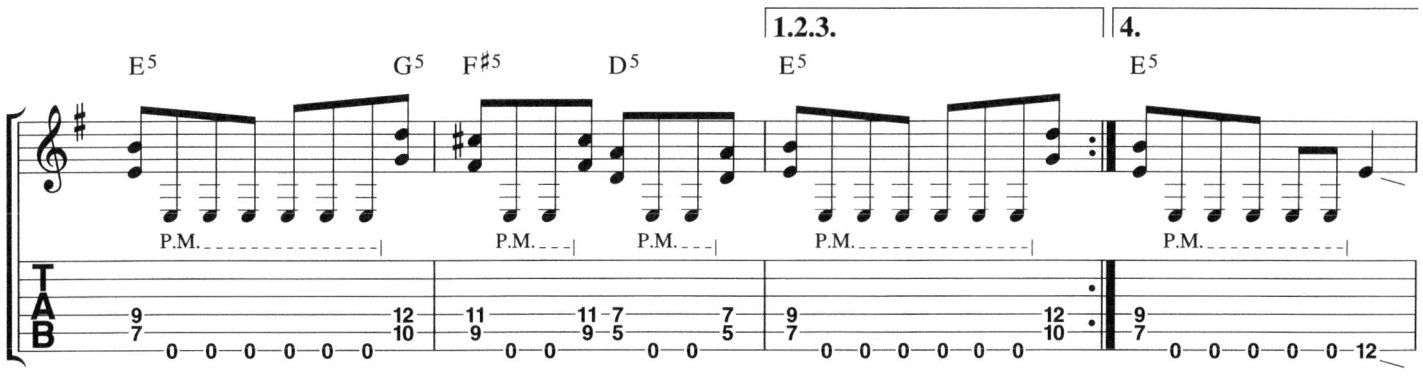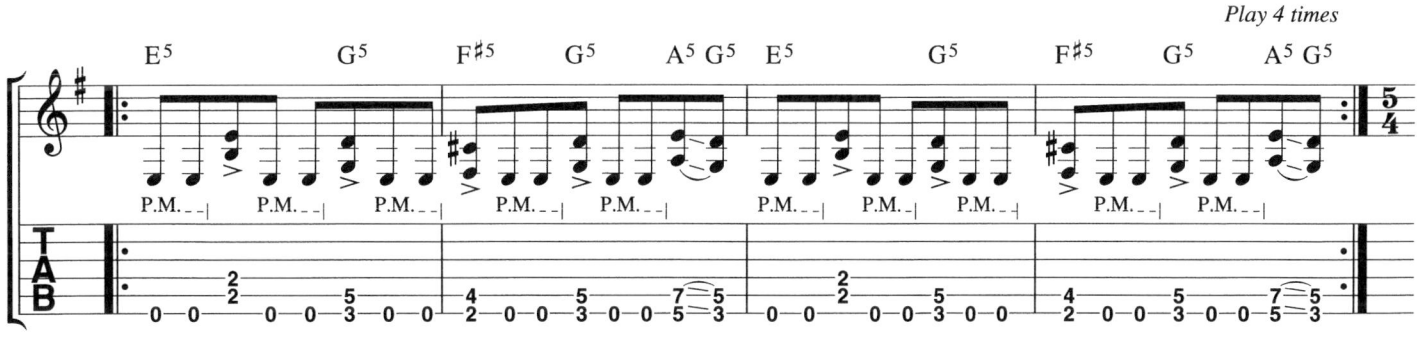

the memory remains

Words & Music by James Hetfield & Lars Ulrich

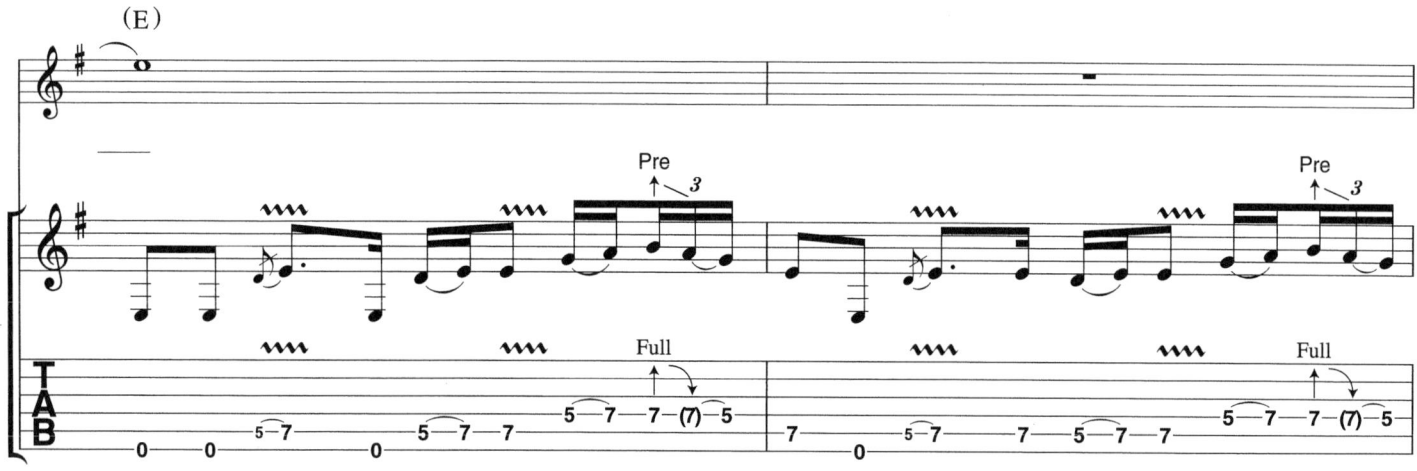

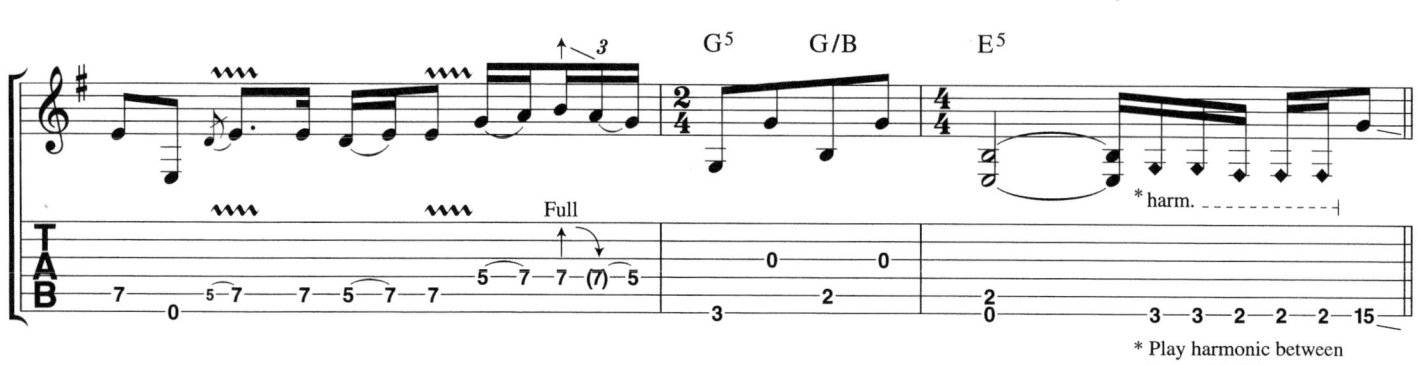

*Play harmonic between 2nd and 3rd frets

whiskey in the jar

Traditional. Arranged by Eric Bell, Brian Downey & Phil Lynott

© Copyright 1972 PolyGram Music Publishing Limited, 47 British Grove, London W4
d/b/a Pippin The Friendly Ranger Music Comapny Limited.
All Rights Reserved. International Copyright Secured.

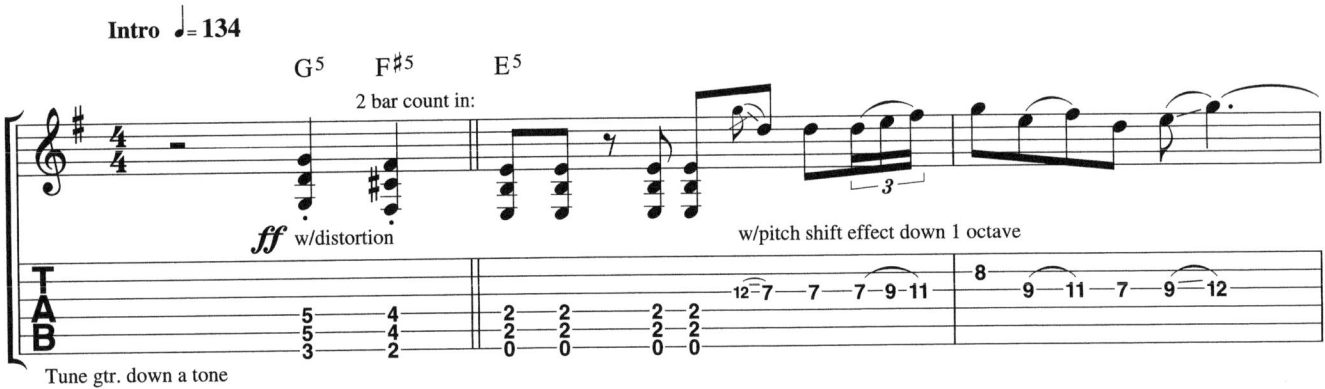

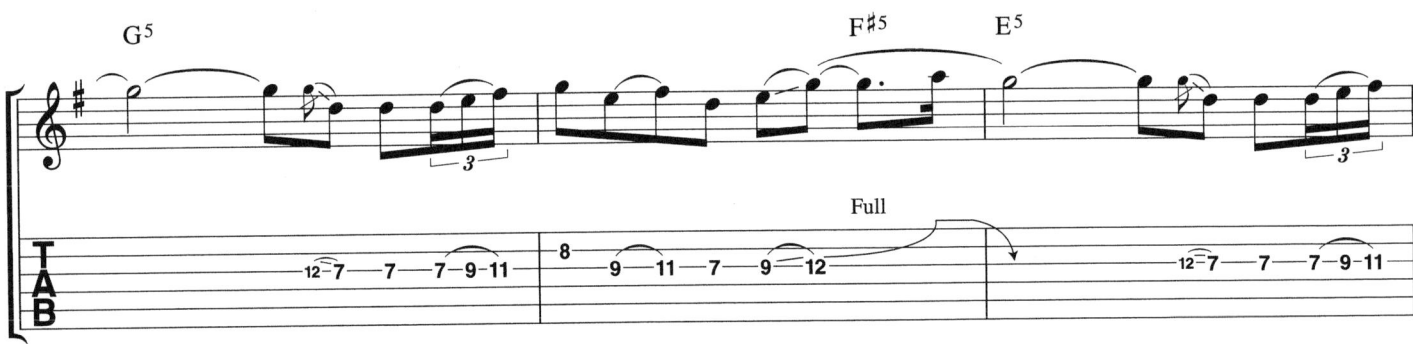

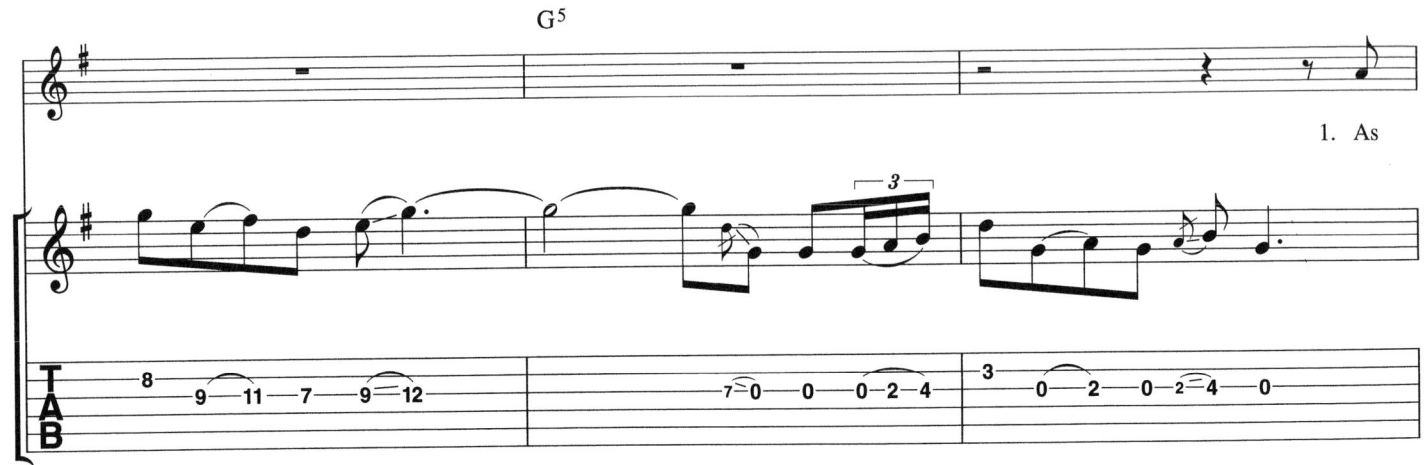

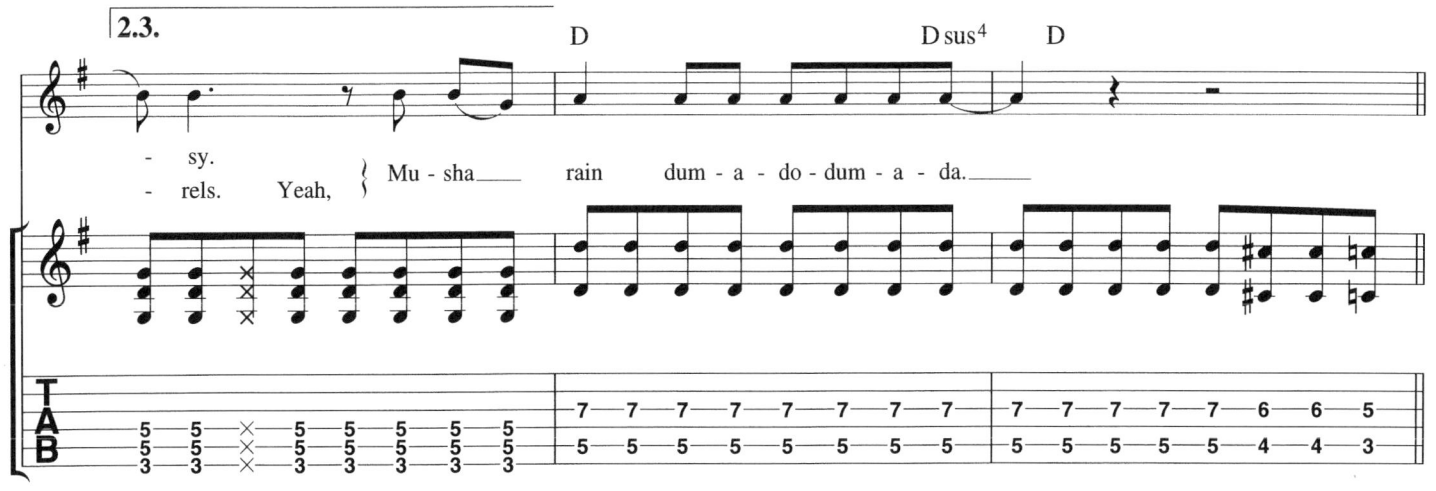
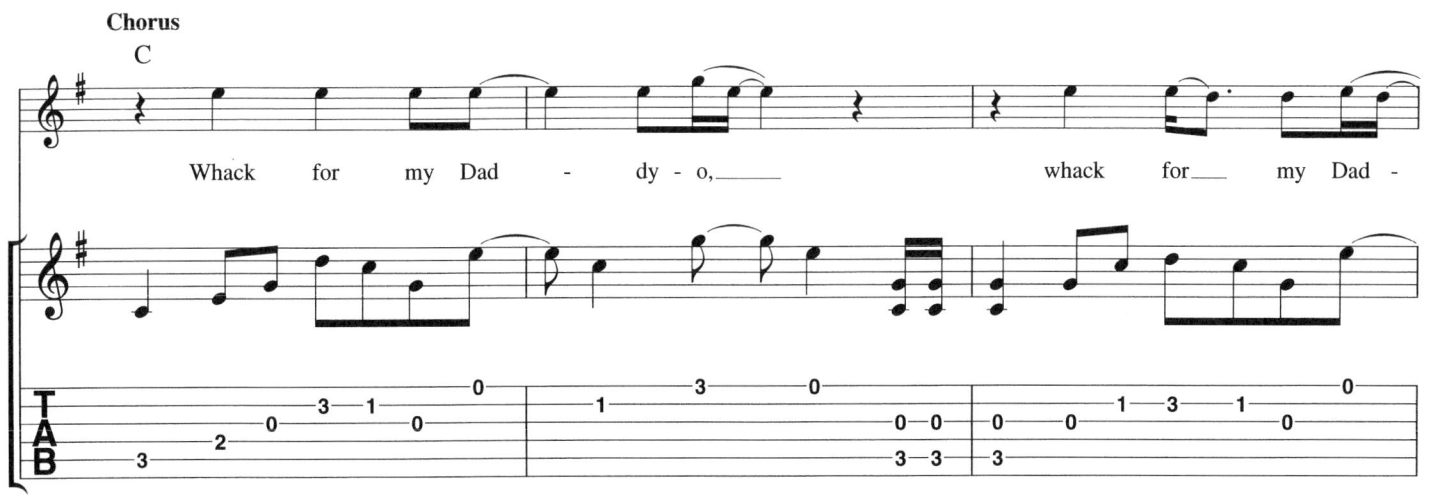
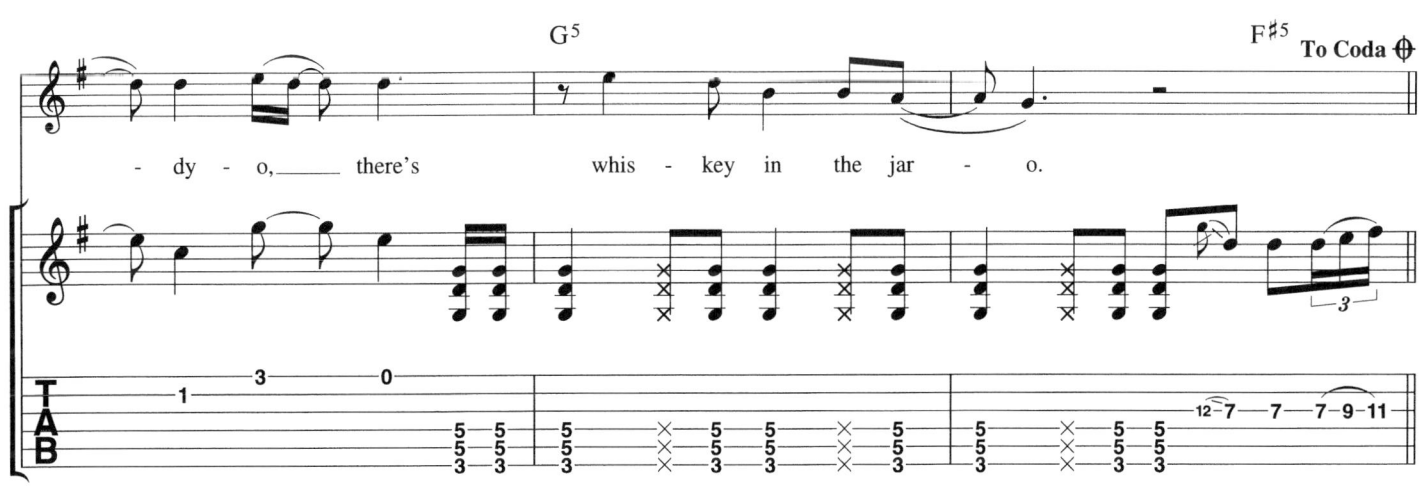
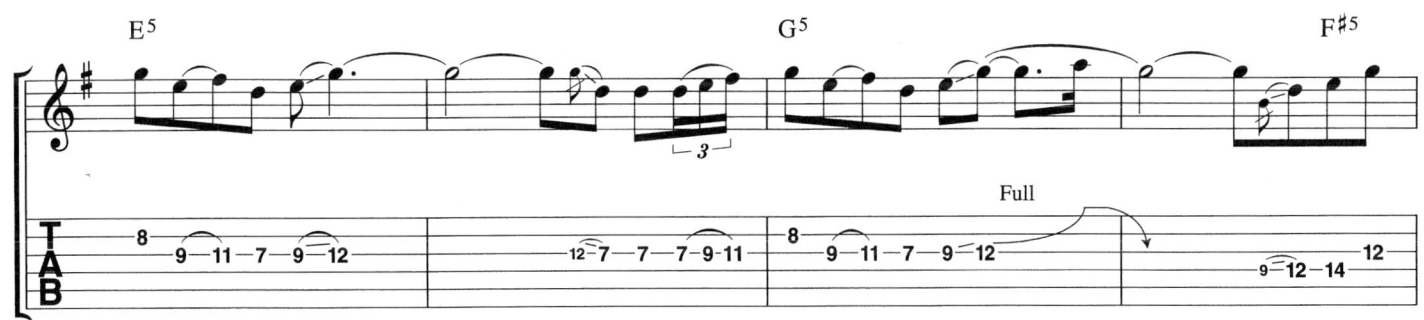

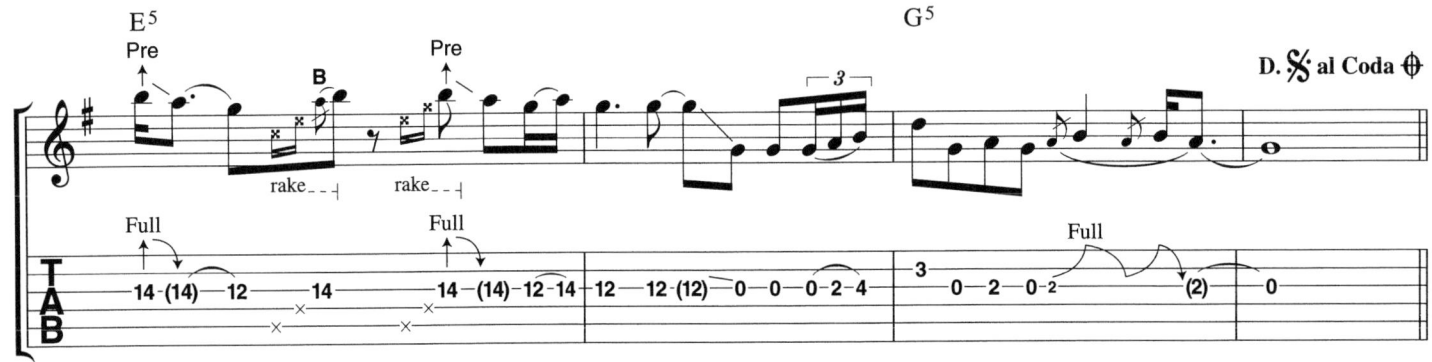

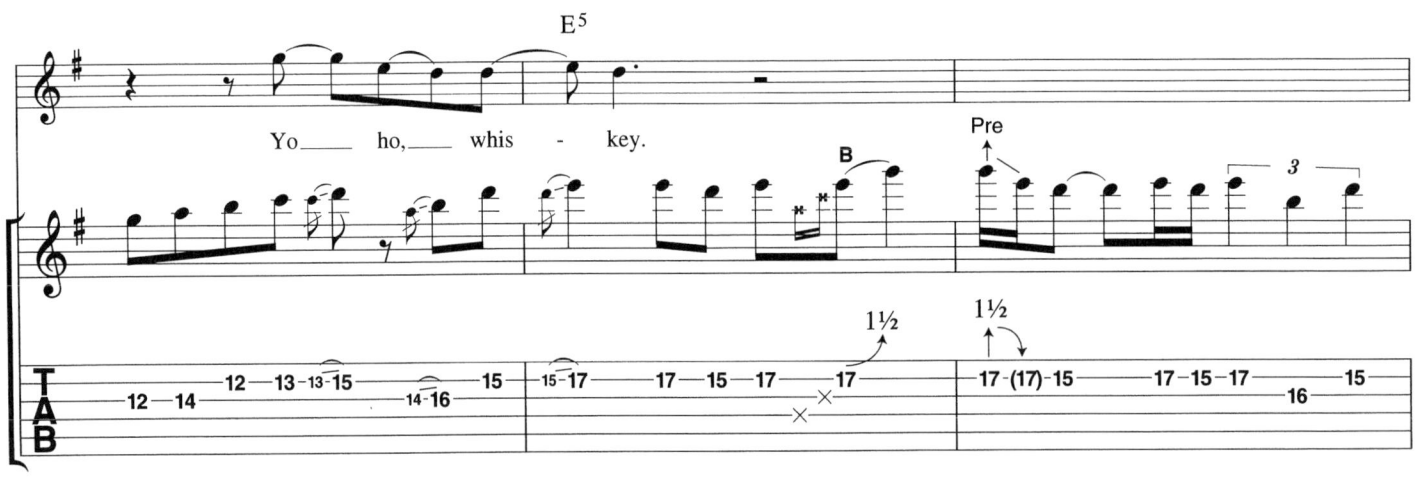
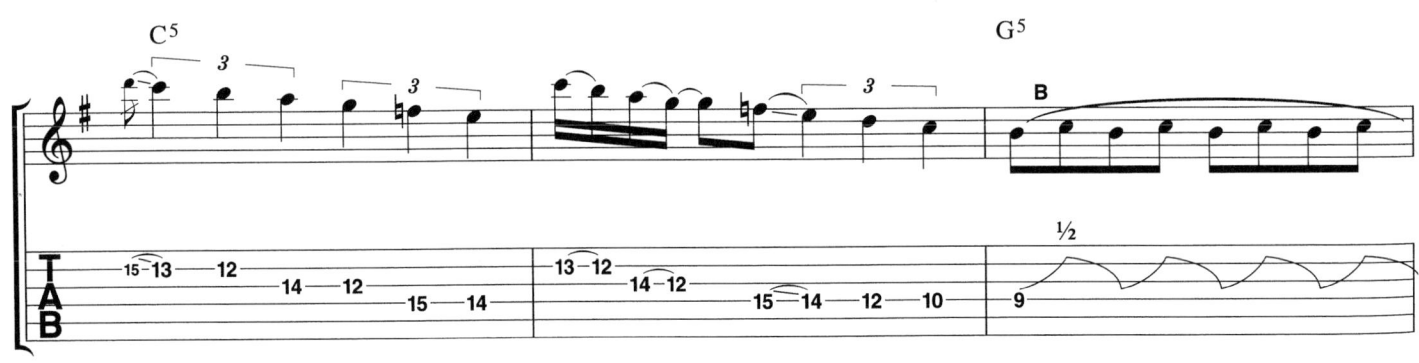

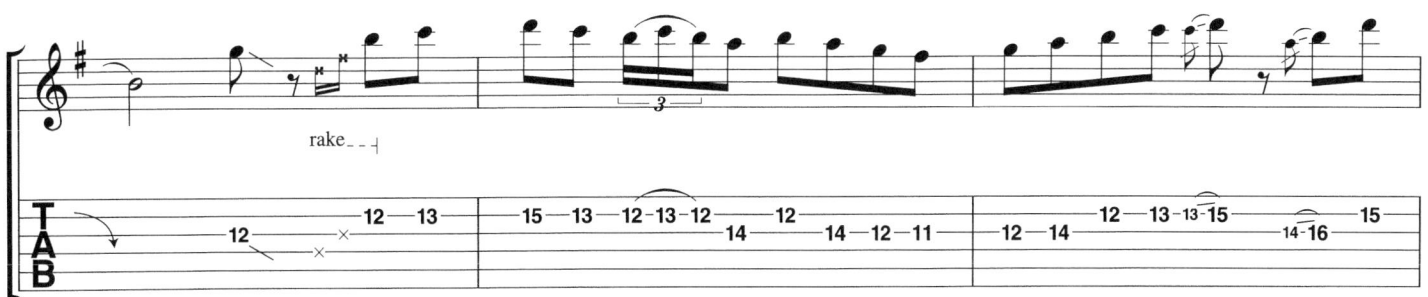
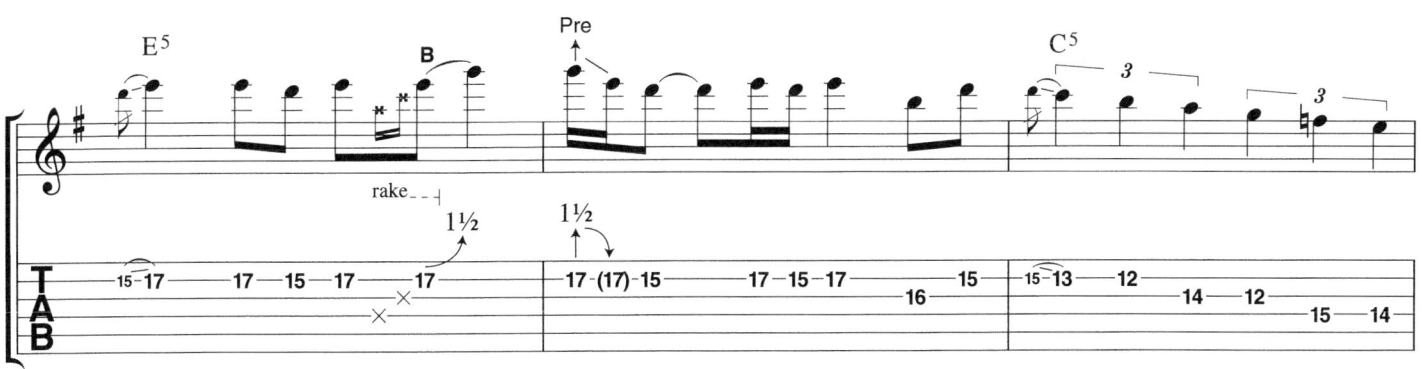
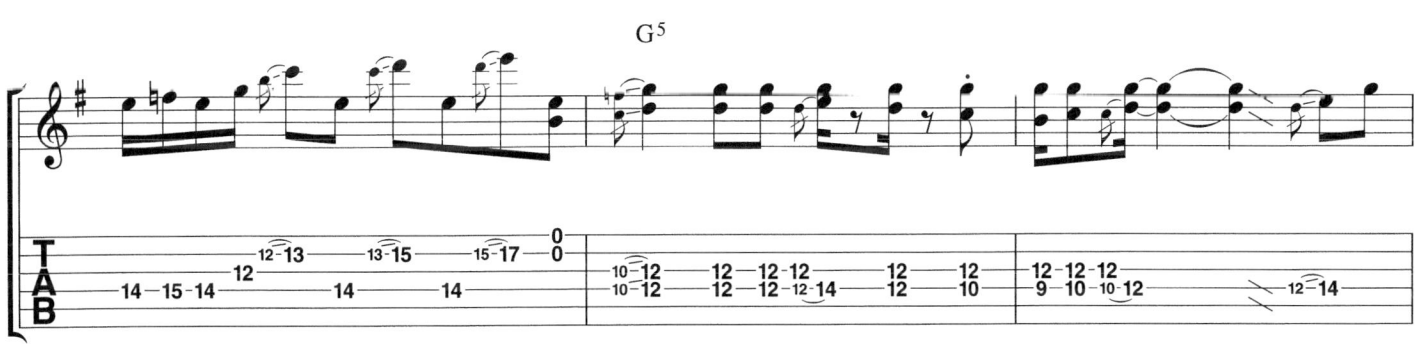
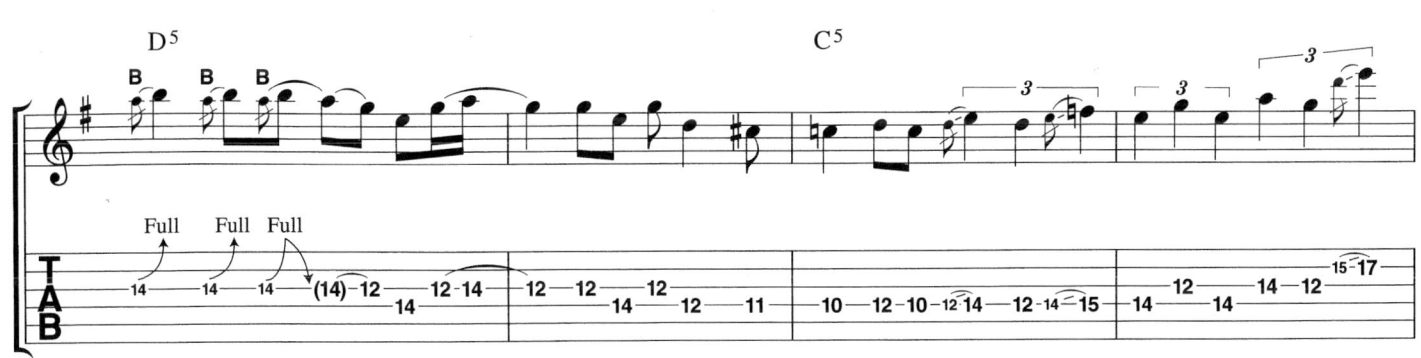

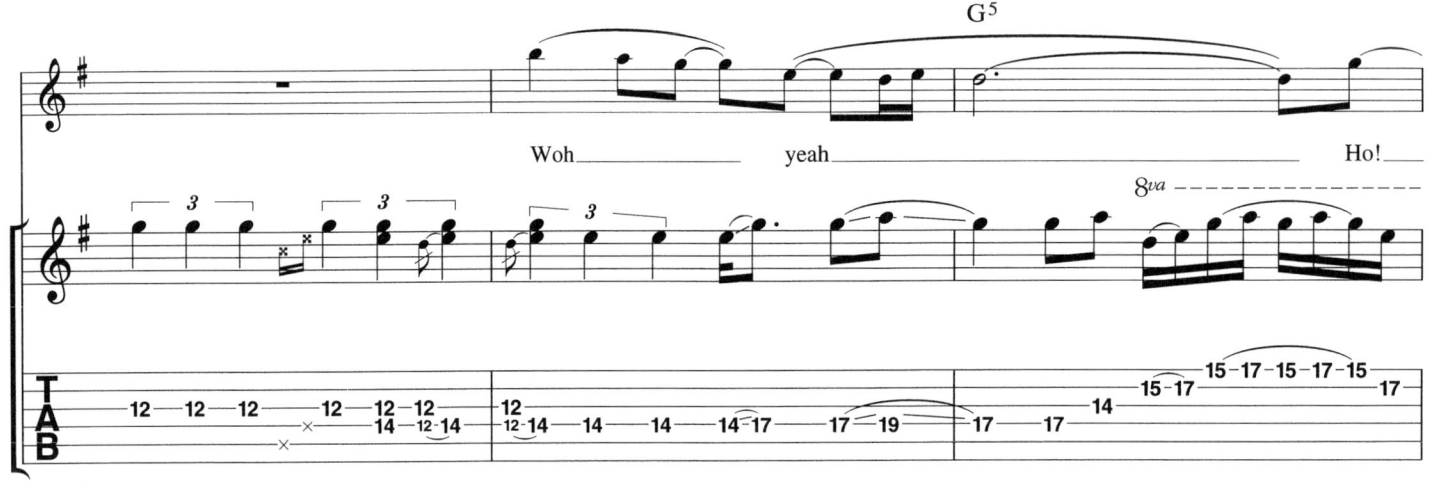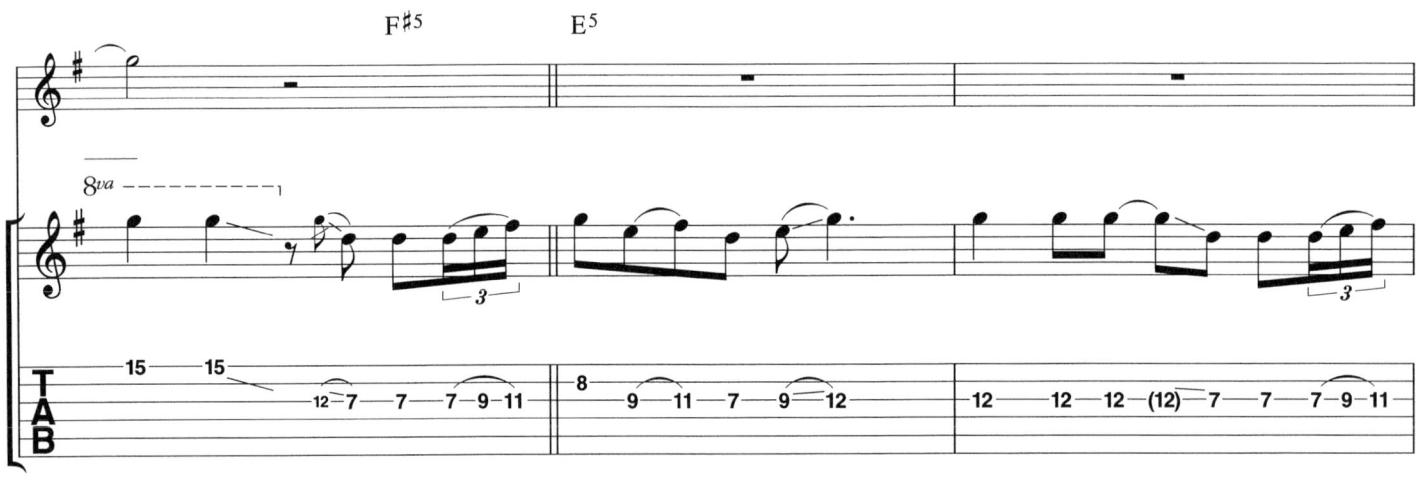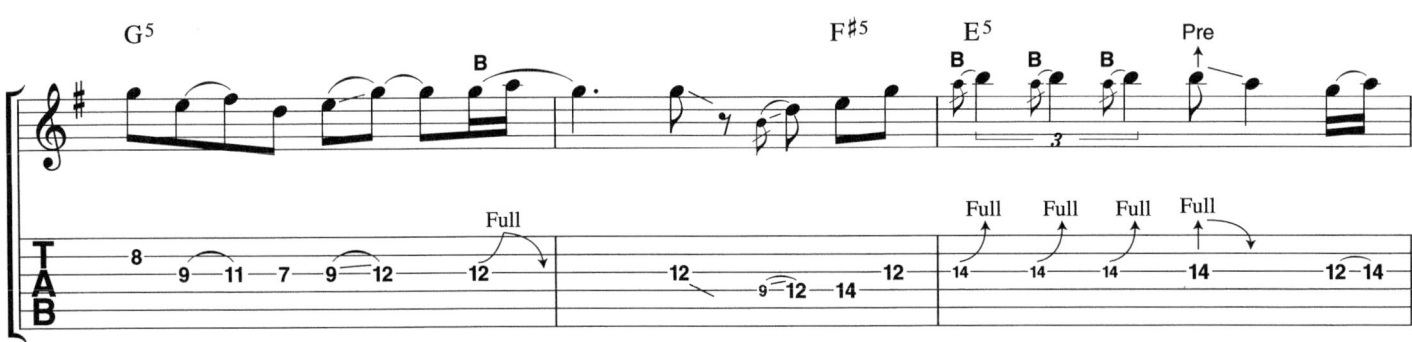

guitar tablature explained
Guitar music can be notated three different ways: on a musical stave, in tablature, and in rhythm slashes

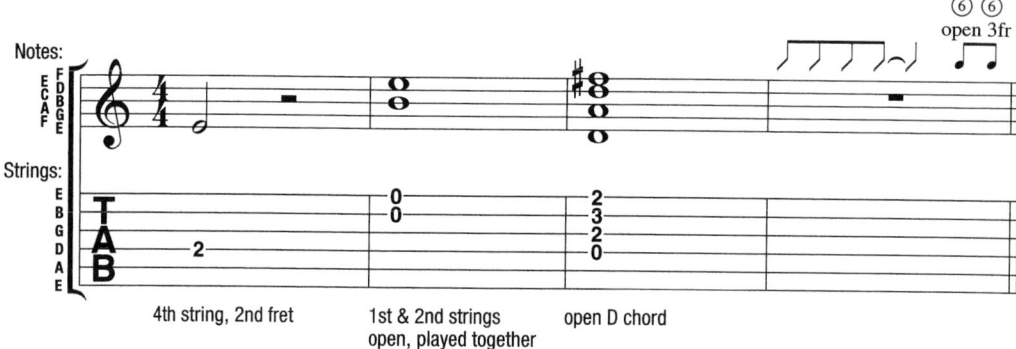

RHYTHM SLASHES are written above the stave. Strum chords in the rhythm indicated. Round noteheads indicate single notes.

THE MUSICAL STAVE shows pitches and rhythms and is divided by lines into bars. Pitches are named after the first seven letters of the alphabet.

TABLATURE graphically represents the guitar fingerboard. Each horizontal line represents a string, and each number represents a fret.

definitions for special guitar notation

SEMI-TONE BEND: Strike the note and bend up a semi-tone (1/2 step).

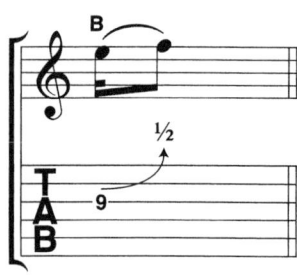

WHOLE-TONE BEND: Strike the note and bend up a whole-tone (whole step).

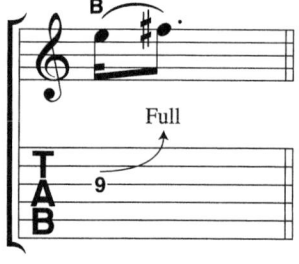

GRACE NOTE BEND: Strike the note and bend as indicated. Play the first note as quickly as possible.

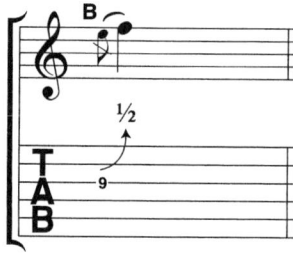

QUARTER-TONE BEND: Strike the note and bend up a 1/4 step.

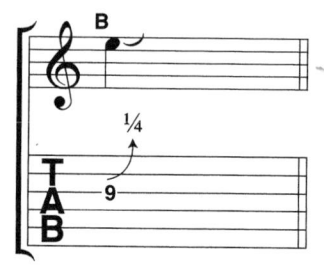

BEND & RELEASE: Strike the note and bend up as indicated, then release back to the original note.

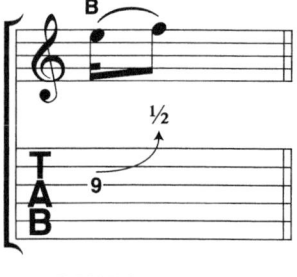

COMPOUND BEND & RELEASE: Strike the note and bend up and down in the rhythm indicated.

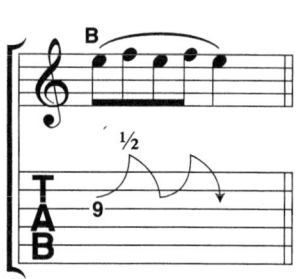

PRE-BEND: Bend the note as indicated, then strike it.

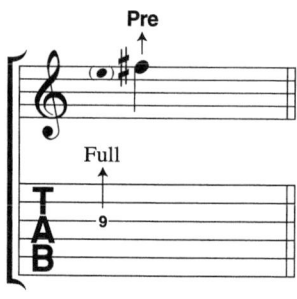

PRE-BEND & RELEASE: Bend the note as indicated. Strike it and release the note back to the original pitch.

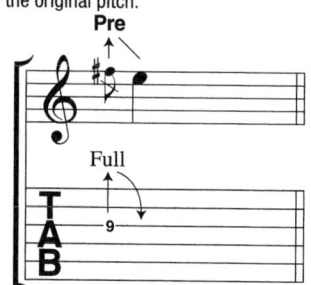

UNISON BEND: Strike the two notes simultaneously and bend the lower note up to the pitch of the higher.

BEND & RESTRIKE: Strike the note and bend as indicated then restrike the string where the symbol occurs.

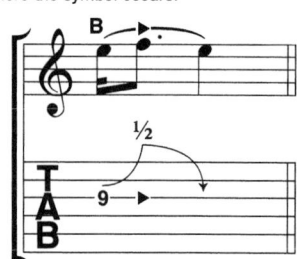

BEND, HOLD AND RELEASE: Same as bend and release but hold the bend for the duration of the tie.

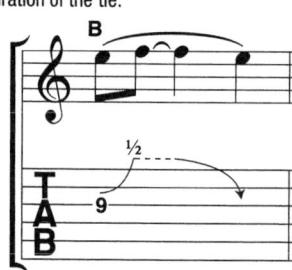

BEND AND TAP: Bend the note as indicated and tap the higher fret while still holding the bend.

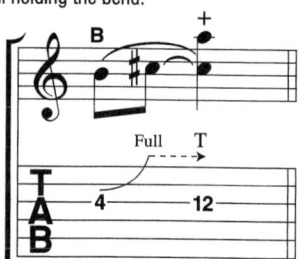

VIBRATO: The string is vibrated by rapidly bending and releasing the note with the fretting hand.

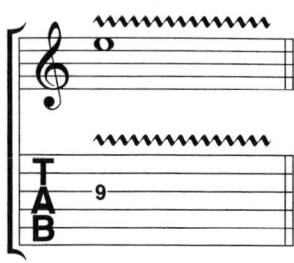

HAMMER-ON: Strike the first (lower) note with one finger, then sound the higher note (on the same string) with another finger by fretting it without picking.

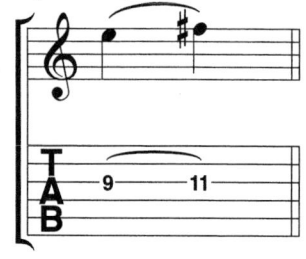

PULL-OFF: Place both fingers on the notes to be sounded, Strike the first note and without picking, pull the finger off to sound the second (lower) note.

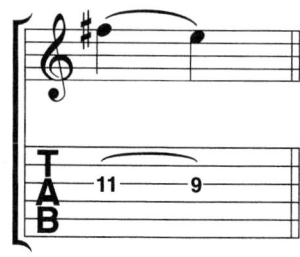

LEGATO SLIDE (GLISS): Strike the first note and then slide the same fret-hand finger up or down to the second note. The second note is not struck.

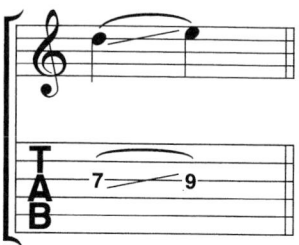

NOTE: The speed of any bend is indicated by the music notation and tempo.

SHIFT SLIDE (GLISS & RESTRIKE): Same as legato slide, except the second note is struck.

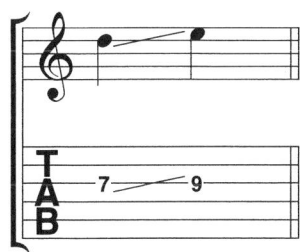

TRILL: Very rapidly alternate between the notes indicated by continuously hammering on and pulling off.

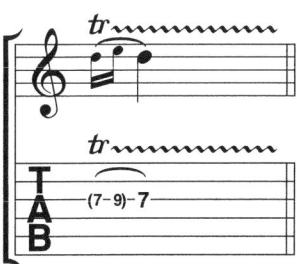

TAPPING: Hammer ("tap") the fret indicated with the pick-hand index or middle finger and pull off to the note fretted by the fret hand.

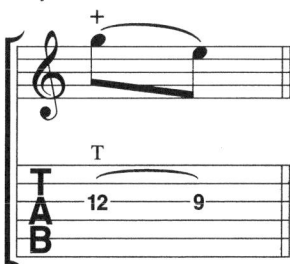

PICK SCRAPE: The edge of the pick is rubbed down (or up) the string, producing a scratchy sound.

MUFFLED STRINGS: A percussive sound is produced by laying the fret hand across the string(s) without depressing, and striking them with the pick hand.

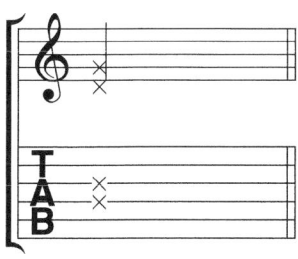

NATURAL HARMONIC: Strike the note while the fret-hand lightly touches the string directly over the fret indicated.

PINCH HARMONIC: The note is fretted normally and a harmonic is produced by adding the edge of the thumb or the tip of the index finger of the pick hand to the normal pick attack.

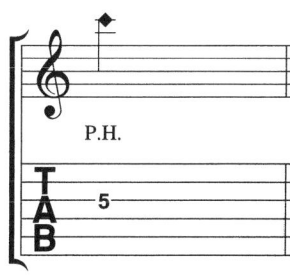

HARP HARMONIC: The note is fretted normally and a harmonic is produced by gently resting the pick hand's index finger directly above the indicated fret (in parentheses) while the pick hand's thumb or pick assists by plucking the appropriate string.

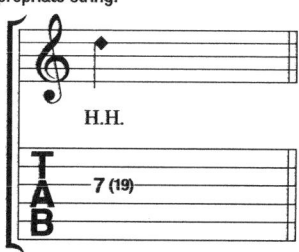

PALM MUTING: The note is partially muted by the pick hand lightly touching the string(s) just before the bridge.

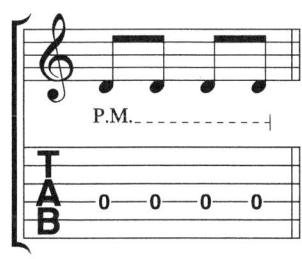

RAKE: Drag the pick across the strings indicated with a single motion.

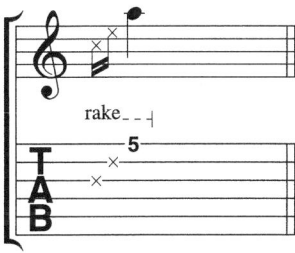

TREMOLO PICKING: The note is picked as rapidly and continuously as possible.

ARPEGGIATE: Play the notes of the chord indicated by quickly rolling them from bottom to top.

SWEEP PICKING: Rhythmic downstroke and/or upstroke motion across the strings.

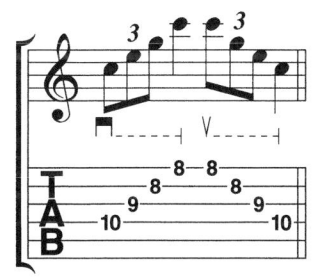

VIBRATO DIVE BAR AND RETURN: The pitch of the note or chord is dropped a specific number of steps (in rhythm) then returned to the original pitch.

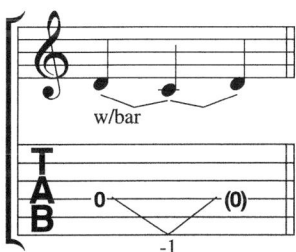

VIBRATO BAR SCOOP: Depress the bar just before striking the note, then quickly release the bar.

VIBRATO BAR DIP: Strike the note and then immediately drop a specific number of steps, then release back to the original pitch.

additional musical definitions

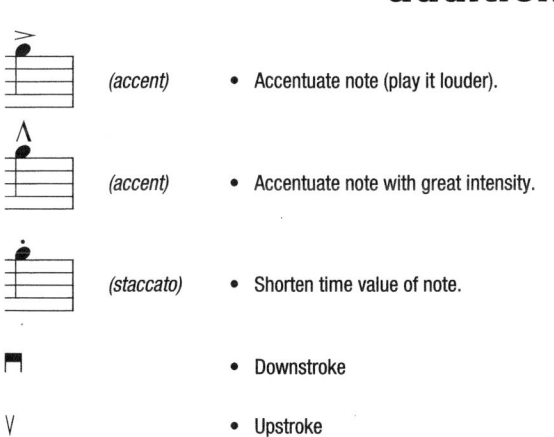

- Accentuate note (play it louder).
- Accentuate note with great intensity.
- Shorten time value of note.
- Downstroke
- Upstroke

NOTE: Tablature numbers in parentheses mean:
1. The note is sustained, but a new articulation (such as hammer on or slide) begins.
2. A note may be fretted but not necessarily played.

D.S. al Coda

D.C. al Fine

tacet

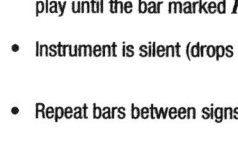

- Go back to the sign (𝄋), then play until the bar marked *To Coda* ⊕ then skip to the section marked ⊕ *Coda*.
- Go back to the beginning of the song and play until the bar marked *Fine* (end).
- Instrument is silent (drops out).
- Repeat bars between signs.
- When a repeated section has different endings, play the first ending only the first time and the second ending only the second time.

Présentation De La Tablature De Guitare

Il existe trois façons différentes de noter la musique pour guitare : à l'aide d'une portée musicale, de tablatures ou de barres rythmiques.

Les BARRES RYTHMIQUES sont indiquées au-dessus de la portée. Jouez les accords dans le rythme indiqué. Les notes rondes indiquent des notes récíles.

La PORTÉE MUSICALE indique les notes et rythmes et est divisée en mesures. Cette division est représentée par des lignes. Les notes sont : do, ré, mi, fa, sol, la, si.

La PORTÉE EN TABLATURE est une représentation graphique des touches de guitare. Chaque ligne horizontale correspond à une corde et chaque chiffre correspond à une case.

Notation Spéciale De Guitare : Définitions

TIRÉ DEMI-TON : Jouez la note et tirez la corde afin d'élever la note d'un demi-ton (étape à moitié).

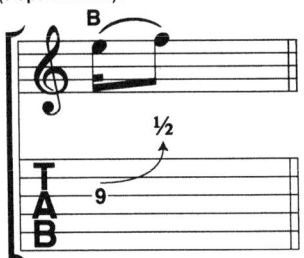

TIRÉ PLEIN : Jouez la note et tirez la corde afin d'élever la note d'un ton entier (étape entière).

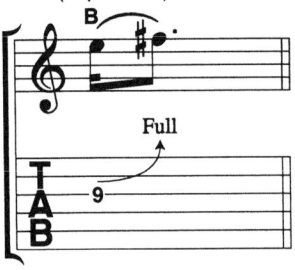

TIRÉ D'AGRÉMENT : Jouez la note et tirez la corde comme indiqué. Jouez la première note aussi vite que possible.

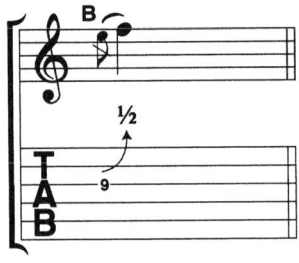

TIRÉ QUART DE TON : Jouez la note et tirez la corde afin d'élever la note d'un quart de ton.

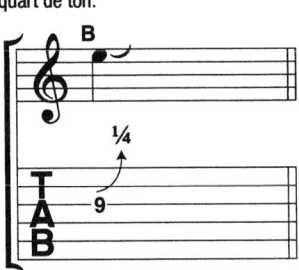

TIRÉ ET LÂCHÉ : Jouez la note et tirez la corde comme indiqué, puis relâchez, afin d'obtenir de nouveau la note de départ.

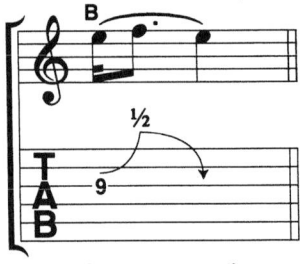

TIRÉ ET REJOUÉ : Jouez la note et tirez la corde comme indiqué puis rejouez la corde où le symbole apparaît.

PRÉ-TIRÉ : Tirez la corde comme indiqué puis jouez cette note.

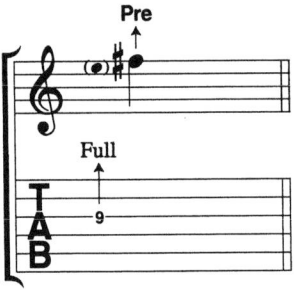

PRÉ-TIRÉ ET LÂCHÉ : Tirez la corde comme indiqué. Jouez la note puis relâchez la corde afin d'obtenir le ton de départ.

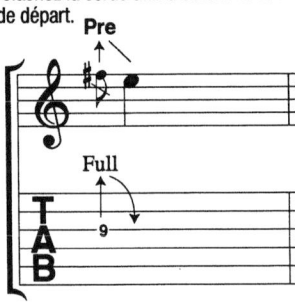

HAMMER-ON: Jouez la première note (plus basse) avec un doigt puis jouez la note plus haute sur la même corde avec un autre doigt, sur le manche mais sans vous servir du médiator.

PULL-OFF: Positionnez deux doigts sur les notes à jouer. Jouez la première note et sans vous servir du médiator, dégagez un doigt pour obtenir la deuxième note, plus basse.

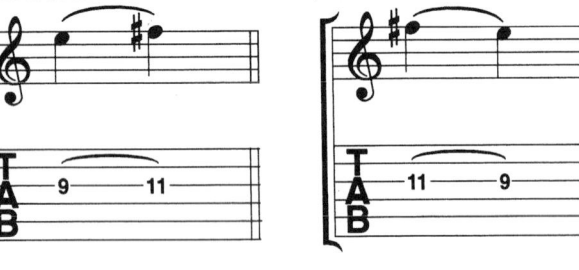

GLISSANDO : Jouez la première note puis faites glisser le doigt le long du manche pour obtenir la seconde note qui, elle, n'est pas jouée.

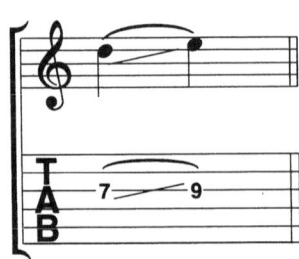

GLISSANDO ET REJOUÉ : Identique au glissando à ceci près que la seconde note est jouée.

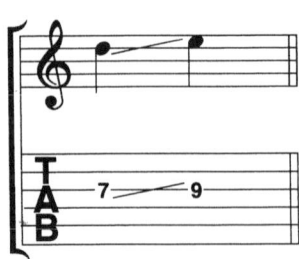

HARMONIQUES NATURELLES : Jouez la note tandis qu'un doigt effleure la corde sur le manche correspondant à la case indiquée.

PICK SCRAPE (SCRATCH) : On fait glisser le médiator le long de la corde, ce qui produit un son éraillé.

ÉTOUFFÉ DE LA PAUME : La note est partiellement étouffée par la main (celle qui se sert du médiator). Elle effleure la (les) corde(s) juste au-dessus du chevalet.

CORDES ÉTOUFFÉES : Un effet de percussion produit en posant à plat la main sur le manche sans relâcher, puis en jouant les cordes avec le médiator.

NOTE: La vitesse des tirés est indiquée par la notation musicale et le tempo.

Erläuterung zur Tabulaturschreibweise

Es gibt drei Möglichkeiten, Gitarrenmusik zu notieren: im klassichen Notensystem, in Tabulaturform oder als rhythmische Akzente.

RHYTHMISCHE AKZENTE werden über dem Notensystem notiert. Geschlagene Akkorde werden rhythmisch dargestellt. Ausgeschriebene Noten stellen Einzeltöne dar.

Im **NOTENSYSTEM** werden Tonhöhe und rhythmischer Verlauf festgelegt; es ist durch Taktstriche in Takte unterteilt. Die Töne werden nach den ersten acht Buchstaben des Alphabets benannt.
Beachte: "B" in der anglo-amerikanischen Schreibweise entspricht dem deutschen "H"!

DIE TABULATUR ist die optische Darstellung des Gitarrengriffbrettes. Jeder horizontalen Linie ist eine bestimmte Saite zugeordnet, jede Zahl bezeichnet einen Bund.

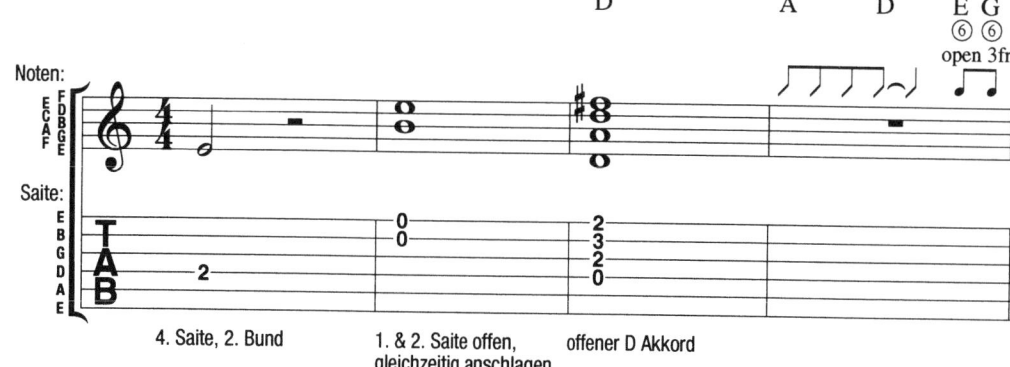

Erklärungen zur speziellen Gitarennotation

HALBTON-ZIEHER: Spiele die Note und ziehe dann um einen Halbton höher (Halbtonschritt).

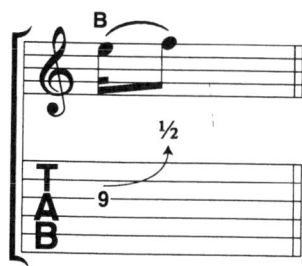

GANZTON-ZIEHER: Spiele die Note und ziehe dann einen Ganzton höher (Ganztonschritt).

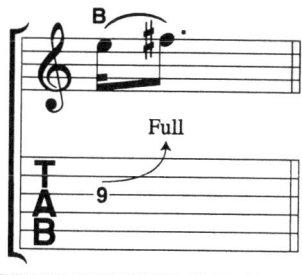

ZIEHER MIT VORSCHLAG: Spiele die Note und ziehe wie notiert. Spiele die erste Note so schnell wie möglich.

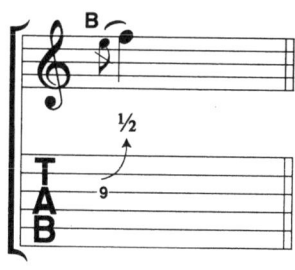

VIERTELTON-ZIEHER: Spiele die Note und ziehe dann einen Viertelton höher (Vierteltonschritt).

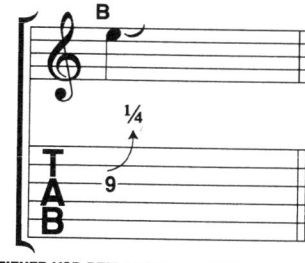

ZIEHEN UND ZURÜCKGLEITEN: Spiele die Note und ziehe wie notiert; lasse den Finger dann in die Ausgangsposition zurückgleiten. Dabei wird nur die erste Note angeschlagen.

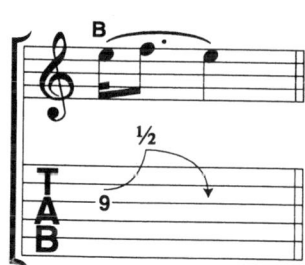

ZIEHEN UND NOCHMALIGES ANSCHLAGEN: Spiele die Note und ziehe wie notiert, schlage die Saite neu an, wenn das Symbol "▶" erscheint und lasse den Finger dann zurückgleiten.

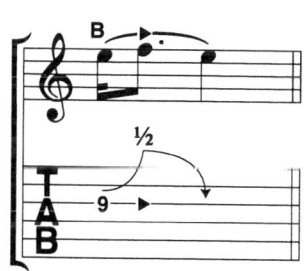

ZIEHER VOR DEM ANSCHLAGEN: Ziehe zuerst die Note wie notiert; schlage die Note dann an.

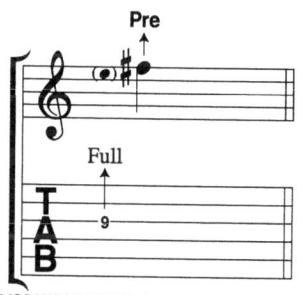

ZIEHER VOR DEM ANSCHLAGEN MIT ZURÜCKGLEITEN: Ziehe die Note wie notiert; schlage die Note dann an und lasse den Finger auf die Ausgangslage zurückgleiten.

AUFSCHLAGTECHNIK: Schlage die erste (tiefere) Note an; die höhere Note (auf der selben Saite) erklingt durch kräftiges Aufschlagen mit einem anderen Finger der Griffhand.

ABZIEHTECHNIK: Setze beide Finger auf die zu spielenden Noten und schlage die erste Note an. Ziehe dann (ohne nochmals anzuschlagen) den oberen Finger der Griffhand seitlich - abwärts ab, um die zweite (tiefere) Note zum klingen zu bringen.

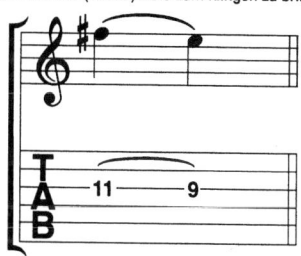

GLISSANDOTECHNIK: Schlage die erste Note an und rutsche dann mit dem selben Finger der Griffhand aufwärts oder abwärts zur zweiten Note. Die zweite Note wird nicht angeschlagen.

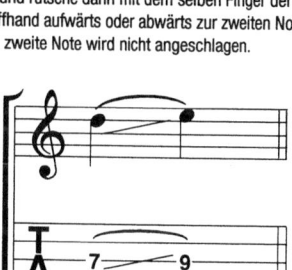

GLISSANDOTECHNIK MIT NACHFOLGENDEM ANSCHLAG: Gleiche Technik wie das gebundene Glissando, jedoch wird die zweite Note angeschlagen.

NATÜRLICHES FLAGEOLETT: Berühre die Saite über dem angegebenen Bund leicht mit einem Finger der Griffhand. Schlage die Saite an und lasse sie frei schwingen.

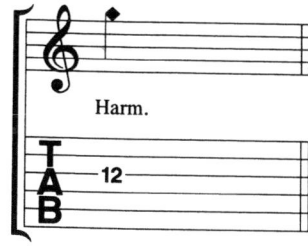

PICK SCRAPE: Fahre mit dem Plektrum nach unten über die Saiten - klappt am besten bei umsponnenen Saiten.

DÄMPFEN MIT DER SCHLAGHAND: Lege die Schlaghand oberhalb der Brücke leicht auf die Saite(n).

DÄMPFEN MIT DER GRIFFHAND: Du erreichst einen percussiven Sound, indem du die Griffhand leicht über die Saiten legst (ohne diese herunterzudrücken) und dann mit der Schlaghand anschlägst.

ANMERKUNG: Das Tempo der Zieher und Glissandos ist abhängig von der rhythmischen Notation und dem Grundtempo.